What Does
God Say
About That?

What Does God Say About That?

**POLITICS, RACE, HEAVEN, HELL,
THE ENVIRONMENT, MONEY,**
and hundreds more!

BETHANY HOUSE PUBLISHERS
a division of Baker Publishing Group
Minneapolis, Minnesota

© 2013 by Bethany House Publishers

Compiled by Aaron Sharp

Published by Bethany House Publishers
11400 Hampshire Avenue South
Bloomington, Minnesota 55438
www.bethanyhouse.com

Bethany House Publishers is a division of
Baker Publishing Group, Grand Rapids, Michigan

Printed in the United States of America

Library of Congress Cataloging-in-Publication Data
    What does God say about that? : politics, race, heaven, hell, the environment, money, and hundreds more.
       p. cm.
    Summary: "A collection of Bible quotes covering a wide variety of timely issues and topics" —provided by the publisher.
      ISBN 978-0-7642-1056-3 (pbk. : alk. paper)
      1. Bible—Indexes. I. Bethany House Publishers.
    BS432.W49 2013
    220.3—dc23   2012039403

The internet addresses, email addresses, and phone numbers in this book are accurate at the time of publication. They are provided as a resource. Baker Publishing Group does not endorse them or vouch for their content or permanence.

Cover design by Eric Walljasper

13   14   15   16   17   18   19   7   6   5   4   3   2   1

Topics

Introduction

To find out what God says about a topic, all we have to do is look to the Bible. For thousands of years people of faith have recognized that the Scriptures provide for both eternal life and the sustenance that is required to live everyday life in the here and now. In the words of nineteenth-century pastor Charles Haddon Spurgeon, "Keep upon the foundation of the Scriptures, and you stand safely and have an answer for those who question you, yea, and an answer which you may render at the bar of God; but once you allow your own whim, or fancy or taste or your notion of what is proper and right to rule you instead of the word of God, and you have entered upon a dangerous course, and unless the grace of God prevent, boundless mischief may ensue."*

The Bible, its knowledge, and its wisdom have guided kings, pastors, presidents, missionaries, and common people through every circumstance known to humanity. President Theodore Roosevelt valued its sixty-six books so much that he said, "A thorough knowledge of the Bible is worth more than a college education."†

Those who have learned that what appears on the Bible's pages are more than mere words are those who have found God's revealed source of life and truth. The words and sentiments of the Scriptures have sustained soldiers,

---

* Eric Hayden, *The Unforgettable Spurgeon: Reflections on His Life and Writings* (Greenville, SC: Emerald House, 1997), 42.
†George Grant, *The Courage and Character of Theodore Roosevelt: A Hero Among Leaders* (Nashville: Cumberland House, 2005), 167.

slaves, the persecuted, mothers, fathers, those experiencing life's highest peaks, and those enduring the world's lowest valleys. It is no wonder then that Helen Keller's words resonate loudly today: "Unless we form the habit of going to the Bible in bright moments as well as in trouble, we cannot fully respond to its consolations because we lack equilibrium between light and darkness."

In this book you'll find a short summary of what God has to say about hundreds of topics, followed by key Scripture verses covering each subject. You'll also find a list of additional verses that refer to the issue. The main purpose of this book is to present what God says, not interpret it. It's up to you to apply what God says to your own life.

The topics are arranged alphabetically. You'll find a list of them at the beginning of the book. If there's a particular subject that interests you, you can start there. You may want to browse the list and see what catches your eye, or even start with A and read all the way through to Z. Any way you approach it, you will reap the benefits of knowing what God has to say.

Abortion

The truth of the Bible is timeless, but we face many different issues than did those who lived in the time of Peter and Paul, much less Abraham, Isaac, and Jacob. Modern technology and scientific expertise have given the world many reasons for hope and health, but there are downsides to technology as well. Abortion was more difficult and therefore less common in Bible times. So when we consider what the Bible says about abortion, we are really asking what the Bible says about those in the womb. Today, with sonograms and other modern marvels, we are able to see funny images on a screen that eventually take the shape of a baby, but in the Bible we learn that God sees life.

Key Verses

When men strive together and hit a pregnant woman, so that her children come out, but there is no harm, the one who hit her shall surely be fined, as the woman's husband shall impose on him, and he shall pay as the judges determine. But if there is harm, then you shall pay life for life, eye for eye, tooth for tooth, hand for hand, foot for foot, burn for burn, wound for wound, stripe for stripe.

Exodus 21:22–25 ESV

Oh yes, you shaped me first inside, then out; you formed me in my mother's womb. I thank you, High God—you're breathtaking! Body and soul, I am marvelously made! I worship in adoration—what a creation! You know me inside and out, you know every bone in my body; you know exactly how I was made, bit by bit, how I was sculpted from nothing into something. Like an open book, you watched me grow from conception to birth; all the stages of my life were spread out before you, the days of my life all prepared before I'd even lived one day.

Psalm 139:13–16 THE MESSAGE

Did not he who made me in the womb make them? Did not the same one form us both within our mothers?

Job 31:15 NIV

Additional Notable Verses Concerning Abortion

Genesis 1:20–27; Psalm 22:9–10; 58:3; Isaiah 44:2; 24; Jeremiah 1:5

Addiction

Addiction has become commonplace in the twenty-first century. People become addicted to alcohol, antidepressants, caffeine, coffee, food, gambling, the internet, painkillers, risk, sex, sleeping pills, television, and tobacco. Even though addictions may feel good for a time, there is a better way to live.

Key Verses

Therefore let him who thinks he stands take heed that he does not fall. No temptation has overtaken you but such as is common to man; and God is faithful, who will not allow you to be tempted beyond what you are able, but with the temptation will provide the way of escape also, so that you will be able to endure it.

1 Corinthians 10:12–13 NASB

Blessed is the man who remains steadfast under trial, for when he has stood the test he will receive the crown of life, which God has promised to those who love him.

James 1:12 ESV

Jesus said, "I tell you most solemnly that anyone who chooses a life of sin is trapped in a dead-end life and is, in fact, a slave. A slave is a transient, who can't come and go at will. The Son, though, has an established position, the run of the house. So if the Son sets you free, you are free through and through."

John 8:34–36 THE MESSAGE

Additional Notable Verses Concerning Addiction

Psalms 121:1–2; Proverbs 6:27; 23:20; Isaiah 5:11; Matthew 5:28; 6:3; Romans 5:3–5; 13:14; 1 Corinthians 6:12–20; 8:9; 15:33; Galatians 5:19–21; Ephesians 5:5, 18–20; Colossians 3:5; Titus 2:12; James 1:2–3; 4:7; 1 Peter 2:11; 5:8; 1 John 2:16; 3:8

Adultery

The Bible is not just a list of things to do and things not to do, but God's definition of right and wrong for many areas of life. Marriage and a person's sex life are one of these areas. Sex and the intimacy that is associated with that act is to exist solely between a man and a woman in the context of a marriage. Marriage exists as a bond between two people, and whenever one of the people in a marriage commits adultery, it shatters that bond and clearly violates both God's plan and His will for that relationship. Adultery may not be taken seriously by the world at large, but it is something that the world's Creator takes incredibly seriously.

Key Verses

You shall not commit adultery.

Exodus 20:14 NKJV

You have heard that it was said, "You shall not commit adultery." But I tell you that anyone who looks at a woman lustfully has already committed adultery with her in his heart.

Matthew 5:27–28 NIV

Marriage is to be held in honor among all, and the marriage bed is to be undefiled; for fornicators and adulterers God will judge.

Hebrews 13:4 NASB

Additional Notable Verses Concerning Adultery

Genesis 20:1–18; Numbers 5:11–31; Deuteronomy 5:18; 22:13–30; 2 Samuel 11–12; Job 24:15–18; Proverbs 2:16–19; 5:1–23; 6:20–35; 7:1–27; 9:13–18; 22:14; 23:27–28; 30:18–20; Jeremiah 5:7–8; 23:10; 29:20–23; Ezekiel 18:4–9; Hosea 4:1–2; Matthew 5:30–32; 15:19; 19:9–12; Mark 7:20–21; 10:11–12; Luke 16:18; John 8:1–11; Romans 7:1–13; 13:8–14; 1 Corinthians 5:1–13; 6:8–11; Galatians 5:16–23; Ephesians 5:1–12; 1 Thessalonians 4:1–7; 1 Peter 4:1–5

Adversity

Many people expect that belief in the Bible and following its wisdom would eliminate adversity. The opposite, however, is true. A life of faith in Jesus Christ is one that is full of adversity. For the most part, knowing what the Bible says about adversity will not allow you to avoid it, but God will help you navigate the adversity that is certain to come your way.

Key Verses

But evil does not spring from the soil, and trouble does not sprout from the earth. People are born for trouble as readily as sparks fly up from a fire.

Job 5:6–7 NLT

A friend loves at all times, and a brother is born for adversity.

Proverbs 17:17 NKJV

In the day of prosperity be happy, but in the day of adversity consider—God has made the one as well as the other so that man will not discover anything that will be after him.

Ecclesiastes 7:14 NASB

I have told you these things, so that in Me you may have [perfect] peace and confidence. In the world you have tribulation and trials and distress and frustration; but be of good cheer [take courage; be confident, certain, undaunted]! For I have overcome the world. [I have deprived it of power to harm you and have conquered it for you.]

John 16:33 AMP

Additional Notable Verses Concerning Adversity

Genesis 3:16–19; 15:12–15; 50:20; Exodus 1:1–13; Numbers 11:1; Deuteronomy 8:1–9; 1 Kings 9:9; 2 Chronicles 7:22; Job 2:10–11; 4:8; 14:1; Psalms 30:5; 49:5; 89:30–32; 94:13; 119:75; 126:5–6; Proverbs 3:12; 13:17,21; Micah 7:7–9; Lamentations 3:33; Matthew 5:1–12; 24:8–13; John 16:16–22; Romans 8:18–25, 27–29; 2 Corinthians 4:15–18; 1 Thessalonians 3:1–4; 2 Timothy 3:10–17; Hebrews 12:1–17; James 5:13–17; 1 Peter 1:3–8; 4:12–19; 5:6–10

Alcohol

Just asking the question "What does the Bible say about alcohol?" can be almost as controversial as the answers to some other questions. Few topics generate the level of emotion and passion of this one.

Those whose lives and families have been forever damaged by alcohol abuse may find it very difficult to separate what the Scriptures actually say from their own experience. Those who have never endured the pain of substance abuse can find it difficult to see why there is such angst over something as simple as a little drink. An issue this contentious and emotional necessitates careful study of the Scriptures.

Key Verses

Use the money to buy anything you want: cattle, sheep, wine, or beer—anything that looks good to you. You and your family can then feast in the Presence of God, your God, and have a good time.

Deuteronomy 14:26 THE MESSAGE

Do not get drunk with wine, for that is dissipation, but be filled with the Spirit.

Ephesians 5:18 NASB

Do not, for the sake of food, destroy the work of God. Everything is indeed clean, but it is wrong for anyone to make another stumble by what he eats. It is good not to eat meat or drink wine or do anything that causes your brother to stumble.

Romans 14:20–21 ESV

Woe to those who are mighty heroes at drinking wine and men of strength in mixing alcoholic drinks!

Isaiah 5:22 AMP

Additional Notable Verses Concerning Alcohol

Genesis 14:18; Deuteronomy 7:13; 11:14; 14:23–26; Esther 5:6; 7:1–2; Job 1:13; Psalm 4:7; 104:14–15; Proverbs 3:9–10; 20:1; 21:17; 23:29–35; 31:4–7; Isaiah 25:6; Jeremiah 31:12; 48:33; Daniel 10:3; Hosea 2:8–9; Joel 2:19–24; 3:18; Luke 7:33–34; John 2:1–11; 1 Corinthians 6:9–10; 11:17–22; Galatians 5:19–21; Ephesians 5:15–21; 1 Timothy 5:23

Ambition

Ambition can be a good or a bad thing. When it is ambition to reach the world for the Gospel, to glorify God, to worship God, or to influence people for right, it is a very good thing. When it is ambition for more money, more prestige, a better position in life, or the desire to win at all costs, then it is a very bad thing. The difference biblically is a matter of motivation. Biblical examples of ambition show us that ambition can change the world, but it can also destroy a life.

Key Verses

What good is it for someone to gain the whole world, and yet lose or forfeit their very self?

Luke 9:25 NIV

But we urge you, brethren, to excel still more, and to make it your ambition to lead a quiet life and attend to your own business and work with your hands, just as we commanded you, so that you will behave properly toward outsiders and not be in any need.

1 Thessalonians 4:10–12 NASB

Who is wise and understanding among you? By his good conduct let him show his works in the meekness of wisdom. But if you have bitter jealousy and selfish ambition in your hearts, do not boast and be false to the truth. This is not the wisdom that comes down from above, but is earthly, unspiritual, demonic. For where jealousy and selfish ambition exist, there will be disorder and every vile practice. But the wisdom from above is first pure, then peaceable, gentle, open to reason, full of mercy and good fruits, impartial and sincere.

James 3:13–17 ESV

Additional Notable Verses Concerning Ambition

Genesis 11:1–9; Psalm 49:11–20; 131:1–2; Proverbs 17:19; Isaiah 14:12–15; Ezekiel 31:10–11; Matthew 4:8–10; 16:26; 18:1–5; 20:20–28; 23:11–12; Mark 10:35–45; 12:38–40; Luke 22:24–30; John 5:44; 1 Timothy 2:1–2; James 4:1–2; 1 John 2:16; 3 John 1:9–10

Angels

Periodically angels have become popular in modern culture. When this happens, these beings almost never resemble what we actually know about angels from God's Word.

The angelic beings who serve a holy and just God, and even those who betrayed the Almighty in favor of rebellion, are powerful and mighty beings. The angels who are faithful to God are equal parts messenger, warrior, servant, worshiper, and protector.

Far from caricatures carrying harps or pitchforks, angels are very real and a most serious friend or foe.

Key Verses

The angel of the Lord encamps around those who fear Him, and rescues them.

Psalm 34:7 NASB

Praise the Lord! Praise the Lord from the heavens; praise him in the heights! Praise him, all his angels; praise him, all his hosts!

Psalm 148:1–2 ESV

And did he ever say anything like this to an angel? Sit alongside me here on my throne until I make your enemies a stool for your feet. Isn't it obvious that all angels are sent to help out with those lined up to receive salvation?

Hebrews 1:13–14 THE MESSAGE

Do not let anyone disqualify you by making you humiliate yourself and worship angels. Such people enter into visions, which fill them with foolish pride because of their human way of thinking.

Colossians 2:18 NCV

Additional Notable Verses Concerning Angels

Numbers 22:22–35; 2 Samuel 14:20; 24:1–17; Nehemiah 9:6; Job 38:1–7; Psalm 68:17; 91:11–12; 103:20–21; 104:4; Isaiah 6:1–7; Daniel 8:15–27; 9:21–23; 12:6–7; Matthew 1:20–25; 13:36–43; 24:29–31; 25:31; 26:51–54; 28:1–9; Mark 8:38; Luke 1:1–38; 2:8–21; 15:10; 22:39–43; John 1:50–51; Acts 1:1–11; 7:53; 8:26; 10:1–7; 12:7–11; 27:23; Ephesians 1:18–23; 3:9–10; Philippians 2:9–11; Colossians 1:16; 1 Thessalonians 4:16; 2 Thessalonians 1:7; 1 Timothy 3:16; 5:21; Hebrews 1:1–14; 2:1–4; 12:22; 1 Peter 1:12; 3:21–22; 2 Peter 2:11; Jude 1:9; Revelation 12:7; 19:10; 22:9

Anger

Too often we categorize concepts as positive or negative without ever considering that the issue may be more multifaceted than we have realized. Anger is one of these concepts that, although we know better, we tend to simply file away in categories labeled "sin," "wrong," or "bad." The picture that the Bible paints of anger, however, is a much more subtle and complex one.

The example of Jesus, as well as periodic urgings of biblical writers for the reader to respond in anger, lets us know that there are times and places in which we should indeed be angry. Humanity's biggest problem with anger is that all too often we are mad at the wrong times and places, we show our anger in the wrong ways, and we direct our anger at the wrong people.

Key Verses

Whoever is patient has great understanding, but one who is quick-tempered displays folly.

Proverbs 14:29 NIV

A soft answer turns away wrath, but grievous words stir up anger.

Proverbs 15:1 AMP

Know this, my beloved brothers: let every person be quick to hear, slow to speak, slow to anger; for the anger of man does not produce the righteousness of God.

James 1:19–20 ESV

Additional Notable Verses Concerning Anger

Genesis 4:5–8; Exodus 32; Job 5:2, Psalm 37:8; 78:38; 90:11; 103:8; Proverbs 6:34; 12:16; 15:18; 16:32; 19:11, 19; 22:24–25; 25:28; 27:3–4; 29:8–11, 22; Ecclesiastes 7:9; Jonah 4:1–4; Nahum 1:2, Matthew 5:22; 21:12–16; Romans 12:19; 1 Corinthians 13:4–5; 2 Corinthians 12:20; Galatians 5:19–21; Ephesians 4:26–32; Colossians 3:8; 1 Timothy 2:8; Titus 1:7

Animals

I n the biblical world animals were not usually pets as they often are today. Animals were transportation, sustenance, and fellow workers. They exist in biblical accounts overwhelmingly for practical purposes. Twice in the Bible animals even speak. The first is the serpent in the Garden of Eden (Genesis 3), and the second is Balaam's donkey (Numbers 22). Other than these two exceptions, animals are biblical history's silent characters. It can be easy to conclude that since they have little to say, God is uninterested in them and their lives. Nothing could be further from what God says in His Word.

Key Verses

And God made the beasts of the earth according to their kinds and the livestock according to their kinds, and everything that creeps on the ground according to its kind. And God saw that it was good.

Genesis 1:25 ESV

Sing to the Lord with thanksgiving; sing praises to our God on the lyre, who covers the heavens with clouds, who provides rain for the earth, who makes grass to grow on the mountains. He gives to the beast its food, and to the young ravens which cry.

Psalm 147:7–9 NASB

Good people are good to their animals; the "good-hearted" bad people kick and abuse them.

Proverbs 12:10 THE MESSAGE

Look at the birds. They don't plant or harvest or store food in barns, for your heavenly Father feeds them. And aren't you far more valuable to him than they are?

Matthew 6:26 NLT

Additional Notable Verses Concerning Animals

Genesis 1:20–25, 30; 2:18–20; 8:1–19; 9:1–5; Exodus 21:28–36; 22:1–4; 23:5; Numbers 22:22–35; Deuteronomy 25:4; Job 12:10; 35:11; 38:41; 39:1–30; Psalm 36:6; 50:7–11; 104:20–25; 147:7–11, Proverbs 6:6–8; 30:25–28; Ecclesiastes 3:18–21; Isaiah 35:8–10; 65:25; Joel 1:18–20; Matthew 10:26–33; Luke 12:4–7, 24; 14:5; 1 Corinthians 9:9; 1 Timothy 5:18; James 3:7

Anxiety

Worry is the deep dark secret of many Christians. The idea that we should not worry is one that everyone agrees with and almost no one practices. A massive amount of sermons, books, and counseling sessions all tell us that anxiety is not only negative but can also be deadly to a person's physical, mental, and spiritual well-being.

Even though we know that anxiety is harmful, we continue to worry. Even though we know that the Scriptures tell us that God is in control, it is still a struggle to have victory over thoughts that constantly seek to discourage and confuse God's people. Some people have even gotten so used to worrying that to them it is almost comforting. Worry does not need to stay a dirty little secret. More than just warning us against it, the Bible teaches how to overcome worry.

Key Verses

Anxiety in a man's heart weighs it down, but a good word makes it glad.

Proverbs 12:25 NASB

Be anxious for nothing, but in everything by prayer and supplication, with thanksgiving, let your requests be made known to God; and the peace of God, which surpasses all understanding, will guard your hearts and minds through Christ Jesus.

Philippians 4:6–7 NKJV

Be humble under God's powerful hand so he will lift you up when the right time comes. Give all your worries to him, because he cares about you.

1 Peter 5:6–7 NCV

Additional Notable Verses Concerning Anxiety

Psalm 32:8–10; 94:19; 139:23; Isaiah 35:4; Jeremiah 17:8; Matthew 6:24–34; Luke 10:41–42; John 14:1–4; Hebrews 13:5–6

Art

When God's Spirit was present, the characters of the Bible did amazing things. They slew giants, raised people from the dead, won wars, saw the blind given sight, and witnessed a multitude of other things that would easily qualify as incredible. The moving of the Spirit of God, however, is not limited to awe-inspiring miracles. Awe-inspiring works by painters, carpenters, stone masons, seamstresses, and artists of all stripes were just as motivated and empowered by the Spirit of God, yet we seldom recognize them for exactly what they are. Creativity and skill are signs of God at work!

Key Verses

Moses told the Israelites, "See, God has selected Bezalel son of Uri, son of Hur, of the tribe of Judah. He's filled him with the Spirit of God, with skill, ability, and know-how for making all sorts of things, to design and work in gold, silver, and bronze; to carve stones and set them; to carve wood, working in every kind of skilled craft. And he's also made him a teacher, he and Oholiab son of Ahisamach, of the tribe of Dan. He's gifted them with the know-how needed for carving, designing, weaving, and embroidering in blue, purple, and scarlet fabrics, and in fine linen. They can make anything and design anything."

Exodus 35:30–35 THE MESSAGE

David told the leaders of the Levites to appoint their fellow Levites as musicians to make a joyful sound with musical instruments: lyres, harps and cymbals.

1 Chronicles 15:16 NIV

But now, O Lord, you are our Father; we are the clay, and you are our potter; we are all the work of your hand.

Isaiah 64:8 ESV

Additional Notable Verses Concerning Art

Genesis 4:18–22; 9:20; Exodus 28:1–43; 30:1–38; 31:1–11; 35:20–35; 1 Kings 7; 1 Chronicles 22:13–16; 2 Chronicles 2:11–15; 24:1–13; Proverbs 31:10–31; Jeremiah 18:1–11

Astrology

Humanity has been looking for meaning and a purpose for life's events for its entire history. Those who chose to follow God found meaning in Him, and in His Word, but there were others who foolishly chose to find meaning in other places. They searched for reason and tried to make sense of the world that they lived in, even when things seemed to be spinning out of control.

Some of these people who rejected God as the Creator and Sustainer of all things found something else to give them a reasonable explanation for why things happened as they did. They found a cosmic force at work in the sky. The worship and searching of the sky for answers is one of the oldest false religions in existence. The words of Scripture warn against it just as much today as they did then.

Key Verses

And beware lest you raise your eyes to heaven, and when you see the sun and the moon and the stars, all the host of heaven, you be drawn away and bow down to them and serve them, things that the Lord your God has allotted to all the peoples under the whole heaven.

Deuteronomy 4:19 ESV

This is what the Lord says: "Do not act like the other nations, who try to read their future in the stars. Do not be afraid of their predictions, even though other nations are terrified by them."

Jeremiah 10:2 NLT

Additional Notable Verses Concerning Astrology

Genesis 1:14; Leviticus 19:31; Deuteronomy 4:19–20; 17:1–6; 18:9–12; 2 Kings 21:1–9; Job 9:1–13; 26:1–13; 38:31–41; Psalm 8:1–9; 19:1–6; 147:1–5; Isaiah 47:10–15; Jeremiah 8:1–3; 27:1–11; Daniel 1:17–20; 2:24–30; 4:4–7; Amos 5:8; Micah 5:8–15; Galatians 5:19–21

Beauty

What one person finds beautiful another sees as only average. The one constant with regard to beauty is that it lasts for only a short time. Whether it is the beauty of a person or of a rose, it will only be here for a moment.

Repeatedly throughout the Bible the reader is cautioned against viewing beauty as more than it really is. Beauty is great, but there are things far more permanent and satisfying.

Key Verses

But the Lord said to Samuel, "Don't judge by his appearance or height, for I have rejected him. The Lord doesn't see things the way you see them. People judge by outward appearance, but the Lord looks at the heart."

1 Samuel 16:7 NLT

Charm is deceitful and beauty is passing, but a woman who fears the Lord, she shall be praised.

Proverbs 31:30 NKJV

He has made everything beautiful in its time. Also, he has put eternity into man's heart, yet so that he cannot find out what God has done from the beginning to the end.

Ecclesiastes 3:11 ESV

Training your body helps you in some ways, but serving God helps you in every way by bringing you blessings in this life and in the future life, too.

1 Timothy 4:8 NCV

What matters is not your outer appearance—the styling of your hair, the jewelry you wear, the cut of your clothes—but your inner disposition. . . . The holy women of old were beautiful before God that way, and were good, loyal wives to their husbands.

1 Peter 3:3, 5 THE MESSAGE

Additional Notable Verses Concerning Beauty

Genesis 12:10–20; Esther 2:1–18; Psalm 27; 50:1–2; 139:14; Song of Solomon 1; 4; Isaiah 52:7; Zechariah 9:16–17

Bible

There is no greater source of information about someone than his or her autobiography. Historical figures who have penned their own stories have left later generations a lasting testament to who they were, what they did, and why they did what they did.

In many ways the Bible exists as God's autobiography. God's Spirit moved men to write the sixty-six books contained in our Bibles to communicate himself to humanity. Why does God allow bad things to happen to good people, or why did He send His Son to die in our place? Instead of taking someone else's word for it, why not just ask the author himself?

Key Verses

The grass withers, the flower fades, when the breath of the Lord blows upon it; surely [all] the people are like grass. The grass withers, the flower fades, but the word of our God will stand forever.

Isaiah 40:7–8 AMP

All Scripture is given by inspiration of God, and is profitable for doctrine, for reproof, for correction, for instruction in righteousness, that the man of God may be complete, thoroughly equipped for every good work.

2 Timothy 3:16–17 NKJV

For the word of God is living and active and sharper than any two-edged sword, and piercing as far as the division of soul and spirit, of both joints and marrow, and able to judge the thoughts and intentions of the heart. And there is no creature hidden from His sight, but all things are open and laid bare to the eyes of Him.

Hebrews 4:12–13 NASB

Additional Notable Verses Concerning the Bible

Deuteronomy 4:2; 12:32; Joshua 1:8–9; Psalm 1; 12:6; 19; 119; Proverbs 30:5–6; Isaiah 55:11; Jeremiah 1:9; Matthew 4:4; 5:18; Luke 8:1–15; John 5:39; 10:34–39; 21:25; Romans 15:4; 2 Thessalonians 2:15; 1 Peter 1:23–25; 2 Peter 3:14–16

Birth Control

In the world of the Bible, pharmacies were not on every street corner the way that they are now in many modern cities. In that time, if one wanted to practice family planning, there was but one good method of achieving it: abstinence. Aside from this fact, there were also a number of benefits to large families, such as additional sources of income and people who could protect and serve the family's interests. Additionally, with high infant mortality rates, losing multiple children before they reached adulthood was commonplace.

Today, modern conveniences and medical advances have given parents both the opportunity to better plan families, as well as to see many more of their children reach adulthood. There are, however, two biblical concerns that must be ever present when considering birth control. First, to God all life is valuable and only He has the right to give or end life. Second, the human life that God is so zealous about begins when that life is conceived.

Key Verses

God blessed them and said to them, Be fruitful, multiply, and fill the earth, and subdue it [using all its vast resources in the service of God and man]; and have dominion over the fish of the sea, the birds of the air, and over every living creature that moves upon the earth.

Genesis 1:28 AMP

Behold, children are a heritage from the Lord, the fruit of the womb a reward. Like arrows in the hand of a warrior are the children of one's youth. Blessed is the man who fills his quiver with them! He shall not be put to shame when he speaks with his enemies in the gate.

Psalm 127:3–5 ESV

Additional Notable Verses Concerning Birth Control
Genesis 9:1–10; 38:1–10; Psalm 139:13–16

The Body

From the earliest days, people have struggled to understand the body. When people think about sin they are almost always picturing something done with the body. If you tell a lie, build an idol, or get in a fistfight, you do so with your body. It is easy to see, then, why some people could decide that the body is evil and wicked, and the soul is actually the good part of you that God saves.

But that conclusion is wrong according to God's Word. The body can be used by our sin nature as an instrument for sin and wickedness, but it can just as easily be used by the Holy Spirit as an implement of love, mercy, and grace.

Key Verses

You made all the delicate, inner parts of my body and knit me together in my mother's womb. Thank you for making me so wonderfully complex! Your workmanship is marvelous—how well I know it.

Psalm 139:13–14 NLT

Some of you say, "We can do anything we want to." But I tell you that not everything is good for us. So I refuse to let anything have power over me. You also say, "Food is meant for our bodies, and our bodies are meant for food." But I tell you that God will destroy them both. We are not supposed to do indecent things with our bodies. We are to use them for the Lord who is in charge of our bodies. . . . You surely know that your body is a temple where the Holy Spirit lives. The Spirit is in you and is a gift from God. You are no longer your own. God paid a great price for you. So use your body to honor God.

1 Corinthians 6:12–13, 19–20 CEV

Additional Notable Verses Concerning the Body

Genesis 1:26–27; Leviticus 19:28; Psalm 51:5; Matthew 6:25–26; Romans 1:24–25; 12:1–8; 1 Corinthians 3:10–17; 9:24–27; 15; 2 Corinthians 5:1–10; Philippians 1:20–22; 3:18–21; 1 Thessalonians 4:3–5; 1 Timothy 4:8–9; James 2:26; 1 Peter 3:3–4

Borrowing

"If you would know the value of money, go and try to borrow some; for he that goes a borrowing goes a sorrowing."* This quote is one of the many dealing with money by American founding father Benjamin Franklin. It is sound and practical advice, but all too often it is wisdom that is foreign to our everyday lives.

The Bible, much like Franklin, does not take a positive outlook on the process and possibility of borrowing. Instead of banning borrowing or lending under all circumstances, the Bible presents borrowing as an unwise action with possible severely negative complications. It turns out that Franklin's idea that it is better to go without than to "go sorrowing" was one he actually borrowed from the Bible.

Key Verses

The rich rules over the poor, and the borrower is servant to the lender.
Proverbs 22:7 NKJV

Do not be one who shakes hands in pledge or puts up security for debts; if you lack the means to pay, your very bed will be snatched from under you.
Proverbs 22:26–27 NIV

Owe nothing to anyone—except for your obligation to love one another. If you love your neighbor, you will fulfill the requirements of God's law.
Romans 13:8 NLT

Additional Notable Verses Concerning Borrowing
Exodus 22:14; Deuteronomy 15:6; 28:44–45; Psalm 37:21; Proverbs 3:27–28; Nehemiah 5:1–13; Matthew 5:38–42

---

*Richard (Philomath) Saunders, *Poor Richard Improved: Being an Almanack and Ephemeris . . . for the Year of our Lord 1758* (Philadelphia: Printed and Sold by B. Franklin and D. Hall) (Yale University Library).

Business

Human beings were designed for business and industry. The desire and competency to undertake a project and see it through to completion is as old as Adam's naming of the animals. Many of the great characters of the Bible were involved in business in one way or another. Abraham, Isaac, Jacob, and Boaz all excelled in business ventures.

Most businessmen and women tend to focus on the bottom line, but that is not how God views business. There is nothing wrong with making money, and that is why businesses exist. There is, however, a right way and a wrong way to do business.

Key Verses

Dishonest scales are an abomination to the Lord, but a just weight is His delight.

Proverbs 11:1 NKJV

Whatever your hand finds to do, do it with all your might; for there is no activity or planning or knowledge or wisdom in Sheol where you are going.

Ecclesiastes 9:10 NASB

No one can serve two masters. The person will hate one master and love the other, or will follow one master and refuse to follow the other. You cannot serve both God and worldly riches.

Matthew 6:24 NCV

Don't you remember the rule we had when we lived with you? "If you don't work, you don't eat." And now we're getting reports that a bunch of lazy good-for-nothings are taking advantage of you. This must not be tolerated. We command them to get to work immediately—no excuses, no arguments—and earn their own keep. Friends, don't slack off in doing your duty.

2 Thessalonians 3:10–13 THE MESSAGE

Additional Notable Verses Concerning Business

Leviticus 19:9–13; 23:22; 25:8–17, 35–55; Deuteronomy 15:1–23; 25:4; 1 Corinthians 10:31; Colossians 3:23–24; 1 Timothy 6:10

Child Abuse

Children should grow up knowing that their parents love them, want the best for them, and would do anything to protect them from harm. One would hope that one of the few things on which everyone could agree would be the care and protection of children. Unfortunately, the world at large—and even some parents—inconceivably ignores and even abuses these most innocent of God's creation.

When one of these horrific man-made tragedies occurs, God's Word is very clear. Not only is the harming of a child something that God takes very seriously, it is also something that He takes very personally. To harm a child is to harm someone God views not only as innocent, but also as His. To participate in such a wicked action is to assure oneself of the judgment of Almighty God.

Key Verses

Even if my father and mother should desert me, you will take care of me.

Psalm 27:10 CEV

But if you cause one of these little ones who trusts in me to fall into sin, it would be better for you to be thrown into the sea with a large millstone hung around your neck.

Mark 9:42 NLT

Fathers, do not provoke your children to anger, but bring them up in the discipline and instruction of the Lord.

Ephesians 6:4 ESV

Additional Notable Verses Concerning Child Abuse

Exodus 21:22–25; Leviticus 18:25; Matthew 18:5–6; 19:13–15; Luke 17:2; Colossians 3:21

Children

To the parent stressed out trying to pay bills, change diapers, drop children off at soccer practice, make PTA meetings, and survive the rest of life, raising children can sometimes feel like a burden. To the church member in the pew straining to hear the sermon over the noises of a rambunctious child, that child feels like a nuisance. Yet when it comes to children, we sometimes forget that we are only seeing the smallest glimmer of what God sees.

Key Verses

Don't you see that children are God's best gift? the fruit of the womb his generous legacy? Like a warrior's fistful of arrows are the children of a vigorous youth. Oh, how blessed are you parents, with your quivers full of children! Your enemies don't stand a chance against you; you'll sweep them right off your doorstep.

Psalm 127:3–5 The Message

Hear, my son, your father's instruction and do not forsake your mother's teaching; indeed, they are a graceful wreath to your head and ornaments about your neck.

Proverbs 1:8–9 NASB

Then the people brought their little children to Jesus so he could put his hands on them and pray for them. His followers told them to stop, but Jesus said, "Let the little children come to me. Don't stop them, because the kingdom of heaven belongs to people who are like these children." After Jesus put his hands on the children, he left there.

Matthew 19:13–15 NCV

Children, obey your parents in everything, for this pleases the Lord.

Colossians 3:20 ESV

Additional Notable Verses Concerning Children

Genesis 15:1–6; Exodus 20:12; Deuteronomy 21:18–21; 27:1–16; 31:9–13; 1 Samuel 1:1–20; 2:12–36; 3:1–21; 2 Chronicles 34:1–3; Psalm 8:2; 148:12–13; Proverbs 3:1–4; 6:20; 10:1; 13:1; 15:5; 17:25; 19:26–27; 22:15; 24:21–22; 28:7; 29:17; 30:11–17; Ecclesiastes 12:1–7; Matthew 15:21–28; Mark 5:21–43; 7:1–13; Ephesians 6:1–3; Hebrews 12:4–11

Church

We often have the wrong mental picture when we hear the word *church*. We might think of buildings or massive cathedrals. Perhaps we even picture a preacher, a group of deacons, pews, offering plates, or a litany of other objects. The church is not an organization, but a body. It is not a building, but a bride. These aren't the images that advertisers would choose first for the church, but they are the ones that God gave us in His Word. That is what makes them worth our time and attention.

Key Verses

And I tell you that you are Peter, and on this rock I will build my church, and the gates of Hades will not overcome it.

Matthew 16:18 NIV

Again I say to you, if two of you agree on earth about anything they ask, it will be done for them by my Father in heaven. For where two or three are gathered in my name, there am I among them.

Matthew 18:19–20 ESV

So guard yourselves and God's people. Feed and shepherd God's flock—his church, purchased with his own blood—over which the Holy Spirit has appointed you as elders.

Acts 20:28 NLT

You Gentiles are no longer strangers and foreigners. You are citizens with everyone else who belongs to the family of God. You are like a building with the apostles and prophets as the foundation and with Christ as the most important stone. Christ is the one who holds the building together and makes it grow into a holy temple for the Lord. And you are part of that building Christ has built as a place for God's own Spirit to live.

Ephesians 2:19–22 CEV

Additional Notable Verses Concerning the Church

Acts 2; Romans 16:17; 1 Corinthians 11; 12:12–31; 2 Corinthians 12:11–21; Ephesians 1:19–23; 4:1–16; Colossians 3:1–13; 1 Timothy 3:1–16; 5; Titus 1–3; Hebrews 13:17; 1 Peter 5:1–11; Revelation 1–3

Civil Disobedience

The Bible clearly teaches that we are to obey governments and civil authorities. The Bible also clearly teaches us that our obedience to God is to be the most important thing in our lives. When the governments of men command us to disobey the Word of God, Christians must consider civil disobedience. It is then and only then that the command to obey human authorities can be set aside in favor of the superior commandment.

Key Verses

Peter and the apostles replied: "We don't obey people. We obey God."

Acts 5:29 CEV

Every person is to be in subjection to the governing authorities. For there is no authority except from God, and those which exist are established by God. Therefore whoever resists authority has opposed the ordinance of God; and they who have opposed will receive condemnation upon themselves. For rulers are not a cause of fear for good behavior, but for evil. Do you want to have no fear of authority? Do what is good and you will have praise from the same; for it is a minister of God to you for good. But if you do what is evil, be afraid; for it does not bear the sword for nothing; for it is a minister of God, an avenger who brings wrath on the one who practices evil. Therefore it is necessary to be in subjection, not only because of wrath, but also for conscience' sake.

Romans 13:1–5 NASB

Submit yourselves for the Lord's sake to every human authority: whether to the emperor, as the supreme authority, or to governors, who are sent by him to punish those who do wrong and to commend those who do right. For it is God's will that by doing good you should silence the ignorant talk of foolish people.

1 Peter 2:13–15 NIV

Additional Notable Verses Concerning Civil Disobedience

Exodus 1–2; Esther 3–7; Daniel 1; 3; 6; Matthew 22:15–22; Mark 15:1–5; Luke 20:1–8; Acts 4:18–20; 7; 1 Timothy 2:1–2; Titus 3:1

Community

The Scriptures teach us that our community of believers functions as our brothers in arms. Without our community of believers, we would be isolated and vulnerable to the enemy's attacks. With our community, we have safety and security to survive Satan's attempts to defeat us.

Key Verses

How wonderful, how beautiful, when brothers and sisters get along! It's like costly anointing oil flowing down head and beard, flowing down Aaron's beard, flowing down the collar of his priestly robes. It's like the dew on Mount Hermon flowing down the slopes of Zion. Yes, that's where God commands the blessing, ordains eternal life.

Psalm 133 THE MESSAGE

And He said to him, "'You shall love the lord your God with all your heart, and with all your soul, and with all your mind.' This is the great and foremost commandment. The second is like it, 'You shall love your neighbor as yourself.' On these two commandments depend the whole Law and the Prophets."

Matthew 22:37–40 NASB

Brethren, if any person is overtaken in misconduct or sin of any sort, you who are spiritual [who are responsive to and controlled by the Spirit] should set him right and restore and reinstate him, without any sense of superiority and with all gentleness, keeping an attentive eye on yourself, lest you should be tempted also. Bear (endure, carry) one another's burdens and troublesome moral faults, and in this way fulfill and observe perfectly the law of Christ (the Messiah) and complete what is lacking [in your obedience to it].

Galatians 6:1–2 AMP

And let us consider how to stir up one another to love and good works, not neglecting to meet together, as is the habit of some, but encouraging one another, and all the more as you see the Day drawing near.

Hebrews 10:24–25 ESV

Additional Notable Verses Concerning Community

John 17; Acts 2:42–47; Romans 12:3–13; 1 Thessalonians 5:14; 1 John 1:5–7; 2:9–11

Compassion

Today we speak of compassion as "coming from the heart." At the time and places in which the Bible was written, the guts rather than the heart were thought of as the place where emotion originated. When we see a passage, for example, saying that Jesus was "moved with compassion," the word being used for *move* is the same one used to mean move one's bowels.

This idea might make you cringe a little bit, but if you can get past the visual image, there is something about it that makes a lot of sense. Compassion is not something that is passive; it is an action. There is no such thing as a compassionate observer. Compassion requires movement. To show compassion is not to exhibit an emotion, but rather to run to the aid of the one in need.

Key Verses

The Lord answered, "Could a mother forget a child who nurses at her breast? Could she fail to love an infant who came from her own body? Even if a mother could forget, I will never forget you."

Isaiah 49:15 CEV

The people saw them going, and many recognized them and ran there together on foot from all the cities, and got there ahead of them. When Jesus went ashore, He saw a large crowd, and He felt compassion for them because they were like sheep without a shepherd; and He began to teach them many things.

Mark 6:33–34 NASB

Summing up: Be agreeable, be sympathetic, be loving, be compassionate, be humble. That goes for all of you, no exceptions. No retaliation. No sharp-tongued sarcasm. Instead, bless—that's your job, to bless. You'll be a blessing and also get a blessing.

1 Peter 3:8–9 THE MESSAGE

But whoso hath this world's good, and seeth his brother have need, and shutteth up his bowels of compassion from him, how dwelleth the love of God in him?

1 John 3:17 KJV

Additional Notable Verses Concerning Compassion

2 Samuel 9; 17:27–29; Proverbs 19:17; Matthew 9:36; 10:42; 14:14; Luke 10:25–37; 15; 19:41–42; Romans 12:15; 1 Corinthians 12:25–26; 2 Corinthians 1:3–7; Galatians 6:2; Ephesians 4:32; Colossians 3:12–17; Hebrews 5:1–10; 13:3; 2 Peter 3:9

Competition

Sometimes it seems like the world is one big competition. Employees compete for raises, children compete for attention, and students compete for class rank. Then everyone comes home, and to relax they watch a group of people compete in sports. With competition seeping into every area of life, it is no wonder that some people are just worn out from all of the winning and losing.

How refreshing it is to come to the Bible and to see that the spiritual life is not a competition. Sure, there are rewards, but those are not based on how well you stacked up against the competition, but rather on how much you did with what God gave you.

Key Verses

You've all been to the stadium and seen the athletes race. Everyone runs; one wins. Run to win. All good athletes train hard. They do it for a gold medal that tarnishes and fades. You're after one that's gold eternally. I don't know about you, but I'm running hard for the finish line. I'm giving it everything I've got. No sloppy living for me! I'm staying alert and in top condition. I'm not going to get caught napping, telling everyone else all about it and then missing out myself.

1 Corinthians 9:24–27 THE MESSAGE

The answer is, if you eat or drink, or if you do anything, do it all for the glory of God.

1 Corinthians 10:31 NCV

Do nothing from selfishness or empty conceit, but with humility of mind regard one another as more important than yourselves; do not merely look out for your own personal interests, but also for the interests of others.

Philippians 2:3–4 NASB

Additional Notable Verses Concerning Competition
Psalm 108:13; Ecclesiastes 2:22–26; Matthew 6:33; Galatians 6:2–4; 6:14; Colossians 3:17; 3:23–25; James 4:6

Confession

What makes the Bible's approach to sin and wrongdoing so unique is that more than merely admitting to sin or saying "I'm sorry," confession says that the one confessing agrees with God about his or her sin. To truly repent from sin we must not just accept negative consequences; we must change our minds.

The word translated "confess" is also translated "acknowledge" in many places. God repeatedly states that if we acknowledge Him, He will acknowledge us.

Key Verses

Then I acknowledged my sin to you and did not cover up my iniquity. I said, "I will confess my transgressions to the Lord." And you forgave the guilt of my sin.

Psalm 32:5 NIV

Because if you acknowledge and confess with your lips that Jesus is Lord and in your heart believe (adhere to, trust in, and rely on the truth) that God raised Him from the dead, you will be saved. For with the heart a person believes (adheres to, trusts in, and relies on Christ) and so is justified (declared righteous, acceptable to God), and with the mouth he confesses (declares openly and speaks out freely his faith) and confirms [his] salvation.

Romans 10:9–10 AMP

If we say we have no sin, we deceive ourselves, and the truth is not in us. If we confess our sins, he is faithful and just to forgive us our sins and to cleanse us from all unrighteousness.

1 John 1:8–9 ESV

Additional Notable Verses Concerning Confession

Leviticus 16; 26:40–42; Numbers 5:5–7; 1 Kings 8:33–36; 2 Chronicles 6:24–27; Psalm 38:18; Isaiah 26:13; Matthew 9:6–8; 10:32–33; Luke 12:8–12; John 1:43–51; 9:22–38; 11:17–27; 12:27–43; Philippians 2:9–11; 2 Timothy 2:11–13; James 5:16; 1 John 2:22–23; 4:1–21; Revelation 3:5

Confidence

George Herman "Babe" Ruth never lacked for confidence as a baseball player. One legendary story of the 1932 World Series, which baseball historians hotly debate, says that "The Babe" even pointed his bat to the outfield fence before a pitch, predicting a home run. On the very next pitch Ruth smacked the ball well over 400 feet, and the tale of his "called shot" has grown over the years.

To the world, Babe Ruth's home run prediction—if it did indeed happen—is the perfect example of confidence. To the biblical record, an action such as Babe's is not confidence, but foolishness. True confidence does not reside in our own talents and abilities, but rather it finds its source and focus in God. Confidence in anything but the Almighty is misplaced.

Key Verses

Some trust in chariots and some in horses, but we trust in the name of the Lord our God.

Psalm 20:7 NIV

For the Lord will be your confidence and will keep your foot from being caught.

Proverbs 3:26 NASB

In the fear of the Lord one has strong confidence, and his children will have a refuge.

Proverbs 14:26 ESV

Not that we are sufficient of ourselves to think of anything as being from ourselves, but our sufficiency is from God.

2 Corinthians 3:5 NKJV

Additional Notable Verses Concerning Confidence

Nehemiah 6:16; Job 4:6; 22:29; Psalm 27:1–3; 71:5; 78:7; Proverbs 25:19; Isaiah 32:17; Ezekiel 29:16; 2 Corinthians 1:12–22; 3:1–6; Philippians 3:1–11; 1 Timothy 3:13; 6:17; Hebrews 3:6; 4:16; 10:19, 35; James 4:13–15; 1 John 3:20–22; 4:17; 5:14

Conflict Resolution

L ife will never have a shortage of conflicts. When Job, certainly no stranger to difficulties, says, "Man, who is born of woman, is short-lived and full of turmoil" (14:1 NASB), there are plenty of people who are tempted to utter a loud "Amen!" At times, life can seem like one conflict after another, or even just one big, long conflict.

Rather than advising us to skirt our problems or to push them away, God's Word directs us to meet our problems directly. We are to deal with them in ways that honor and glorify God, even if those ways are not always pleasant for us.

Key Verses

A gentle response defuses anger, but a sharp tongue kindles a temper-fire.
Proverbs 15:1 THE MESSAGE

One day Jesus said to his disciples, "There will always be temptations to sin, but what sorrow awaits the person who does the tempting! It would be better to be thrown into the sea with a millstone hung around your neck than to cause one of these little ones to fall into sin. So watch yourselves! "If another believer sins, rebuke that person; then if there is repentance, forgive. Even if that person wrongs you seven times a day and each time turns again and asks forgiveness, you must forgive."
Luke 17:1–4 NLT

Never pay back evil for evil to anyone. Respect what is right in the sight of all men. If possible, so far as it depends on you, be at peace with all men. Never take your own revenge, beloved, but leave room for the wrath of God, for it is written, "Vengeance is mine, I will repay," says the Lord.
Romans 12:17–19 NASB

Additional Notable Verses Concerning Conflict Resolution
Leviticus 19:17–18; Proverbs 18:19; Matthew 5:9, 21–26; 18:15–35; Luke 6:27–36; 1 Corinthians 6:1–11; 13; Ephesians 4:26–32; Colossians 3:11–14

Contentment

Self-help books and motivational speakers do not make money urging people to be content with their lives. When you think about it, not much of our world would be the same if everyone listed contentment as one of their goals. Products in stores are designed to capitalize on people's lack of contentment. You must drive a particular car, eat at a particular restaurant, or use a particular phone because if you do not, other people will have something that you do not have.

Our modern world may not value contentment, but it is something that God finds very valuable. You will not see it advertised on your television, but contentment is something worth obtaining.

Key Verses

The Lord gives perfect peace to those whose faith is firm.

Isaiah 26:3 CEV

I am not saying this because I am in need, for I have learned to be content whatever the circumstances. I know what it is to be in need, and I know what it is to have plenty. I have learned the secret of being content in any and every situation, whether well fed or hungry, whether living in plenty or in want. I can do all this through him who gives me strength.

Philippians 4:11–13 NIV

Yet true godliness with contentment is itself great wealth. After all, we brought nothing with us when we came into the world, and we can't take anything with us when we leave it. So if we have enough food and clothing, let us be content.

1 Timothy 6:6–8 NLT

Let your conduct be without covetousness; be content with such things as you have. For He Himself has said, "I will never leave you nor forsake you."

Hebrews 13:5 NKJV

Additional Notable Verses Concerning Contentment
Psalm 37:16; Proverbs 17:1; Ecclesiastes 5:10; Matthew 6:19–24; Luke 3:14; 12:13–21; 2 Corinthians 12:10; Philippians 3:7–8; 4:19

Counsel

Many law firms have lawyers on staff who are referred to as "of counsel." These are attorneys who are employed by the firm, but are neither associates nor partners. These attorneys practice law, but their function is that of an advisory nature. These attorneys will not bring the case to trial, but their role as advisors is indispensable to the firm's ability to function.

Those who are not attorneys would do well to learn a lesson from the legal profession. It would be wise for all of God's children to have a group of people in their lives who function as their own personal "of counsel." These people will not be able to make your decisions for you or live your life for you, but their role as advisors will be indispensable to your ability to navigate life.

Key Verses

Blessed is the man who walks not in the counsel of the wicked, nor stands in the way of sinners, nor sits in the seat of scoffers; but his delight is in the law of the Lord, and on his law he meditates day and night.

Psalm 1:1–2 ESV

The Lord nullifies the counsel of the nations; He frustrates the plans of the peoples. The counsel of the Lord stands forever, the plans of His heart from generation to generation.

Psalm 33:10–11 NASB

Let the wise listen to these proverbs and become even wiser. Let those with understanding receive guidance.

Proverbs 1:5 NLT

Additional Notable Verses Concerning Counsel

Exodus 18; 2 Samuel 15:13–37; 17:1–29; 1 Kings 12:1–20; Ezra 10:3; Job 12:13; Psalm 2:1–3; 73:24; Proverbs 1:20–33; 8; 13:10; 19:20–21; 21:30; 27:9

Courage

You can find out a lot about a concept by looking at who talks about it. Take courage, for example. Do a little research and you will find that Martin Luther King, Jr., Albert Einstein, Abraham Lincoln, Winston Churchill, Confucius, Mark Twain, Benjamin Franklin, William Shakespeare, C. S. Lewis, Steve Jobs, John Wayne, Aristotle, and hundreds more had something to say about courage.

For the believer, courage is more than just the difference between average and successful. It is the quality that the Holy Spirit uses to take timid children of God and turn them into bold people willing to speak the truth despite untold adversity.

Key Verses

Be brave and strong! Don't be afraid of the nations on the other side of the Jordan. The Lord your God will always be at your side, and he will never abandon you.

Deuteronomy 31:6 CEV

Be of good courage, and He shall strengthen your heart, all you who hope in the Lord.

Psalm 31:24 NKJV

These things I have spoken to you, so that in Me you may have peace. In the world you have tribulation, but take courage; I have overcome the world.

John 16:33 NASB

For God did not give us a spirit of timidity (of cowardice, of craven and cringing and fawning fear), but [He has given us a spirit] of power and of love and of calm and well-balanced mind and discipline and self-control.

2 Timothy 1:7 AMP

Additional Notable Verses Concerning Courage

Joshua 1:1–9; 1 Samuel 17:1–54; 1 Chronicles 22:11–13; 28:20; 2 Chronicles 32:1–8; Psalm 27:14; Isaiah 35:4; Daniel 10:19; Haggai 2:4; Matthew 9:1–8, 18–26; 14:23–33; Mark 6:45–52; 15:43; Acts 23:1–11; 27:14–44; 1 Corinthians 16:13; 2 Corinthians 5:6–10; Ephesians 6:10–20; Philippians 1:12–14, 27–28

Covenant

Biblical covenants, like those between God and Abraham, God and David, as well as God and Israel, are not mere handshakes or loose associations. These covenants are legally binding and carry the force of contracts. That is why it is so important to note that God's relationship with His people is based on covenants that He has entered into. When God makes a promise, His Word is sure, and He never goes back on a covenant.

Key Verses

He's God, our God, in charge of the whole earth. And he remembers, remembers his Covenant—for a thousand generations he's been as good as his word. It's the Covenant he made with Abraham, the same oath he swore to Isaac, the very statute he established with Jacob, the eternal Covenant with Israel, namely, "I give you the land. Canaan is your hill-country inheritance."
Psalm 105:7–11 THE MESSAGE

What I mean is this: The law, introduced 430 years later, does not set aside the covenant previously established by God and thus do away with the promise.
Galatians 3:17 NIV

Now may the God of peace who brought up our Lord Jesus from the dead, that great Shepherd of the sheep, through the blood of the everlasting covenant, make you complete in every good work to do His will, working in you what is well pleasing in His sight, through Jesus Christ, to whom be glory forever and ever. Amen.
Hebrews 13:20–21 NKJV

Additional Notable Verses Concerning Covenant(s)
Genesis 15:7–18; 17:1–14; 26:26–33; 28:10–22; 1 Samuel 18:1–5; 2 Samuel 23:1–7; Nehemiah 13:23–31; Psalm 74:18–20; 89:1–37; 106; 111:9; Isaiah 42:6; 54:10; 55:1–3; 59; 61; Jeremiah 31:31–34; 33:19–22; 34:8–22; 50:1–5; Ezekiel 16; 17:11–24; Micah 7:7–20; Malachi 2:1–9; 3:1; Luke 1:67–80; Romans 11:26–31; Galatians 3; Ephesians 2:12; Hebrews 6:13–20; 8:1–9:28; 10:26–31; 12:18–24

Creation

All types of people are involved in creation. Artists, builders, seam-stresses, and myriad other people expend much effort to create brilliant works of art and other tremendous fabrications. There is one thing that all of these creations have in common. From quilts to cathedrals, all man-made creations require that substance and matter already be in existence.

When God does a work of creation He does not require that the substance of his creation already be in existence. When God created the world, it was what theologians refer to as *ex nihilo* or "out of nothing." When we create, we can only use what is available to us. When God creates, He has no such limitations.

Key Verses

In the beginning God created the heavens and the earth.
Genesis 1:1 NKJV

He is the image of the invisible God, the firstborn of all creation. For by Him all things were created, both in the heavens and on earth, visible and invisible, whether thrones or dominions or rulers or authorities—all things have been created through Him and for Him. He is before all things, and in Him all things hold together.
Colossians 1:15–17 NASB

By faith we understand that the entire universe was formed at God's command, that what we now see did not come from anything that can be seen.
Hebrews 11:3 NLT

Additional Notable Verses Concerning Creation
Genesis 1:1–2:25; Exodus 20:11; 31:17; Job 26:12–14; Psalm 8:3–4; 19:1–6; 104:5; 124:8; 136:5; 148:4–6; Proverbs 16:4; Isaiah 40:25–31; 45:18; Matthew 19:1–6; John 1:1–4; Romans 1; 2 Corinthians 4:6; 1 Timothy 4:4; 2 Peter 3:5; Revelation 4:11

Crime

Scarcely have the pages of the Bible begun to turn and the story turns into a police procedural. The story of Cain and Abel in Genesis chapter four takes the history of mankind from Adam and Eve violating God's laws to Cain committing murder.

Not long after Cain's murder of his brother, human beings display a cunning ability to lie, cheat, steal, commit violence, and violate pretty much every law ever written. By the end of the book of Genesis it is clear that humans beings violate God's standard of perfection and commit heinous acts against one another as well. The Bible makes no secret about the true state of humanity. We are all far from innocent.

Key Verses

But your own lifeblood I will avenge; I will avenge it against both animals and other humans. Whoever sheds human blood, by humans let his blood be shed, because God made humans in his image reflecting God's very nature.

Genesis 9:5–6 THE MESSAGE

Never take your own revenge, beloved, but leave room for the wrath of God, for it is written, "Vengeance is mine, I will repay," says the Lord.

Romans 12:19 NASB

Or do you not know that the unrighteous will not inherit the kingdom of God? Do not be deceived: neither the sexually immoral, nor idolaters, nor adulterers, nor men who practice homosexuality, nor thieves, nor the greedy, nor drunkards, nor revilers, nor swindlers will inherit the kingdom of God. And such were some of you. But you were washed, you were sanctified, you were justified in the name of the Lord Jesus Christ and by the Spirit of our God.

1 Corinthians 6:9–11 ESV

Additional Notable Verses Concerning Crime
Exodus 20:1–17; 22:1–31; Matthew 5:38–42; Luke 10:30–37; Romans 13:1–7

Criticism

Criticism can be very difficult to handle. It takes a very mature and grounded person to be able to handle fierce criticism with grace, dignity, and even humor. Former British Prime Minister Margaret Thatcher was no stranger to criticism. She dealt with it so often that she was once quoted as saying, "If my critics saw me walking over the Thames they would say it was because I couldn't swim."*

Most of us do not have the self-restraint and wisdom of Margaret Thatcher. When we are criticized, we want to strike back, to react, to put critics in their place. Though criticizing the critics may make us feel better temporarily, it is the exact opposite of what God's Word teaches.

Key Verses

A soft answer turns away wrath, but grievous words stir up anger. The tongue of the wise utters knowledge rightly, but the mouth of the [self-confident] fool pours out folly.

Proverbs 15:1–2 AMP

Don't condemn others, and God won't condemn you. God will be as hard on you as you are on others! He will treat you exactly as you treat them. You can see the speck in your friend's eye, but you don't notice the log in your own eye. How can you say, "My friend, let me take the speck out of your eye," when you don't see the log in your own eye? You're nothing but show-offs! First, take the log out of your own eye. Then you can see how to take the speck out of your friend's eye.

Matthew 7:1–5 CEV

Put on then, as God's chosen ones, holy and beloved, compassionate hearts, kindness, humility, meekness, and patience, bearing with one another and, if one has a complaint against another, forgiving each other; as the Lord has forgiven you, so you also must forgive.

Colossians 3:12–13 ESV

Additional Notable Verses Concerning Criticism
Joshua 1:9; 2 Kings 2:23–24; Proverbs 9:9–10; 12:1; Ephesians 4:2, 26–27; Colossians 4:6; 1 Peter 2:23

---

*Editors of New Word City, *Margaret Thatcher: A Life* (New Word City, 2011).

Cruelty

Dictionary definitions of cruelty always include the idea of intentionally causing pain or harm to other people or even animals. This intentional causing of pain actually gives the cruel person enjoyment. Cruelty is a special brand of evil that not only does wrong but also finds pleasure and delight in the pain that it has caused.

It should come as no surprise that God is not only opposed to cruelty but has also promised to meet cruelty with judgment. Whenever someone attempts to be cruel, they will suffer the consequences—both the natural results of their actions and God's intervention to make sure that the cruel learn their lesson.

Key Verses

When you're kind to others, you help yourself; when you're cruel to others, you hurt yourself.

Proverbs 11:17 THE MESSAGE

The godly care for their animals, but the wicked are always cruel.

Proverbs 12:10 NLT

Additional Notable Verses Concerning Cruelty

Genesis 34; 49:7; 50:15–21; Deuteronomy 25:4; Job 30:21; Proverbs 5:1–9; Isaiah 13:9; 19:4; Jeremiah 6:22–23; 30:14; 50:42; Lamentations 4:3

Dancing

The topic of dancing shows us why it is so important to study what the Bible actually says. Throughout the twentieth and twenty-first centuries, Christians—particularly those in America—have struggled with imposing their own standards on people rather than God's standards.

Dancing in the Scriptures was something that, depending on how and why it was done, could honor and glorify God. Done for the wrong purposes and for the wrong reasons, it was something that could offend and bring dishonor.

Key Verses

Let them praise his name in dance; strike up the band and make great music! And why? Because God delights in his people, festoons plain folk with salvation garlands!

Psalm 149:3–4 THE MESSAGE

Praise the Lord! Praise God in his sanctuary; praise him in his mighty heaven! Praise him for his mighty works; praise his unequaled greatness! Praise him with a blast of the ram's horn; praise him with the lyre and harp! Praise him with the tambourine and dancing; praise him with strings and flutes! Praise him with a clash of cymbals; praise him with loud clanging cymbals. Let everything that breathes sing praises to the Lord! Praise the Lord!

Psalm 150 NLT

Additional Notable Verses Concerning Dancing

Exodus 15:1–21; 2 Samuel 6:12–23; 1 Chronicles 15:25–29; Psalm 30:11; Ecclesiastes 3:1–4; Jeremiah 31:1–14; Lamentations 5:15; Matthew 11:16–19

Dating

A trip through your local bookstore will yield no shortage of books and resources on dating. There are books that tell you how to date, books that tell you not to date, books that tell you the purpose of dating, books about whom to date, and even books that tell you to date yourself. Those interested in the topic may very quickly realize that they have more books on dating than actual dates.

Even though relationships, how they come about, and how they progress have changed a lot since Adam first met Eve, the Scriptures have a lot of wisdom for the person seeking a mate. Over the thousands of years since Moses penned the story of the first couple, the important things have stayed the same. Keeping God first, keeping yourself pure, and sacrificing yourself for the other person are all just as foundational today as they were then. And a relationship with God's Word as the foundation is well on its way to success.

Key Verses

He who finds a wife finds a good thing, and obtains favor from the Lord.
Proverbs 18:22 NKJV

Daughters of Jerusalem, I charge you by the gazelles and by the does of the field: Do not arouse or awaken love until it so desires.
Song of Solomon 2:7 NIV

For this is the will of God, your sanctification: that you abstain from sexual immorality; that each one of you know how to control his own body in holiness and honor, not in the passion of lust like the Gentiles who do not know God.
1 Thessalonians 4:3–5 ESV

Love each other with genuine affection, and take delight in honoring each other.
Romans 12:10 NLT

Additional Notable Verses Concerning Dating
Proverbs 4:23; Matthew 5:27–30; 1 Corinthians 6:12–20; 7; 13; 2 Corinthians 6:14–15; 1 Timothy 5:2

Death

There are few experiences that are truly universal. How ironic that death, the thing that so many try to avoid and some even refuse to acknowledge, is the one thing that is inescapable by all. It should come as no surprise, then, that God's Word has much to say about the end of life. Why people die, what happens when we die, and how to live life before death are all things that the Scriptures are very concerned about. Thankfully, not only is death universal, but the Bible's wisdom about it is too.

Key Verses

God, my shepherd! I don't need a thing. You have bedded me down in lush meadows, you find me quiet pools to drink from. True to your word, you let me catch my breath and send me in the right direction. Even when the way goes through Death Valley, I'm not afraid when you walk at my side. Your trusty shepherd's crook makes me feel secure.

Psalm 23:1–4 THE MESSAGE

For none of us lives to himself, and none of us dies to himself. For if we live, we live to the Lord, and if we die, we die to the Lord. So then, whether we live or whether we die, we are the Lord's.

Romans 14:7–8 ESV

And as it is appointed for men to die once, but after this the judgment, so Christ was offered once to bear the sins of many. To those who eagerly wait for Him He will appear a second time, apart from sin, for salvation.

Hebrews 9:27–28 NKJV

Additional Notable Verses Concerning Death

Genesis 3:19; Job 14; Psalm 39:4–5; 115:17; Proverbs 14:32; Ecclesiastes 3:2; 9:5–6; 12:1–8; Ezekiel 18:32; Matthew 10:28; Luke 20:27–38; John 11:1–44; Romans 5:6–21; 6; 14:5–9; 1 Corinthians 15; 2 Corinthians 5:1–10; Philippians 1:21; 1 Thessalonians 4:13–18; 1 Timothy 6:7; 1 Peter 2:24; Revelation 1:18; 21:1–8

Death Penalty

Through the years everything from the dunce cap to the guillotine has been used in an attempt to deter one type of behavior or another. At the core of a just society a punishment would not be primarily meant to dispense revenge to an offender, but rather to set down a standard of behavior with consequences for offenses.

Since the time of Noah the taking of a person's life as a form of punishment was part of biblical revelation. Even though the death penalty was prescribed, there are few instances of it actually being implemented in the Scriptures. Though it was at times justified, even in cases of the most heinous offenses grace and forgiveness were still possibilities.

Key Verses

Whoever kills a human being will be killed by a human being, because God made humans in his own image.

Genesis 9:6 NCV

But if there is further damage, then you must give life for life—eye for eye, tooth for tooth, hand for hand, foot for foot, burn for burn, wound for wound, bruise for bruise.

Exodus 21:23–25 THE MESSAGE

They have become filled with every kind of wickedness, evil, greed and depravity. They are full of envy, murder, strife, deceit and malice. They are gossips, slanderers, God-haters, insolent, arrogant and boastful; they invent ways of doing evil; they disobey their parents; they have no understanding, no fidelity, no love, no mercy. Although they know God's righteous decree that those who do such things deserve death, they not only continue to do these very things but also approve of those who practice them.

Romans 1:29–32 NIV

Additional Notable Verses Concerning the Death Penalty

Exodus 20:13; 21:12–36; Leviticus 24:10–23; Numbers 35:15–34; Deuteronomy 13:1–11; 19:7–13; Matthew 5:38–42; Acts 25:10–11; Romans 12:19

Decision Making

One of the most beneficial aspects of the Bible is that its characters exist as examples, encouragements, and warnings to all those who come after them. These examples can teach us what to do, what not to do, and much more.

There is much to learn from the examples of biblical characters in the area of decision making. From Abraham and King Saul we learn that fear can force us to make bad decisions (Genesis 20; 1 Samuel 15). From Daniel we learn that consistency of character helps us to make wise decisions (Daniel 6). And from Jesus we learn that our actions and decisions reveal what is in our hearts (Luke 6:45).

The Bible can teach us how to make our decisions, but the one thing it cannot do is make our decisions for us. That is up to us.

Key Verses

Thy word is a lamp unto my feet, and a light unto my path.
Psalm 119:105 KJV

Trust in the Lord with all your heart and do not lean on your own understanding. In all your ways acknowledge Him, and He will make your paths straight.
Proverbs 3:5–6 NASB

If any of you need wisdom, you should ask God, and it will be given to you. God is generous and won't correct you for asking.
James 1:5 CEV

Additional Notable Verses Concerning Decision Making
Joshua 24:15; 1 Kings 3:5–15; Nehemiah 1:1–11; Job 2:9–10; Proverbs 11:14; 14:12; Jeremiah 29:11; 1 Corinthians 10:31; Galatians 6:7–8; Hebrews 11:6; 1 Peter 1:13; 5:8; 1 John 5:14

Demons

Demons are a subject that one must study carefully. As C. S. Lewis said, "There are two equal and opposite errors into which our race can fall about the devils. One is to disbelieve in their existence. The other is to believe, and to feel an excessive and unhealthy interest in them. They themselves are equally pleased by both errors and hail a materialist or a magician with the same delight."*

In the pages of Scripture we find exactly what God wanted us to know about the forces of evil. We should know what His Word says, but we should also be careful to stop studying where the Bible stops revealing.

Key Verses

They provoked Him to jealousy with foreign gods; with abominations they provoked Him to anger. They sacrificed to demons, not to God, to gods they did not know, to new gods, new arrivals that your fathers did not fear.

Deuteronomy 32:16–17 NKJV

For our struggle is not against flesh and blood, but against the rulers, against the powers, against the world forces of this darkness, against the spiritual forces of wickedness in the heavenly places.

Ephesians 6:12 NASB

You say you have faith, for you believe that there is one God. Good for you! Even the demons believe this, and they tremble in terror.

James 2:19 NLT

Additional Notable Verses Concerning Demons

Leviticus 20:27; Psalm 106:37; Daniel 10:11–13; Matthew 8:28–34; 12:22–30; 25:41; Mark 3:10–12; 5:1–20; 6:7; 9:14–29; Acts 16:16–20; Romans 8:31–39; 1 Corinthians 10:18–20; 2 Corinthians 11:3–4; 2 Peter 2:1–9; 1 John 4:1–2; Jude 1:6; Revelation 12:7–9; 16:12–16

---

*C. S. Lewis, The Screwtape Letters: With Screwtape Proposes a Toast (San Francisco: HarperSanFrancisco, 2001), ix.

Despair

I n the classic book *Pilgrim's Progress,* the main character, Christian, and his companion, Hopeful, encounter the Giant Despair on their way to their destination, the Celestial City. The giant imprisons the two travelers, throwing them in the dungeon of his castle, where they are beaten and starved and the giant urges them to commit suicide.

Though John Bunyan wrote of Christian's struggle with Despair well over three centuries ago, it is very similar to the struggles of many people today. Despair can seem like a giant far too large to overcome. It beats you down and seems to constantly have the upper hand. In *Pilgrim's Progress,* Christian and Hopeful escape from the Giant Despair using a key called Promise. The key to overcoming despair is to cling to God's promises in His Word in the same way.

Key Verses

My days come and go swifter than the click of knitting needles, and then the yarn runs out—an unfinished life! God, don't forget that I'm only a puff of air! These eyes have had their last look at goodness. And your eyes have seen the last of me; even while you're looking, there'll be nothing left to look at.

Job 7:6–8 THE MESSAGE

The righteous cry out, and the Lord hears them; he delivers them from all their troubles. The Lord is close to the brokenhearted and saves those who are crushed in spirit. The righteous person may have many troubles, but the Lord delivers him from them all; he protects all his bones, not one of them will be broken.

Psalm 34:17–20 NIV

Additional Notable Verses Concerning Despair
Job 24:22; Psalm 27:13–14; 42; 126:4–5; 142; Isaiah 61:1–3; Lamentations 3:18; John 16:33; 2 Corinthians 4:7–12; 12:1–10

Disabilities

When God created the world, it was perfect. All was without blemish and just as the Creator intended—then sin entered the world.

The Scriptures teach us that disabilities are caused by sin. Not the sin of the individual, but the sin of Adam and Eve. They also teach that because of the sin that entered the world all humanity is disabled, even if they do not know it.

Key Verses

Then the Lord said to him, "Who has made man's mouth? Who makes him mute, or deaf, or seeing, or blind? Is it not I, the Lord?"

Exodus 4:11 ESV

You shall not curse the deaf or put a stumbling block before the blind, but you shall [reverently] fear your God. I am the Lord.

Leviticus 19:14 AMP

As Jesus walked along, he saw a man who had been blind since birth. Jesus' disciples asked, "Teacher, why was this man born blind? Was it because he or his parents sinned?"

"No, it wasn't!" Jesus answered. "But because of his blindness, you will see God work a miracle for him. As long as it is day, we must do what the one who sent me wants me to do. When night comes, no one can work. While I am in the world, I am the light for the world."

After Jesus said this, he spit on the ground. He made some mud and smeared it on the man's eyes. Then he said, "Go and wash off the mud in Siloam Pool." The man went and washed in Siloam, which means "One Who Is Sent." When he had washed off the mud, he could see.

John 9:1–7 CEV

Additional Notable Verses Concerning Disabilities

2 Samuel 9:1–13; Matthew 11:4–5; Mark 2:1–12; 7:32–37; 8:22–26; Luke 14:12–14; John 5:1–14; 2 Corinthians 12:7–10

Disappointment

Everyone who lives on planet earth, in a world that has fallen away from God and is full of sin and sinners, will eventually experience disappointment.

Disappointment has no cure, but it does have an antidote. Hopes and dreams that are dependent on frail human beings will always fall short, but a faith that rests upon the God of the Bible will ultimately be fulfilled.

Key Verses

But You are holy, O You Who dwell in [the holy place where] the praises of Israel [are offered]. Our fathers trusted in You; they trusted (leaned on, relied on You, and were confident) and You delivered them. They cried to You and were delivered; they trusted in, leaned on, and confidently relied on You, and were not ashamed or confounded or disappointed.

Psalm 22:3–5 AMP

Not only that, we rejoice in our sufferings, knowing that suffering produces endurance, and endurance produces character, and character produces hope, and hope does not put us to shame, because God's love has been poured into our hearts through the Holy Spirit who has been given to us.

Romans 5:3–5 ESV

That is the way we should live, because God's grace that can save everyone has come. It teaches us not to live against God nor to do the evil things the world wants to do. Instead, that grace teaches us to live in the present age in a wise and right way and in a way that shows we serve God. We should live like that while we wait for our great hope and the coming of the glory of our great God and Savior Jesus Christ.

Titus 2:11–13 NCV

Additional Notable Verses Concerning Disappointment
Romans 8:18–30; Philippians 4:6–7; 1 Peter 5:6–7

Discernment

We live in a world that prides itself on the ability to hide the truth. Frequently professional athletes are caught using performance-enhancing drugs, magazine cover photographs of famous people are doctored, and our television screens are deluged with scripted programs that purport to be reality shows.

For the believer, it is not just the world of advertising and entertainment that seeks to fool you. No, there is an entire world system, including Satan and his forces, that seeks to trick the child of God into believing lies and disbelieving God's truth. It is only through knowing the truth of Scripture that we can truly begin to see through the deceptions.

Key Verses

Now therefore, O kings, show discernment; take warning, O judges of the earth.

Psalm 2:10 NASB

And this is my prayer: that your love may abound more and more in knowledge and depth of insight, so that you may be able to discern what is best and may be pure and blameless for the day of Christ, filled with the fruit of righteousness that comes through Jesus Christ—to the glory and praise of God.

Philippians 1:9–11 NIV

Dear friends, do not believe everyone who claims to speak by the Spirit. You must test them to see if the spirit they have comes from God. For there are many false prophets in the world. This is how we know if they have the Spirit of God: If a person claiming to be a prophet acknowledges that Jesus Christ came in a real body, that person has the Spirit of God.

1 John 4:1–2 NLT

Additional Notable Verses Concerning Discernment

1 Kings 3:1–9; Psalm 119:66; Proverbs 2:3; 1 Corinthians 2:6, 10–15; 2 Corinthians 11:1–15; Colossians 2:8; 1 Timothy 6:3–5; Hebrews 4:12; 5:14

Discipleship

J esus' words in Matthew 28:19–20, "Go therefore and make disciples of all the nations, baptizing them in the name of the Father and the Son and the Holy Spirit, teaching them to observe all that I commanded you; and lo, I am with you always, even to the end of the age" (NASB) are called the Great Commision, the mission statement for those who follow Christ. Despite the popularity of these verses, and the frequency with which they are quoted, it seems that we often miss the point. At the core of this "mission statement" is the idea of discipleship.

Key Verses

And he said to all, "If anyone would come after me, let him deny himself and take up his cross daily and follow me. For whoever would save his life will lose it, but whoever loses his life for my sake will save it. For what does it profit a man if he gains the whole world and loses or forfeits himself? For whoever is ashamed of me and of my words, of him will the Son of Man be ashamed when he comes in his glory and the glory of the Father and of the holy angels."

Luke 9:23–26 ESV

Anyone who comes to me but refuses to let go of father, mother, spouse, children, brothers, sisters—yes, even one's own self!—can't be my disciple. Anyone who won't shoulder his own cross and follow behind me can't be my disciple. Is there anyone here who, planning to build a new house, doesn't first sit down and figure the cost so you'll know if you can complete it? If you only get the foundation laid and then run out of money, you're going to look pretty foolish. Everyone passing by will poke fun at you: "He started something he couldn't finish."

Luke 14:26–30 THE MESSAGE

Additional Notable Verses Concerning Discipleship
Matthew 7:12; 10:32–39; 16:24–28; 28:18–20; Mark 3:13–15; Luke 9:43–62; John 8:31–32; 13:34–35; 15:1–17; 21:15–19; Galatians 5:24; 2 Timothy 2:2

Discipline

The English word *discipline* is one of those funny words that is both a noun and a verb.

The word can have the connotation of punishment, but even then it has the idea of correcting (disciplining) in order to encourage and bring a person to a place of becoming mature (disciplined).

Whether the discipline being handed out is by God, parents, or governments, the end result from a biblical perspective is to bring people into a state of being self-controlled, even if it requires disciplining them to do it.

Key Verses

Blessed is the one you discipline, Lord, the one you teach from your law; you grant them relief from days of trouble, till a pit is dug for the wicked. For the Lord will not reject his people; he will never forsake his inheritance.

Psalm 94:12–14 NIV

Whoever spares the rod hates his son, but he who loves him is diligent to discipline him.

Proverbs 13:24 ESV

Don't you realize that in a race everyone runs, but only one person gets the prize? So run to win! All athletes are disciplined in their training. They do it to win a prize that will fade away, but we do it for an eternal prize. So I run with purpose in every step. I am not just shadowboxing. I discipline my body like an athlete, training it to do what it should. Otherwise, I fear that after preaching to others I myself might be disqualified.

1 Corinthians 9:24–27 NLT

But have nothing to do with worldly fables fit only for old women. On the other hand, discipline yourself for the purpose of godliness; for bodily discipline is only of little profit, but godliness is profitable for all things, since it holds promise for the present life and also for the life to come.

1 Timothy 4:7–8 NASB

Additional Notable Verses Concerning Discipline

Deuteronomy 4:36; Job 5:17; Proverbs 3:11; 6:23; 12:1; 13:1, 18; 15:5, 32; 16:22; 19:18–20, 27; 22:15; 23:12–13; 29:15–17; Ephesians 6:4; Colossians 2:5, Hebrews 12:1–13

Disobedience

At its core, all sin is disobedience.

From the beginning, all mankind was overcome by sin because Adam and Eve willfully chose to disobey a direct command from God. But there is still hope because Christ, as fully God and fully man, lived a sinless life, so He could pay the price for humanity's disobedience.

Key Verses

The serpent was clever, more clever than any wild animal God had made. He spoke to the Woman: "Do I understand that God told you not to eat from any tree in the garden?" The Woman said to the serpent, "Not at all. We can eat from the trees in the garden. It's only about the tree in the middle of the garden that God said, 'Don't eat from it; don't even touch it or you'll die.'" The serpent told the Woman, "You won't die. God knows that the moment you eat from that tree, you'll see what's really going on. You'll be just like God, knowing everything, ranging all the way from good to evil." When the Woman saw that the tree looked like good eating and realized what she would get out of it—she'd know everything!—she took and ate the fruit and then gave some to her husband, and he ate.

Genesis 3:1–6 THE MESSAGE

One man disobeyed God, and many became sinners. In the same way, one man obeyed God, and many will be made right.

Romans 5:19 NCV

As for you, you were dead in your transgressions and sins, in which you used to live when you followed the ways of this world and of the ruler of the kingdom of the air, the spirit who is now at work in those who are disobedient.

Ephesians 2:1–2 NIV

Additional Notable Verses Concerning Disobedience

Genesis 3; Numbers 20:1–13; Deuteronomy 11:26–28; 28; 1 Samuel 12:15; Psalm 78:10, 40; Jeremiah 12:17; John 14:15; Romans 11:27–32; Ephesians 5:6; Colossians 3:6; Titus 1:6; 3:3; Hebrews 2:2; 4:1–13; James 1:14–15; 2 Peter 2:4–10; 1 John 1:9

Diversity

When you read the Bible, there can seem to be a real lack of diversity. It can seem like all of the characters are Jewish, that the most important people are men, and most people were farmers. But that misses the truth.

Consider the genealogy of Jesus as a prime example. There is a Moabitess (Ruth) and a Canaanite (Rahab). There are men listed, of course, but unlike most genealogies of the time, several women are listed. There are kings, a prostitute, businessmen, and priests. What better example of diversity than the Son of God himself?

Key Verses

And as for the outsiders who now follow me, working for me, loving my name, and wanting to be my servants—all who keep Sabbath and don't defile it, holding fast to my covenant—I'll bring them to my holy mountain and give them joy in my house of prayer. They'll be welcome to worship the same as the "insiders," to bring burnt offerings and sacrifices to my altar. Oh yes, my house of worship will be known as a house of prayer for all people.

Isaiah 56:6–7 THE MESSAGE

In this new life, it doesn't matter if you are a Jew or a Gentile, circumcised or uncircumcised, barbaric, uncivilized, slave, or free. Christ is all that matters, and he lives in all of us.

Colossians 3:11 NLT

After these things I looked, and behold, a great multitude which no one could count, from every nation and all tribes and peoples and tongues, standing before the throne and before the Lamb, clothed in white robes, and palm branches were in their hands; and they cry out with a loud voice, saying, "Salvation to our God who sits on the throne, and to the Lamb."

Revelation 7:9–10 NASB

Additional Notable Verses Concerning Diversity

Genesis 12:1–3; Ezekiel 47:21–23; Acts 10; Romans 14; 1 Corinthians 12; Galatians 3:26–29; James 2:1–13

Divorce

Under the best of circumstances marriage is difficult, and few people actually reside under the best of circumstances. Thus divorce becomes a very convenient and prevalent solution to the difficulties put forth by marriage.

God has much to say in His Word about divorce. As with anything, we struggle both with the tendency to be too dogmatic about the issue as well as with the urge to view the whole thing with a sense of relativity. God's Word outlines for us what the designer of marriage thinks about divorce, if and when it is permissible, and what comes next.

Key Verses

"For I hate divorce," says the Lord, the God of Israel, "and him who covers his garment with wrong," says the Lord of hosts. "So take heed to your spirit, that you do not deal treacherously."

Malachi 2:16 NASB

And Pharisees came up to him and tested him by asking, "Is it lawful to divorce one's wife for any cause?" He answered, "Have you not read that he who created them from the beginning made them male and female, and said, 'Therefore a man shall leave his father and his mother and hold fast to his wife, and the two shall become one flesh'? So they are no longer two but one flesh. What therefore God has joined together, let not man separate." They said to him, "Why then did Moses command one to give a certificate of divorce and to send her away?" He said to them, "Because of your hardness of heart Moses allowed you to divorce your wives, but from the beginning it was not so. And I say to you: whoever divorces his wife, except for sexual immorality, and marries another, commits adultery."

Matthew 19:3–9 ESV

Additional Notable Verses Concerning Divorce

Deuteronomy 22:13–21; 24:1–4; Matthew 5:31–32; Mark 10:1–12; Luke 16:18; 1 Corinthians 7:12–16

Doctors

Hippocrates, the father of modern medicine, lived four centuries before Christ. But in Jesus' time leprosy and other dangerous diseases still spread rampantly. Physicians were able to do very little to heal or even to alleviate the pain of illness. This explains why Jesus' words in Mark 2:17 were so revolutionary: "It is not those who are healthy who need a physician, but those who are sick; I did not come to call the righteous, but sinners" (NASB). Unlike the human surgeons of His day, Jesus—humanity's most skilled physician—never loses a patient.

Today God has blessed us with many different types of doctors, and we can usually find a good treatment for what ails us. But still the Lord is the greatest physician of all.

Key Verses

In the thirty-ninth year of his reign Asa was afflicted with a disease in his feet. Though his disease was severe, even in his illness he did not seek help from the Lord, but only from the physicians.

2 Chronicles 16:12 NIV

For my dear broken people, I'm heartbroken. I weep, seized by grief. Are there no healing ointments in Gilead? Isn't there a doctor in the house? So why can't something be done to heal and save my dear, dear people?

Jeremiah 8:21–22 THE MESSAGE

He said to them, "You will surely say this proverb to Me, 'Physician, heal yourself! Whatever we have heard done in Capernaum, do also here in Your country.'" Then He said, "Assuredly, I say to you, no prophet is accepted in his own country."

Luke 4:23–24 NKJV

Our dear doctor Luke sends you his greetings, and so does Demas.

Colossians 4:14 CEV

Additional Notable Verses Concerning Doctors
Genesis 50:2; Mark 5:25–26

Doubt

Because they are opposites, you might think that where faith exists doubt is nowhere to be found. The truth, however, is that very often faith and doubt are both present in the same person.

Abraham is a prime example of this. At times Abraham was a giant of faith, and several times in the New Testament (Romans 4:1–3; Hebrews 11:8–10; James 2:21–24) Abraham is lifted up as an ideal example of faith. Yet Abraham was the same man who at times doubted that God could give him a child (Genesis 15:2; 16:1–16) and that God could keep him safe and provide for him (Genesis 12:1–20; 20:1–18). Maybe there is hope for the rest of us after all.

Key Verses

Then Jesus told them, "I tell you the truth, if you have faith and don't doubt, you can do things like this and much more. You can even say to this mountain, 'May you be lifted up and thrown into the sea,' and it will happen. You can pray for anything, and if you have faith, you will receive it."

Matthew 21:21–22 NLT

If any of you lacks wisdom, you should ask God, who gives generously to all without finding fault, and it will be given to you. But when you ask, you must believe and not doubt, because the one who doubts is like a wave of the sea, blown and tossed by the wind. That person should not expect to receive anything from the Lord. Such a person is double-minded and unstable in all they do.

James 1:5–8 NIV

But you, beloved, building yourselves up in your most holy faith and praying in the Holy Spirit, keep yourselves in the love of God, waiting for the mercy of our Lord Jesus Christ that leads to eternal life. And have mercy on those who doubt.

Jude 1:20–22 ESV

Additional Notable Verses Concerning Doubt
Matthew 14:22–36; Mark 9:14–29; 11:22–24; Luke 24:35–48; John 20:24–29; Romans 14:23; Jude 1:20–22

Dreams

or most of us, dreams are haphazard and crazy. But in the Bible God often gave people dreams and spoke to them in visions through their dreams. These prophetic dreams play a rather large role in the history of the Old Testament.

Does God still speak through dreams? God can always reveal himself in any way He chooses, but it's important to be discerning. If you think God is speaking to you through a dream, be sure it lines up with what the Bible says.

Key Verses

The saying is true: Bad dreams come from too much worrying, and too many words come from foolish people. If you make a promise to God, don't be slow to keep it. God is not happy with fools, so give God what you promised. It is better not to promise anything than to promise something and not do it. Don't let your words cause you to sin, and don't say to the priest at the Temple, "I didn't mean what I promised." If you do, God will become angry with your words and will destroy everything you have worked for. Many useless promises are like so many dreams; they mean nothing. You should respect God.

Ecclesiastes 5:3–7 NCV

And her [promised] husband Joseph, being a just and upright man and not willing to expose her publicly and to shame and disgrace her, decided to repudiate and dismiss (divorce) her quietly and secretly. But as he was thinking this over, behold, an angel of the Lord appeared to him in a dream, saying, Joseph, descendant of David, do not be afraid to take Mary [as] your wife, for that which is conceived in her is of (from, out of) the Holy Spirit.

Matthew 1:19–20 AMP

Additional Notable Verses Concerning Dreams
Genesis 20:1–9; 28:10–22; 31:1–29; 37:1–11; 40:1–41:39; Numbers 12:6; Deuteronomy 13:1–4; Judges 7; 1 Kings 3:1–15; Job 7:14; Jeremiah 23:32; 29:8; Daniel 2:1–45; 4:1–37; 7; Joel 2:28–29; Matthew 2; 27:19; Acts 2:16–18; 16:6–10

Drugs

The real issue with something like a drug—whether it be marijuana, alcohol, or caffeine—is control. For the Christian there is no wiggle room when it comes to control. The Holy Spirit is to be in control of our lives at all times, and we sin when we attempt to take back control or give it to a substance.

Key Verses

Or do you not know that your body is a temple of the Holy Spirit within you, whom you have from God? You are not your own, for you were bought with a price. So glorify God in your body.

1 Corinthians 6:19–20 ESV

Because we have these promises, dear friends, let us cleanse ourselves from everything that can defile our body or spirit. And let us work toward complete holiness because we fear God.

2 Corinthians 7:1 NLT

But you, brethren, are not in darkness, that the day would overtake you like a thief; for you are all sons of light and sons of day. We are not of night nor of darkness; so then let us not sleep as others do, but let us be alert and sober. For those who sleep do their sleeping at night, and those who get drunk get drunk at night. But since we are of the day, let us be sober, having put on the breastplate of faith and love, and as a helmet, the hope of salvation.

1 Thessalonians 5:4–8 NASB

Therefore, with minds that are alert and fully sober, set your hope on the grace to be brought to you when Jesus Christ is revealed at his coming.

1 Peter 1:13 NIV

Additional Notable Verses Concerning Drugs

Romans 13:1–7; 1 Corinthians 3:16–17; 15:34; 2 Timothy 4:5; 1 Peter 1:17–19; 2:13–23; 4:7; 5:8

Dysfunctional Families

I n many ways, to have a family is to have a dysfunctional family. Some families operate more smoothly than others, and there are definitely destructive and harmful family environments.

If anything, the high level of dysfunction of biblical families should encourage parents, children, and siblings alike. Joseph was one of the greatest characters of the Old Testament, but his childhood involved animosity between his father's two wives, who were sisters; favoritism from his father, which caused jealousy from his brothers; his own pride in revealing the dreams that God gave him; and eventually his being sold into slavery by his jealous brothers.

Key Verses

And Sarai said to Abram, "Behold now, the Lord has prevented me from bearing children. Go in to my servant; it may be that I shall obtain children by her." And Abram listened to the voice of Sarai. So, after Abram had lived ten years in the land of Canaan, Sarai, Abram's wife, took Hagar the Egyptian, her servant, and gave her to Abram her husband as a wife. And he went in to Hagar, and she conceived. And when she saw that she had conceived, she looked with contempt on her mistress.

Genesis 16:2–4 ESV

Absalom the son of David had a lovely sister, whose name was Tamar; and Amnon the son of David loved her. Amnon was so distressed over his sister Tamar that he became sick; for she was a virgin. And it was improper for Amnon to do anything to her.

2 Samuel 13:1–2 NKJV

Additional Notable Verses Concerning Dysfunctional Families
Genesis 4; 16; 19; 27; 29:1–30; Judges 11:29–40; 1 Samuel 2–4; 2 Samuel 13

Encouragement

Reputations tend to stick with us. If you doubt this, consider "Doubting Thomas." Of course, there are those, unlike Thomas, who obtain their reputation for good reasons. In Acts 4:36 (NCV) we learn, "One of the believers was named Joseph, a Levite born in Cyprus. The apostles called him Barnabas (which means 'one who encourages')."

Encouragement—what a fantastic thing to be known for. Barnabas was so intent and purposeful in encouraging others that it became his reputation. People like Barnabas have an indispensable role in the lives of others, and the Scriptures tell us that we need more people like him.

Key Verses

Encourage the exhausted, and strengthen the feeble. Say to those with anxious heart, "Take courage, fear not. Behold, your God will come with vengeance; the recompense of God will come, but He will save you."

Isaiah 35:3–4 NASB

The church in Jerusalem heard about all of this, so they sent Barnabas to Antioch. Barnabas was a good man, full of the Holy Spirit and full of faith. When he reached Antioch and saw how God had blessed the people, he was glad. He encouraged all the believers in Antioch always to obey the Lord with all their hearts, and many people became followers of the Lord.

Acts 11:22–24 NCV

So speak encouraging words to one another. Build up hope so you'll all be together in this, no one left out, no one left behind. I know you're already doing this; just keep on doing it. And now, friends, we ask you to honor those leaders who work so hard for you, who have been given the responsibility of urging and guiding you along in your obedience. Overwhelm them with appreciation and love!

1 Thessalonians 5:11–13 THE MESSAGE

Additional Notable Verses Concerning Encouragement
Deuteronomy 1:38; 3:28; 2 Samuel 11:25; Ezra 6:22; Daniel 11:1; Acts 15:31; Romans 15:4–5; Philippians 2:1; Colossians 4:8–11; 1 Thessalonians 3:2; Titus 2:4; Hebrews 3:13; 6:18

End Times

The world is increasingly fascinated with its own demise. More and more movies, television shows, and books tell stories of end-of-the-world scenarios. The potential causes of the end of time are many. Terrorists, diseases, the weather, World War III, technology, nuclear meltdowns, and natural disasters such as earthquakes are among the things we are to fear.

Believers know that even through events such as the world has never seen, Jesus will never leave them nor forsake them. The end of the world is coming, but for believers it will only be the beginning.

Key Verses

I will answer them before they even call to me. While they are still talking about their needs, I will go ahead and answer their prayers! The wolf and the lamb will feed together. The lion will eat hay like a cow. But the snakes will eat dust. In those days no one will be hurt or destroyed on my holy mountain. I, the Lord, have spoken!

Isaiah 65:24–25 NLT

Therefore you also be ready, for the Son of Man is coming at an hour you do not expect.

Matthew 24:44 NKJV

And after He had said these things, He was lifted up while they were looking on, and a cloud received Him out of their sight. And as they were gazing intently into the sky while He was going, behold, two men in white clothing stood beside them. They also said, "Men of Galilee, why do you stand looking into the sky? This Jesus, who has been taken up from you into heaven, will come in just the same way as you have watched Him go into heaven."

Acts 1:9–11 NASB

Additional Notable Verses Concerning the End Times

Isaiah 59–63; Ezekiel 27–39; Daniel 2:1–45; 7–12; Matthew 24; Mark 13; Luke 21:10–36; 1 Corinthians 15:50–58; 1 Thessalonians 4:13–18; 5:1–11; 2 Thessalonians 2:1–12; 1 Timothy 4:1–5; Titus 2:12–13; Hebrews 9:28; James 5:8; 2 Peter 3:3–19; 1 John 2:18–23; Revelation 1–22

Enemies

To live a life without an enemy would be a blessed existence. You might even expect that those who live a life that honors God would be free of enemies, but that is rarely the case. There are times when our lives glorify God and as a result we have peace, but there are also many times that our seeking to do the right thing only angers those who live lives that violate God's principles.

Throughout the revelation of the Scriptures we see God's people dealing with their enemies. King David in particular seemed to have many enemies, and his attempts to deal with them gave us many of the passages in the book of Psalms. Those psalms have been a comfort to untold numbers of believers for thousands of years. When enemies arise, the temptation to strike at them is profound, but before you react, run to the Scriptures. They just might change your plans.

Key Verses

It is God who avenges me, and subdues the peoples under me; He delivers me from my enemies. You also lift me up above those who rise against me; You have delivered me from the violent man.

Psalm 18:47–48 NKJV

When a man's ways please the Lord, he makes even his enemies to be at peace with him.

Proverbs 16:7 ESV

Don't rejoice when your enemies fall; don't be happy when they stumble. For the Lord will be displeased with you and will turn his anger away from them. Don't fret because of evildoers; don't envy the wicked.

Proverbs 24:17–19 NLT

Bless those who persecute you; bless and do not curse.

Romans 12:14 NIV

Additional Notable Verses Concerning Enemies

Exodus 23:4–5; 2 Samuel 16:5–14; Psalm 35; 59:1; 60:12; 61:3; 64:1; 136:23–25; Proverbs 25:21; Matthew 5:43–48; Luke 6:27–36; Acts 7:60; Romans 12:18–20

The Environment

The environment is a tremendous concern in the modern world. For the most part this is a very good thing. We should take our God-given role as stewards of creation seriously. But we must be careful to remember the order of the hierarchy in which Scripture places the environment.

God's Word teaches that humanity is to rule creation. The earth is to be taken care of and used by human beings. Taking care of the earth is important, but human beings are given a higher priority. Though it is important, the environment can never rise to the level of God, and humanity is only in the position that we are in because God gave us that authority.

Key Verses

Then God said, "Let us make man in our image, after our likeness. And let them have dominion over the fish of the sea and over the birds of the heavens and over the livestock and over all the earth and over every creeping thing that creeps on the earth."

Genesis 1:26 ESV

You gave them charge of everything you made, putting all things under their authority—the flocks and the herds and all the wild animals, the birds in the sky, the fish in the sea, and everything that swims the ocean currents.

Psalm 8:6–8 NLT

God claims Earth and everything in it, God claims World and all who live on it. He built it on Ocean foundations, laid it out on River girders.

Psalm 24:1–2 THE MESSAGE

Every wild animal honors me, even jackals and owls. I provide water in deserts—streams in thirsty lands for my chosen people.

Isaiah 43:20 CEV

Additional Notable Verses Concerning the Environment

Genesis 2; Psalm 96:10–13; 104:25–30; Matthew 6:26; John 1:1–3; 2 Peter 3:11–13; Revelation 21:1

Envy

Though the idea was probably not original with him, Shakespeare was one of the first to articulate in English the idea of being "green with envy." In the play *Othello*, one of the characters makes the statement, "O! Beware, my lord, of jealousy; it is the green-eyed monster which doth mock the meat it feeds on."

The idea of envy or jealousy being a "green-eyed monster" is one that the human writers of the Bible would have been fond of. Envy is destructive. It wants what it does not have, and is never content to remain as it is. The Scriptures show us that the person who carries envy in his or her heart is a ticking time bomb. Envy won't settle for remaining in a person's heart. It will seek to have its desires fulfilled, and it will destroy all who stand in its way.

Key Verses

Peace of mind means a healthy body, but jealousy will rot your bones.
Proverbs 14:30 NCV

Wrath is fierce and anger is a flood, but who can stand before jealousy?
Proverbs 27:4 NASB

Love endures long and is patient and kind; love never is envious nor boils over with jealousy, is not boastful or vainglorious, does not display itself haughtily.
1 Corinthians 13:4 AMP

Additional Notable Verses Concerning Envy

Exodus 34:14; Job 5:2; Psalm 73:2–3; 106:16–18; Proverbs 3:31; 23:17; 24:1, 19; Ezekiel 35:11; Matthew 27:18; Mark 7:20–23; 15:10; Acts 7:9; 13:45; 17:5; Romans 1:29; 13:13; 1 Corinthians 3:3; 2 Corinthians 12:20; Galatians 5:19–26; 1 Timothy 6:3–4; Titus 3:3; James 3:13–18; 4:5; 1 Peter 2:1

Equality

When we say that two things are equal, we are really saying that they are the same in some respect. If someone said that Alex is Tom's equal in tennis, then we know that Alex is just as good as Tom at that game. It does not mean that Alex and Tom and are the same height, the same race, or the same age. In fact, Alex may even be a girl!

When the Scriptures refer to equality, it is with respect to value, merit, and worth to God. There are no second-class citizens in God's kingdom. Jesus' death on the cross has made all God's children equal. That does not mean that we can all sing the same, that everyone will be a preacher, or that we should all be leaders. It does mean that each one of us has the same access to God, and that we are loved by Him. In God's family there are no black sheep.

Key Verses

God created man in His own image, in the image of God He created him; male and female He created them.

Genesis 1:27 NASB

When a foreigner resides among you in your land, do not mistreat them. The foreigner residing among you must be treated as your native-born. Love them as yourself, for you were foreigners in Egypt. I am the Lord your God.

Leviticus 19:33–34 NIV

For as many of you as were baptized into Christ have put on Christ. There is neither Jew nor Greek, there is neither slave nor free, there is no male and female, for you are all one in Christ Jesus. And if you are Christ's, then you are Abraham's offspring, heirs according to promise.

Galatians 3:27–29 ESV

Additional Notable Verses Concerning Equality
Romans 2:9–11; Philippians 2:5–11; 1 Peter 1:17–21; Revelation 5:9–10

Eternal Life

As finite human beings it can be a little overwhelming to try to wrap our brains around the concepts of eternity and eternal life. We punch time clocks, flip calendars, and set alarms on our phones to remind us when to go to the doctor's office and pick up the dry cleaning. So trying to imagine a time when there will be no time can really make our heads spin.

One thing that characterizes life here on earth is its temporal nature. Plants, animals, and humans all die, and all too often they die too soon. The life that Christ provided for believers is completely different in its nature. Death and dying will be no more—they will be swallowed up in life.

Key Verses

He who believes in the Son has everlasting life; and he who does not believe the Son shall not see life, but the wrath of God abides on him.

John 3:36 NKJV

God's law was given so that all people could see how sinful they were. But as people sinned more and more, God's wonderful grace became more abundant. So just as sin ruled over all people and brought them to death, now God's wonderful grace rules instead, giving us right standing with God and resulting in eternal life through Jesus Christ our Lord.

Romans 5:20–21 NLT

You cannot fool God, so don't make a fool of yourself! You will harvest what you plant. If you follow your selfish desires, you will harvest destruction, but if you follow the Spirit, you will harvest eternal life.

Galatians 6:7–8 CEV

Additional Notable Verses Concerning Eternal Life

Matthew 19:16–30; 25:31–46; Mark 10:17–31; Luke 10:25–37; 18:18–30; John 3:14–16; 4:13–14; 5:24, 39; 6:22–71; 10:27–28; 12:25; 17:1–5; Acts 13:42–52; Romans 6:20–23; 1 Timothy 1:15–16; 6:12; Titus 1:1–3; 3:7; 1 John 1:1–4; 2:20–25; 3:15; 5:10–13, 20; Jude 1:20–23

Evangelism

Though there is not a lack of understanding about why to evangelize, there is often a lack of participation in the process. This is why the Bible shows us all about evangelism. It shows us that it is part of our mission and calling as children of God. It tells us that saving people is really God's work, but He has allowed us to be used by Him in this process to reach others and earn rewards in heaven.

Key Verses

Go therefore and make disciples of all nations, baptizing them in the name of the Father and of the Son and of the Holy Spirit.

Matthew 28:19 ESV

But you will receive power when the Holy Spirit has come upon you; and you shall be My witnesses both in Jerusalem, and in all Judea and Samaria, and even to the remotest part of the earth.

Acts 1:8 NASB

Even though I am free of the demands and expectations of everyone, I have voluntarily become a servant to any and all in order to reach a wide range of people: religious, nonreligious, meticulous moralists, loose-living immoralists, the defeated, the demoralized—whoever. I didn't take on their way of life. I kept my bearings in Christ—but I entered their world and tried to experience things from their point of view. I've become just about every sort of servant there is in my attempts to lead those I meet into a God-saved life. I did all this because of the Message. I didn't just want to talk about it; I wanted to be in on it!

1 Corinthians 9:19–23 THE MESSAGE

Additional Notable Verses Concerning Evangelism

Isaiah 45:22; Matthew 4:23; 9:35–38; 10; 11:1–6; 24:14; Mark 1:1–20; Luke 3:18; 19:1–10; John 8:24; 14:6; Acts 2:14–42; 8:25–40; 14; Romans 1:1–17; 10; 1 Corinthians 1:17; 2 Timothy 4:5; 1 Peter 3:15; 2 Peter 3:9

Evil

I t is easy to get so busy just living life that we can sometimes forget our theology for days at a time. We can become so focused on our jobs, our families, mowing the lawn, and spring cleaning that we forget that there is another, unseen world in which we also exist. And even though it may often hide or disguise itself, evil is very real and active.

Evil's active presence and its tendency to disguise itself is seen very plainly on the pages of Scripture. Over and over again we find the words of the apostle Paul true: "Satan himself masquerades as an angel of light" (2 Corinthians 11:14 NIV). With all of this deception and deceit we must be careful not to become so focused on everyday life here on planet earth that we forget the spiritual realm where angels of light are not what they appear to be.

Key Verses

Lord, every morning you hear my voice. Every morning, I tell you what I need, and I wait for your answer. You are not a God who is pleased with the wicked; you do not live with those who do evil.

Psalm 5:3–4 NCV

Abstain from every form of evil.
1 Thessalonians 5:22 NASB

Let no man say when he is tempted, I am tempted of God: for God cannot be tempted with evil, neither tempteth he any man.

James 1:13 KJV

Additional Notable Verses Concerning Evil

Genesis 2–3; 8:21; 50:20; 2 Samuel 14:17; Psalm 23:4; 35:12; Proverbs 3:7; 6:16–19; 17:13; Ecclesiastes 12:14; Jeremiah 2:13; Matthew 6:13; John 3:16–20; Romans 12:17–21; 1 Timothy 6:10; James 3:8; 1 Peter 3:8–9

Faith

I f one were asked to summarize the entirety of the Bible's teachings into one word, a good choice would be *faith*.

It is hard to overestimate faith as a biblical concept because it inhabits almost everything that occurs in the Scriptures. When Abraham follows God, it is because of his faith. When Moses leads the children of Israel to the Promised Land it is by faith, and when the children of Israel fail to possess the Promised Land it is due to a lack of faith. By faith David slew a giant and Daniel survived the lion's den. It was faith that led the apostles to proclaim the Good News of Jesus to the world, and so on and so on until we arrive at our tiny little sliver in time and our faith.

Key Verses

Look at the proud; his soul is not straight or right within him, but the [rigidly] just and the [uncompromisingly] righteous man shall live by his faith and in his faithfulness.

Habakkuk 2:4 AMP

The apostles said to the Lord, "Increase our faith!" And the Lord said, "If you had faith like a grain of mustard seed, you could say to this mulberry tree, 'Be uprooted and planted in the sea,' and it would obey you."

Luke 17:5–6 ESV

Faith is the confidence that what we hope for will actually happen; it gives us assurance about things we cannot see . . . And it is impossible to please God without faith. Anyone who wants to come to him must believe that God exists and that he rewards those who sincerely seek him.

Hebrews 11:1, 6 NLT

Additional Notable Verses Concerning Faith

Psalm 146; Matthew 9:1–7; 17:18–20; Luke 7:36–50; 22:31–32; Acts 14:24–28; Romans 5:1–11; 10:17; 1 Corinthians 13:2; 15:14; 2 Corinthians 5:6–10; Galatians 2:20; Ephesians 2:8–10; 4:1–7; 6:16; Colossians 2:5; 1 Thessalonians 5:1–11; 2 Thessalonians 3:1–5; Hebrews 11; 12:1–2; James 1:5–6; 5:13–18

False Prophets

Though you would never know it by most artists' renderings, the saints of the Scriptures did not walk around with halos on their heads. One advantage to the halo is that it would have made it very easy to tell the good guys from the bad guys.

When a prophet came into town saying that he had a word from God, the only way to really tell if he was a true or a false prophet was to wait and see if his word came to pass. Although not nearly as fun as a halo, it proved to be a rather effective test.

Key Verses

The Lord said to me: ". . . But a prophet who presumes to speak in my name anything I have not commanded, or a prophet who speaks in the name of other gods, is to be put to death."

You may say to yourselves, "How can we know when a message has not been spoken by the Lord?" If what a prophet proclaims in the name of the Lord does not take place or come true, that is a message the Lord has not spoken. That prophet has spoken presumptuously, so do not be alarmed.

Deuteronomy 18:17, 20–22 NIV

A horrible and shocking thing has happened in this land—the prophets give false prophecies, and the priests rule with an iron hand. Worse yet, my people like it that way! But what will you do when the end comes?

Jeremiah 5:30–31 NLT

Beware of false prophets, who come to you in sheep's clothing but inwardly are ravenous wolves. You will recognize them by their fruits. Are grapes gathered from thornbushes, or figs from thistles?

Matthew 7:15–16 ESV

Beloved, do not believe every spirit, but test the spirits, whether they are of God; because many false prophets have gone out into the world.

1 John 4:1 NKJV

Additional Notable Verses Concerning False Prophets

Numbers 22–24; Deuteronomy 13; 18; 1 Kings 18:1–40; 22:1–40; Jeremiah 28–29; Ezekiel 13; Zechariah 13:1–6; Matthew 24:3–28; Mark 13:14–22; Luke 6:26; 2 Peter 2:1–3; 1 John 4:1–6

Fame

With technology and social media someone can become an internet sensation and then yesterday's news in what seems like the blink of an eye. There were numerous people who gained fame in the Bible. Yet it is the fame of one person with which the Bible is the most concerned. More than telling the stories of Abraham, David, and the apostle Peter, the Scriptures endeavor to make God's name famous. When we seek to make ourselves famous, we are at our worst, but when we seek to make Him famous, we are at our best.

Key Verses

When the queen of Sheba heard about the fame of Solomon and his relationship to the Lord, she came to test Solomon with hard questions.

1 Kings 10:1 NIV

I will set a sign among them and will send survivors from them to the nations: Tarshish, Put, Lud, Meshech, Tubal and Javan, to the distant coastlands that have neither heard My fame nor seen My glory. And they will declare My glory among the nations.

Isaiah 66:19 NASB

And the news about this spread through all that district. As Jesus passed on from there, two blind men followed Him, shouting loudly, Have pity and mercy on us, Son of David! When He reached the house and went in, the blind men came to Him, and Jesus said to them, Do you believe that I am able to do this? They said to Him, Yes, Lord. Then He touched their eyes, saying, According to your faith and trust and reliance [on the power invested in Me] be it done to you; And their eyes were opened. And Jesus earnestly and sternly charged them, See that you let no one know about this. But they went off and blazed and spread His fame abroad throughout that whole district.

Matthew 9:26–31 AMP

Additional Notable Verses Concerning Fame

Joshua 6:27; 1 Kings 4:29–34; 1 Chronicles 14:17; Ezekiel 16:14–16; Matthew 4:24; 5:1–12; 1 Peter 1:22–25

Family

amily—they are probably the best and worst people you know. No one can make you feel so loved and infuriated as your family. Not everyone has a great family, but most people at least have an ideal of what they wish their family was.

In the Scriptures, when God chose a way to reveal to us how we should relate to Him and to one another, He chose the idea of a family. Your dad may be a kind and loving man or he me may be a total jerk, but in God we find a heavenly Father who is perfect in His love for us. Your siblings may be your best friends or they may drive you crazy, but in the person of Jesus Christ we find the perfect firstborn older brother from whom to learn about life. And just think, one day all of God's family will get together in heaven, and we will all be perfect. Now that is a family reunion worth attending!

Key Verses

Therefore a man shall leave his father and his mother and hold fast to his wife, and they shall become one flesh.

Genesis 2:24 ESV

Honor your father and mother. Then you will live a long, full life in the land the Lord your God is giving you.

Exodus 20:12 NLT

Wives, be subject to your husbands, as is fitting in the Lord. Husbands, love your wives and do not be embittered against them. Children, be obedient to your parents in all things, for this is well-pleasing to the Lord. Fathers, do not exasperate your children, so that they will not lose heart.

Colossians 3:18–21 NASB

Additional Notable Verses Concerning Family

Genesis 3:16–19; Deuteronomy 4:9–10; Joshua 24:15; Job 1:5; Psalm 128:3–6; Ephesians 3:14–19; 5:22–33; 1 Timothy 3:4–5, 12; 1 Peter 3:1–7

Fasting

If you participate in a fast and it is just about eating or not eating, then you have missed the most important part of the fast—the spiritual benefits.

Fasting, whether from food or some other activity, is really about getting your attention. It is about taking the time when you typically focus on one thing (food, for example) and focusing instead on God, your relationship with Him, and your own spiritual vitality. People fast in times of great stress and distress because something has so garnered their attention that the time spent in prayer and seeking God is more important than a meal or whatever activity they are fasting from. Fasting is good. Putting your attention on God and keeping it there is even better.

Key Verses

They repay me evil for good, to the bereavement of my soul. But as for me, when they were sick, my clothing was sackcloth; I humbled my soul with fasting, and my prayer kept returning to my bosom.

Psalm 35:12–13 NASB

And when you fast, don't make it obvious, as the hypocrites do, for they try to look miserable and disheveled so people will admire them for their fasting. I tell you the truth, that is the only reward they will ever get. But when you fast, comb your hair and wash your face. Then no one will notice that you are fasting, except your Father, who knows what you do in private. And your Father, who sees everything, will reward you.

Matthew 6:16–18 NLT

Additional Notable Verses Concerning Fasting

1 Samuel 7:6; 2 Samuel 12:16; Esther 4:1–3; 9:28–32; Psalm 69:10; Isaiah 58:3–7; Daniel 6:18; 9:3; Joel 1:14; 2:12; Zechariah 7:5; Matthew 4:2; Mark 2:18–20; Luke 5:33–35; Acts 13:3; 14:23; 2 Corinthians 6:1–10

Fathers

A child with a father who loves him or her has begun life with the most tremendous of advantages. No matter how imperfect that father is, or how many of his own struggles he must overcome, if he truly loves his child and wants the best for that child, he will move heaven and earth to protect and provide for that child. That father's children will go through life knowing that there is someone who is there for them, who loves them, and who will always seek their best interests.

Regrettably, not everyone has that type of father, and they seem to get rarer by the day. God's Word tells us that God himself is ready, willing, and able to step into the void and become a father to those without fathers or with imperfect fathers. The pain of having an unloving dad can be very intense, but the God of the Bible is able to overcome that pain by extending a hand that is loving, just, and caring.

Key Verses

As a father has compassion on his children, so the Lord has compassion on those who fear him.

Psalm 103:13 NIV

My son, do not despise the Lord's discipline or be weary of his reproof, for the Lord reproves him whom he loves, as a father the son in whom he delights.

Proverbs 3:11–12 ESV

Grandparents are proud of their grandchildren, and children should be proud of their parents.

Proverbs 17:6 CEV

Fathers, do not make your children angry, but raise them with the training and teaching of the Lord.

Ephesians 6:4 NCV

Additional Notable Verses Concerning Fathers

Psalm 10:18; 68:5; Proverbs 23:22–25; Malachi 4:6; Matthew 6:6–15; Mark 9:14–29; Luke 6:27–36; Colossians 3:21; Hebrews 12:4–13

Fear

Fear can do crazy things to people. Take a person who suffers from acrophobia (fear of heights) and try to get him or her to ride to the top of a tall building in a glass elevator. That person, who may usually be of sound mind and body, will probably react quite irrationally.

We can look at some fears and laugh if we are not the one with that particular phobia, but most of us have fears of one type or another. God's Word tells us that to fear is to be human, but for the believer in Jesus Christ, fear is something to be overcome by the Spirit of God. Fear and the Holy Spirit cannot coexist for long. It may be an uncomfortable process, but God will not allow us to live a life of fear and doubt.

Key Verses

The Lord is my light and my salvation; whom shall I fear? The Lord is the strength of my life; of whom shall I be afraid?

Psalm 27:1 NKJV

Do not fear, for I am with you; do not anxiously look about you, for I am your God. I will strengthen you, surely I will help you, surely I will uphold you with My righteous right hand.

Isaiah 41:10 NASB

The Spirit we received does not make us slaves again to fear; it makes us children of God. With that Spirit we cry out, "Father."

Romans 8:15 NCV

Where God's love is, there is no fear, because God's perfect love drives out fear. It is punishment that makes a person fear, so love is not made perfect in the person who fears.

1 John 4:18 NCV

Additional Notable Verses Concerning Fear

Genesis 3:10; Psalm 23:4; 112; Proverbs 1:27–29; 3:21–25; 10:24–27; Isaiah 35:4; Matthew 10:26; 1 Corinthians 2:1–5; Ephesians 6:5; 2 Timothy 1:7

Fear of God

Thinking about the "fear of God" can be awkward for us. We tend to focus on God's love, and so fearing Him may seem a bit unnatural. Theologian Charles Haddon Spurgeon discussed this in a commentary on Psalm 111: "To know God so as to walk aright before him is the greatest of all the applied sciences. Holy reverence of God leads us to praise him."*

When we speak of the fear of God, we are not talking about fear in the same way that we fear disaster or mayhem. We are talking about fear in the sense of awesome reverence, or as Spurgeon referred to it, "holy reverence." In this respect, fear of God is something that is very important in the Bible, but not nearly so important in popular culture, even amongst Christians. Maybe it is something that has been ignored far too long.

Key Verses

The [reverent] fear of the Lord is clean, enduring forever; the ordinances of the Lord are true and righteous altogether.

Psalm 19:9 AMP

The fear of the Lord is the beginning of wisdom; all those who practice it have a good understanding. His praise endures forever!

Psalm 111:10 ESV

Things calmed down after that and the church had smooth sailing for a while. All over the country—Judea, Samaria, Galilee—the church grew. They were permeated with a deep sense of reverence for God. The Holy Spirit was with them, strengthening them. They prospered wonderfully.

Acts 9:31 THE MESSAGE

Additional Notable Verses Concerning the Fear of God
Genesis 20:11; Exodus 1:21; 14:29–31; Deuteronomy 4:9–10; 6:24; 10:12–13; Joshua 24:14; Job 28:28; Psalm 22:23; 25:12; 34:9; 112:1; Proverbs 2:1–5; 3:7; 8:13; 9:10; 14:27; 15:16; 23:17; 24:21; 31:30; Ecclesiastes 5:7; Isaiah 11:3; 50:10; Romans 3:18; 2 Corinthians 5:11

*Charles Haddon Spurgeon, *The Treasury of David*, "Psalm 111," www.spurgeon.org/treasury/ps111.htm.

Food

J esus said a lot of radical things, but one of the most radical is found in Mark 7:18–19: "'Do you not understand that whatever goes into the man from outside cannot defile him, because it does not go into his heart, but into his stomach, and is eliminated?' (Thus He declared all foods clean.)" (NASB). To the average Gentile believer Jesus' statement may not seem all that controversial, but to a Jewish audience who adhered to very strict dietary laws, it was earth-shattering.

Jesus essentially taught that food is neither spiritual nor unspiritual; it is just food. The dietary laws and restrictions that God gave the Old Testament Israelites were no longer necessary because Jesus had fulfilled the law and its requirements.

Key Verses

Then God said, "I give you every seed-bearing plant on the face of the whole earth and every tree that has fruit with seed in it. They will be yours for food."

Genesis 1:29 NIV

Every moving thing that is alive shall be food for you; I give all to you, as I gave the green plant. Only you shall not eat flesh with its life, that is, its blood.

Genesis 9:3–4 NASB

That is why I tell you not to worry about everyday life—whether you have enough food and drink, or enough clothes to wear. Isn't life more than food, and your body more than clothing? Look at the birds. They don't plant or harvest or store food in barns, for your heavenly Father feeds them. And aren't you far more valuable to him than they are?

Matthew 6:25–26 NLT

Therefore, whether you eat or drink, or whatever you do, do all to the glory of God.

1 Corinthians 10:31 NKJV

Additional Notable Verses Concerning Food

Genesis 3:6; Leviticus 11; Psalm 111:5; 104:14; 145:15; Proverbs 15:17; 31:15; Ecclesiastes 8:15; Matthew 3:4; Romans 14; 1 Corinthians 8:8

Foot Washing

eople's feet are generally sweaty, stinky, and rough, and that is a description of the good ones. Now imagine if everyone walked everywhere instead of driving, and that instead of wearing shoes everyone wore sandals. Welcome to the first century.

It was in this environment that someone who hosted a gathering would provide the water and a servant for people to have their feet washed when they arrived. Now consider that Christ washed His disciples' feet and said that the same attitude of servitude should be in all of His followers.

Key Verses

Jesus knew that the Father had put him in complete charge of everything, that he came from God and was on his way back to God. So he got up from the supper table, set aside his robe, and put on an apron. Then he poured water into a basin and began to wash the feet of the disciples, drying them with his apron. When he got to Simon Peter, Peter said, "Master, you wash my feet?"

Jesus answered, "You don't understand now what I'm doing, but it will be clear enough to you later."

Peter persisted, "You're not going to wash my feet—ever!"

Jesus said, "If I don't wash you, you can't be part of what I'm doing."

"Master!" said Peter. "Not only my feet, then. Wash my hands! Wash my head!"

Jesus said, "If you've had a bath in the morning, you only need your feet washed now and you're clean from head to toe. My concern, you understand, is holiness, not hygiene. So now you're clean. But not every one of you." (He knew who was betraying him. That's why he said, "Not every one of you.") After he had finished washing their feet, he took his robe, put it back on, and went back to his place at the table.

Then he said, "Do you understand what I have done to you? You address me as 'Teacher' and 'Master,' and rightly so. That is what I am. So if I, the Master and Teacher, washed your feet, you must now wash each other's feet. I've laid down a pattern for you. What I've done, you do."

John 13:3–15 The Message

Additional Notable Verses Concerning Foot Washing
Genesis 19:1–2; Luke 7:36–50

Forgiveness

The root concept behind the primary word for forgiveness in the Bible is interesting. It is the Greek word *aphiemi* (pronounced af-ee'-ay-mee) and its primary meaning is that of sending something or someone away. It was used of a husband divorcing his wife, or of someone getting rid of a debt. The basic idea behind *aphiemi* is that of removing something from your presence.

What a fantastic word picture God has given us for the act of forgiveness. Whenever someone offends you, or hurts your feelings, or does you wrong, respond with *aphiemi*. You could choose to try to get even and get revenge, but instead respond as God did to our sins by choosing to send the offense away and forgive.

Key Verses

Help us, O God of our salvation, for the glory of Your name; and deliver us and forgive our sins for Your name's sake.

Psalm 79:9 NASB

Get rid of all bitterness, rage and anger, brawling and slander, along with every form of malice. Be kind and compassionate to one another, forgiving each other, just as in Christ God forgave you.

Ephesians 4:31–32 NIV

And you, who were dead in your trespasses and the uncircumcision of your flesh, God made alive together with him, having forgiven us all our trespasses, by canceling the record of debt that stood against us with its legal demands. This he set aside, nailing it to the cross.

Colossians 2:13–14 ESV

Additional Notable Verses Concerning Forgiveness

Genesis 37–50; Nehemiah 9:16–21; Psalm 130:1–4; Hosea 1–4; Matthew 6:1–15; 9:1–8; 18:21–35; 26:26–29; Mark 2:1–12; Luke 7:40–50; 23:34; 24:44–47; Acts 10:34–43; Ephesians 1:3–9; Colossians 1:9–14; Hebrews 9:1–22; 1 John 1:9

Fortune-Telling

Knowing the future would be great, wouldn't it? Imagine being able to magically avoid the highway traffic because you knew ahead of time where the bottleneck would be. You could bet on the World Series champion and become filthy rich. If you were full of compassion for your fellow human beings you could even help prevent disasters and criminal acts.

Knowing the future is the promise of the fortune-teller. But according to the Scriptures the promise of the fortune-teller is a false one. Fortune-tellers operate by deception and the power of Satan, and even though they promise a brighter future, your participation with them makes yours darker.

Key Verses

When you enter the land that God, your God, is giving you, don't take on the abominable ways of life of the nations there. Don't you dare sacrifice your son or daughter in the fire. Don't practice divination, sorcery, fortunetelling, witchery, casting spells, holding séances, or channeling with the dead. People who do these things are an abomination to God. It's because of just such abominable practices that God, your God, is driving these nations out before you.

Deuteronomy 18:9–12 The Message

As for the person who turns to mediums and to spiritists, to play the harlot after them, I will also set My face against that person and will cut him off from among his people. . . . Now a man or a woman who is a medium or a spiritist shall surely be put to death. They shall be stoned with stones, their bloodguiltiness is upon them.

Leviticus 20:6, 27 nasb

But as for the cowardly, the faithless, the detestable, as for murderers, the sexually immoral, sorcerers, idolaters, and all liars, their portion will be in the lake that burns with fire and sulfur, which is the second death.

Revelation 21:8 esv

Additional Notable Verses Concerning Fortune-Telling

Exodus 22:18; Deuteronomy 4:19; Leviticus 19:31; 2 Chronicles 33:1–6; Isaiah 8:19; Acts 16:16–21; 19:11–20; Galatians 5:19–21; Revelation 22:14–15

Free Will

There are certain things that are more of a concern to us than they seem to be to God. The free will of humanity is one of those things. The Bible says precious little about whether or not humanity has free will, and if we do how much. Consequently theologians have debated and argued over the concept for hundreds of years. If we decide our theology on what sounds right or what seems like a good idea to us, we are in a very dangerous place. That is why it is important to search the Scriptures on this issue.

Key Verses

Why do you keep calling me "Lord, Lord!" when you don't do what I say?
Luke 6:46 NLT

Jerusalem, Jerusalem, you who kill the prophets and stone those sent to you, how often I have longed to gather your children together, as a hen gathers her chicks under her wings, and you were not willing.
Luke 13:34 NIV

If ye love me, keep my commandments.
John 14:15 KJV

The Spirit and the bride say, "Come!" Let the one who hears this say, "Come!" Let whoever is thirsty come; whoever wishes may have the water of life as a free gift.
Revelation 22:17 NCV

Additional Notable Verses Concerning Free Will
Deuteronomy 30:11–19; John 1:9–12; 15; Romans 10:14–17; 13:1–4

Freedom

To those outside of the Christian faith it can seem that there are an awful lot of restrictions. To its own detriment Christianity has at times overemphasized what believers are to do or not to do. It may seem that rather than abundant life, Jesus just delivered a large book of rules. When this occurs, an unbelieving world looks at Christianity as something akin to house arrest while they themselves are living lives of freedom.

The Bible actually teaches just the opposite. Those who have never placed their faith in Christ may believe themselves to be free, but in reality they are slaves to sin. The Christian is the one who is truly living in freedom. As a child of God, only the believer can truly and fully experience the freedom that comes in Christ.

Key Verses

The Lord God has put his Spirit in me, because the Lord has appointed me to tell the good news to the poor. He has sent me to comfort those whose hearts are broken, to tell the captives they are free, and to tell the prisoners they are released.

Isaiah 61:1 NCV

So Jesus said to the Jews who had believed him, "If you abide in my word, you are truly my disciples, and you will know the truth, and the truth will set you free."

John 8:31–32 ESV

You, my brothers and sisters, were called to be free. But do not use your freedom to indulge the flesh; rather, serve one another humbly in love. For the entire law is fulfilled in keeping this one command: "Love your neighbor as yourself."

Galatians 5:13–14 NIV

[Live] as free people, [yet] without employing your freedom as a pretext for wickedness; but [live at all times] as servants of God.

1 Peter 2:16 AMP

Additional Notable Verses Concerning Freedom
John 8:31–38; Romans 6:15–22; 8:1–30; 14; Galatians 5:1–15; 1 Corinthians 6:12–20; 2 Corinthians 3; James 1:22–25

Friendship

A good friend is an amazing thing to have. Some people go their entire lives without ever finding a tried and true friend. Others have many, many friends, but few if any of them are actually close and dependable.

It is not the number of friends that is important; it is the quality of friendship. Friends will come and go, but the type of friend who will stand by you no matter the adversity is worth his or her weight in gold. The friend who will not be chased away by difficult times is a true friend, and one whom the Scriptures equate to family (Proverbs 18:24). Find those friends and do not let them go.

Key Verses

The Lord would speak to Moses face to face, as one speaks to a friend. Then Moses would return to the camp, but his young aide Joshua son of Nun did not leave the tent.

Exodus 33:11 NIV

I wish for the days when I was strong, when God's close friendship blessed my house.

Job 29:4 NCV

A friend loves at all times, and a brother is born for adversity.

Proverbs 17:17 ESV

This is My commandment, that you love one another, just as I have loved you. Greater love has no one than this, that one lay down his life for his friends. You are My friends if you do what I command you. No longer do I call you slaves, for the slave does not know what his master is doing; but I have called you friends, for all things that I have heard from My Father I have made known to you.

John 15:12–15 NASB

Additional Notable Verses Concerning Friendship

1 Samuel 18:1–4; Job 6:14; 16:20; Psalm 38:11; 55:12–13; Proverbs 16:28; 18:24; 19:4; 25:17; 27:6, 9–10, 14; Ecclesiastes 4:9–12; Matthew 11:19; James 4:4–5

Giving

Most human beings are not naturally selfless. If you doubt this, find an infant and take away his pacifier, or tell him to wait a little while for his next meal, or even take away the blanket that he clutches while he naps. Human beings enter life thinking of themselves and their own wants and desires.

The Scriptures tell us that giving may not come naturally, but for the follower of Christ it must become a way of life. Giving should be done freely, sacrificially, and regularly. Giving should be done to further the cause of the Gospel and to help those who are in need. Giving may not be on the mind of the crying infant, but as we progress from spiritual infancy to adulthood it must become our second nature.

Key Verses

Give generously to the poor, not grudgingly, for the Lord your God will bless you in everything you do. There will always be some in the land who are poor. That is why I am commanding you to share freely with the poor and with other Israelites in need.

Deuteronomy 15:10–11 NLT

Sometimes you can become rich by being generous or poor by being greedy. Generosity will be rewarded: Give a cup of water, and you will receive a cup of water in return.

Proverbs 11:24–25 CEV

But this I say: He who sows sparingly will also reap sparingly, and he who sows bountifully will also reap bountifully. So let each one give as he purposes in his heart, not grudgingly or of necessity; for God loves a cheerful giver. And God is able to make all grace abound toward you, that you, always having all sufficiency in all things, may have an abundance for every good work.

2 Corinthians 9:6–8 NKJV

Additional Notable Verses Concerning Giving

Deuteronomy 16:17; 1 Chronicles 29:9; Proverbs 22:9; 28:27; Matthew 6:1–4; 10:8; Mark 12:41–44; Luke 6:30–38; Acts 20:35; Philippians 4:15–17; James 2:15–16

Goals

The setting of goals can be a very useful thing in the Christian life. Without a goal to reach or a destination to arrive at, you can drift aimlessly, accomplishing little and wasting much of your time and energy. The goals that a Christian should set should be goals that encourage and promote spiritual growth. The goal of being a better child of God tomorrow than you are today is a great one in general. When accompanied by specific goals regarding prayer, Bible study, and other disciplines, goals can and will help you to continue to grow in grace, and you will be a bigger blessing to others in turn.

Key Verses

> You shall not do at all what we are doing here today, every man doing whatever is right in his own eyes; for you have not as yet come to the resting place and the inheritance which the Lord your God is giving you.
>
> Deuteronomy 12:8–9 NASB

> Brethren, I do not count myself to have apprehended; but one thing I do, forgetting those things which are behind and reaching forward to those things which are ahead, I press toward the goal for the prize of the upward call of God in Christ Jesus.
>
> Philippians 3:13–14 NKJV

> But the goal of our instruction is love from a pure heart and a good conscience and a sincere faith.
>
> 1 Timothy 1:5 NASB

Additional Notable Verses Concerning Goals
Habakkuk 2:3; Proverbs 21:5; Luke 13:32; Galatians 1:10

God

Our attempts to describe God inevitably end in failure. No matter what we say, it is not great enough, big enough, or awesome enough. Taking an infinite God and encapsulating Him in finite terms is an impossible task. Hymn writers, musicians, preachers, prophets, and theologians have all attempted the task, and every last one has fallen short.

This is why the Scriptures are so important to our vision of God. Since the books of the Bible were written under the inspiration of God, they are God's words to reveal and describe himself to us.

Key Verses

He is the Rock, His work is perfect; for all His ways are justice, a God of truth and without injustice; righteous and upright is He.

Deuteronomy 32:4 NKJV

Great is the Lord! He is most worthy of praise! No one can measure his greatness.

Psalm 145:3 NLT

God is spirit, and those who worship him must worship in spirit and truth.

John 4:24 ESV

Whoever does not love does not know God, because God is love.

1 John 4:8 NCV

And this is the message [the message of promise] which we have heard from Him and now are reporting to you: God is Light, and there is no darkness in Him at all [no, not in any way].

1 John 1:5 AMP

Additional Notable Verses Concerning God

Exodus 15:1–21; 34:6–7; Numbers 14:18; Joshua 24:1–28; 2 Samuel 7:22; 1 Kings 8:10–66; 2 Chronicles 2:5; Job 11:7–10; 23:8–9; 37:23; Psalm 25:8; 83:18; 90; 99; 102:24–28; 116:5; 139; 145:17; Proverbs 5:21; Isaiah 5:16; 6; 40:28; 44:6; 45:21; 46:3–13; 60:19; Jeremiah 10:10; Nahum 1:2–11; Matthew 5:48; Romans 11:33; 1 Timothy 1:17; Hebrews 12:28–29; 1 Peter 4:19; 1 John 4:7–21

God's Glory

Glory that is ascribed to human beings will ultimately be tarnished. Think of the star athlete who scores the points that allow his team to win the championship. He is given a trophy, perhaps a sports car, and the adulation of thousands of screaming fans. Yet in just a matter of months, if he cannot duplicate his efforts, he will be considered a failure. Before the stadium lights have been turned off, his glory has already begun to fade.

Unlike human glory, God's glory does not fade away. God is the same yesterday, today, and forever. He will not grow old, and his skills will not diminish. Today when you glorify God for His provision for you, you are saying the same thing that God's people have said for thousands of years. Time spent glorifying God is not time wasted; it is time with eternal significance.

Key Verses

The heavens declare the glory of God, and the sky above proclaims his handiwork.

Psalm 19:1 ESV

Whether, then, you eat or drink or whatever you do, do all to the glory of God.

1 Corinthians 10:31 NASB

Now the Lord is the Spirit, and where the Spirit of the Lord is, there is freedom. And we all, who with unveiled faces contemplate the Lord's glory, are being transformed into his image with ever-increasing glory, which comes from the Lord, who is the Spirit.

2 Corinthians 3:17–18 NIV

Additional Notable Verses Concerning God's Glory

Exodus 16:1–12; 24:16; 40:34–38; Numbers 14:1–10; 1 Kings 8:1–11; Psalm 104:31; Proverbs 25:2; Isaiah 40:1–5; 60:1; John 11:1–44; Acts 7:55; Romans 3:23; 5:2; 15:7; 1 Corinthians 11:1–16; 2 Corinthians 1:20; 4:6, 15; Philippians 2:1–11

God's Guidance

I t can be very easy to read the Bible and feel like its characters had it easy. The Israelites needed to know where to go, so God sent a pillar of cloud by day and a pillar of fire by night to show them the way. If only we had pillars of fire, surely we would know which way to go.

It is amazing how quickly we forget that with our own personal copy of the Bible in our hands, we have so much more guidance than the ancient Israelites ever had. There will always be times when we do not know which way to turn, but the Bible gives us much more direction than a pillar of cloud or fire ever could.

Key Verses

The steps of a man are established by the Lord, when he delights in his way; though he fall, he shall not be cast headlong, for the Lord upholds his hand.
Psalm 37:23–24 ESV

For the Lord gives wisdom; from his mouth come knowledge and under-standing. He holds success in store for the upright, he is a shield to those whose walk is blameless, for he guards the course of the just and protects the way of his faithful ones. Then you will understand what is right and just and fair—every good path.

Proverbs 2:6–9 NIV

A man's heart plans his way, but the Lord directs his steps.
Proverbs 16:9 NKJV

So I tell you to ask and you will receive, search and you will find, knock and the door will be opened for you. Everyone who asks will receive, everyone who searches will find, and the door will be opened for everyone who knocks.
Luke 11:9–10 CEV

Additional Notable Verses Concerning God's Guidance

1 Chronicles 16:11; Psalm 32:8; 48:14; Proverbs 1:33; 3:5–6; Isaiah 48:17; 58:11; Jeremiah 10:23; 29:11; 33:3; Matthew 6:33; John 8:12; 16:13

God's Love

We say that we love lots of things: God, our families, pets, and even a pizza from our favorite restaurant. In general, we seem to think that we love an awful lot.

God does not merely love, God *is* love. When we speak of love from God's perspective, it is infinitely different than when we speak of love from our own view of the world. Love is not simply a trait that God exhibits—and exhibits better than we do—love is an integral part of who God is.

Key Verses

Now hope does not disappoint, because the love of God has been poured out in our hearts by the Holy Spirit who was given to us.

Romans 5:5 NKJV

And I am convinced that nothing can ever separate us from God's love. Neither death nor life, neither angels nor demons, neither our fears for today nor our worries about tomorrow—not even the powers of hell can separate us from God's love. No power in the sky above or in the earth below—indeed, nothing in all creation will ever be able to separate us from the love of God that is revealed in Christ Jesus our Lord.

Romans 8:38–39 NLT

Beloved, let us love one another, for love is from God, and whoever loves has been born of God and knows God. Anyone who does not love does not know God, because God is love. In this the love of God was made manifest among us, that God sent his only Son into the world, so that we might live through him. In this is love, not that we have loved God but that he loved us and sent his Son to be the propitiation for our sins.

1 John 4:7–10 ESV

Additional Notable Verses Concerning God's Love

Luke 11:42; John 3:16–21; 5:39–42; 13:34–35; Romans 5:1–11; 2 Corinthians 13:14; 2 Thessalonians 3:5; 1 John 3:17; 4:13–21; 5:1–5; Jude 1:20–21

God's Mercy

When God shows mercy it is different than when we show mercy. Our mercy tends to have limits and constraints, but God's mercy has no limits.

God shows mercy to the people who caused the death of His Son. Not only that, He shows mercy on people who continue to live in sin. The sins that Christ died for are still being committed, and God goes right on showing mercy. Thank goodness God's mercy is different from our own.

Key Verses

God passed in front of him and called out, "God, God, a God of mercy and grace, endlessly patient—so much love, so deeply true—loyal in love for a thousand generations, forgiving iniquity, rebellion, and sin. Still, he doesn't ignore sin. He holds sons and grandsons responsible for a father's sins to the third and even fourth generation."

Exodus 34:6–7 THE MESSAGE

The Lord shows mercy and is kind. He does not become angry quickly, and he has great love.

Psalm 103:8 NCV

Rend your hearts and not your garments and return to the Lord, your God, for He is gracious and merciful, slow to anger, and abounding in loving-kindness; and He revokes His sentence of evil [when His conditions are met].

Joel 2:13 AMP

What shall we say then? Is there injustice on God's part? By no means! For he says to Moses, "I will have mercy on whom I have mercy, and I will have compassion on whom I have compassion." So then it depends not on human will or exertion, but on God, who has mercy.

Romans 9:14–16 ESV

Additional Notable Verses Concerning God's Mercy

Numbers 14:18; 1 Kings 8:23; 1 Chronicles 16:34; Psalm 25:6; 36:5; 52:8; 86:5; 89:28; 103; 106:1; 107:1; 119:156; 136; 145:9; 147:11; Proverbs 28:13; Isaiah 54:7; 55:1–9; 63:9; Jeremiah 3:12; Lamentations 3:32; Daniel 9:9; Micah 7:18–20; Luke 1:75–79; Romans 12:1–2; Ephesians 2:1–5; Titus 3:5; 1 Peter 1:3

God's Power

The idea that God is not just powerful, but all-powerful, is an incredible one to grasp. No matter the problems, God is big enough to handle them. In the Bible we see God showing His power in almost every way imaginable. Over and over again the power of the Almighty accomplishes its purposes, even when incredibly powerful forces on earth and in the spiritual realm oppose Him. God's power always makes sure that God's purposes are complete. Now that is something that will help you sleep at night.

Key Verses

Now you will see that I am the one God! There is no god but me. I send life and death; I can hurt, and I can heal. No one can escape from me.

Deuteronomy 32:39 NCV

God has spoken plainly, and I have heard it many times: Power, O God, belongs to you.

Psalm 62:11 NLT

The steadfast of mind You will keep in perfect peace, because he trusts in You. Trust in the Lord forever, for in God the Lord, we have an everlasting Rock.

Isaiah 26:3–4 NASB

Jesus looked straight at them and said, "There are some things that people cannot do, but God can do anything."

Matthew 19:26 CEV

Additional Notable Verses Concerning God's Power

Genesis 18:14; Exodus 15:6; 2 Chronicles 16:8–9; Job 9; 26:14; 40:6–24; Psalm 8; 21:13; 63:1–2; 66:7; 79:11; 89:13; 102:25; 106:8; 136:12; Isaiah 26:4; 41:10; Jeremiah 10:12; 32:27; Daniel 4:35; Nahum 1:3; Romans 1:16–20; 4:21; 1 Corinthians 1:18–31; 6:14; 2 Corinthians 9:8; Ephesians 3:7; 6:10; Colossians 1:11; 2 Timothy 1:8; 1 Peter 1:5; Revelation 4:11; 5:13; 11:17

God's Presence

Omnipresence is the word that theologians have given to God's ability to be present everywhere at one time. It is one of the most basic and fundamental concepts about God, and it is probably one of the first that little children grasp. Yet it is so basic that we often forget it as we go about everyday life.

That God is ever present is at the core of who the Bible says He is. Over and over again God's Word reiterates that there is nowhere that one can go to hide from God. Adam and Eve, Jonah, and others tried to hide from God, but you cannot hide from a Creator who is everywhere. This also means that no matter our trouble, no matter how deep our despair, God is already there as well.

Key Verses

Honor and majesty are [found] in His presence; strength and joy are [found] in His sanctuary.

1 Chronicles 16:27 AMP

You make known to me the path of life; in your presence there is fullness of joy; at your right hand are pleasures forevermore.

Psalm 16:11 ESV

Where can I go from Your Spirit? Or where can I flee from Your presence?

Psalm 139:7 NASB

Additional Notable Verses Concerning God's Presence
Genesis 3:8; Exodus 33:14; Psalm 9:3; 31:20; 51:11; 68:8; 95:2; 97:5; 100:2; 114:7; 140:13; Zephaniah 1:7; Acts 3:19; Jude 1:24–25

God's Protection

If you live somewhere that gets tornadoes, you fully appreciate a storm cellar. When a funnel cloud sweeping through your neighborhood could take your home with it, you are more than happy to have a refuge. Storms that can cause severe damage are frightening even from inside a shelter, and without it they could be deadly.

Life sends along other types of storms as well. These may not involve wind and rain, but they are no less dangerous. Storms can come in the form of disease, health problems, relational difficulties, and a host of other issues. When these storms come we must run to the Christian's refuge—our God. God promises to protect us, and His power is so much greater than any storm cellar. When the storms come, make sure to take shelter!

Key Verses

In peace I will both lie down and sleep, for You alone, O Lord, make me to dwell in safety.

Psalm 4:8 NASB

The name of the Lord is a fortified tower; the righteous run to it and are safe.

Proverbs 18:10 NIV

But the Lord is faithful, who will establish you and guard you from the evil one.

2 Thessalonians 3:3 NKJV

Additional Notable Verses Concerning God's Protection

Psalm 5:11; 18:2; 20:1; 27; 32:7; 37:28; 40:11; 41:1–3; 59:1; 56:9; 69:29; 91; 97:10; 112:6–8; 116:6; 121; 140; Proverbs 1:33; 2:8–22; 3:23–24; Isaiah 43:2; John 17:1–19; 1 Peter 3:12–14

God's Wrath

Don't make me angry. You wouldn't like me when I'm angry." Those immortal words were uttered by the character David Banner, who transformed into the Incredible Hulk in the TV series of the same name. If we are not careful, we can view God this way. We tell ourselves, "Don't make God angry. You wouldn't like Him when He's angry."

The Word of God tells us that our God is incredibly powerful and that His anger burns against those who have rejected Him. Believers have been saved from God's wrath (Romans 5:9), and now God approaches them as children rather than enemies. God's wrath is a fearsome prospect, and we should have great concern for those who are without God. Thankfully God's wrath will never be something that the Christian has to experience firsthand.

Key Verses

He that believeth on the Son hath everlasting life: and he that believeth not the Son shall not see life; but the wrath of God abideth on him.

John 3:36 KJV

For the wrath of God is revealed from heaven against all ungodliness and unrighteousness of men, who by their unrighteousness suppress the truth.

Romans 1:18 ESV

For God has not destined us for wrath, but for obtaining salvation through our Lord Jesus Christ, who died for us, so that whether we are awake or asleep, we will live together with Him.

1 Thessalonians 5:9–10 NASB

Additional Notable Verses Concerning God's Wrath

Genesis 6–9; 19; Exodus 34:6–7; Deuteronomy 7:1–5; Numbers 16; Isaiah 13:6–16; 53:4–11; Matthew 3:5–12; 24:15–22, 48–51; Luke 21:20–28; John 2:13–17; 2 Corinthians 5:11; 1 Thessalonians 1:9–10; Revelation 6:12–17; 16:1–12; 19:11–16

Good and Evil

Anyone who fails to believe in good and evil obviously does not watch the news. At times it seems that the forces of good are making headway, and at other times it looks like the forces of evil will overwhelm all that is good in the world.

The Bible reads in many ways like a blow-by-blow account of the struggle of good versus evil. From the description of Satan's rebellion, to humanity's fall in the Garden of Eden, to God's ultimate victory, the Scriptures tell us how the battle has gone and where it is going.

Key Verses

Woe to those who call evil good and good evil, who put darkness for light and light for darkness, who put bitter for sweet and sweet for bitter!

Isaiah 5:20 ESV

For a good tree does not bear bad fruit, nor does a bad tree bear good fruit. For every tree is known by its own fruit. For men do not gather figs from thorns, nor do they gather grapes from a bramble bush. A good man out of the good treasure of his heart brings forth good; and an evil man out of the evil treasure of his heart brings forth evil. For out of the abundance of the heart his mouth speaks.

Luke 6:43–45 NKJV

God will reward each of us for what we have done. He will give eternal life to everyone who has patiently done what is good in the hope of receiving glory, honor, and life that lasts forever. But he will show how angry and furious he can be with every selfish person who rejects the truth and wants to do evil. All who are wicked will be punished with trouble and suffering.

Romans 2:6–9 CEV

Additional Notable Verses Concerning Good and Evil

Genesis 3; 50:15–21; Proverbs 2:6–13; Matthew 7:15–23; 15:11–20; 18:6–7; Romans 12:21; Galatians 5:19–23; Revelation 1–22

Government

Citizenry and government always seem to have a very uneasy relationship. Governments all seem to tax too much, participate in unethical activities, become bureaucratic nightmares, and do whatever they can to perpetuate themselves.

Human governments will always be fraught with sinful people who have sinful agendas. Still, God's Word is very specific that Christians are to obey the laws of the land. If and when government contradicts God, those who name the name of Christ are to submit to the higher power. And no matter what governments of men may think, they are not the higher power.

Key Verses

The king gives stability to the land by justice, but a man who takes bribes overthrows it.

Proverbs 29:4 NASB

Be a good citizen. All governments are under God. Insofar as there is peace and order, it's God's order. So live responsibly as a citizen. If you're irresponsible to the state, then you're irresponsible with God, and God will hold you responsible. Duly constituted authorities are only a threat if you're trying to get by with something. Decent citizens should have nothing to fear. . . . That's also why you pay taxes—so that an orderly way of life can be maintained. Fulfill your obligations as a citizen. Pay your taxes, pay your bills, respect your leaders.

Romans 13:1–3; 6–7 THE MESSAGE

Submit yourselves for the Lord's sake to every human authority: whether to the emperor, as the supreme authority, or to governors, who are sent by him to punish those who do wrong and to commend those who do right. For it is God's will that by doing good you should silence the ignorant talk of foolish people. Live as free people, but do not use your freedom as a cover-up for evil; live as God's slaves. Show proper respect to everyone, love the family of believers, fear God, honor the emperor.

1 Peter 2:13–17 NIV

Additional Notable Verses Concerning Government

Proverbs 11:14; 16:12–15; 28:2; 29:14; Ecclesiastes 10:17; Daniel 6:1–4; Acts 5:27–29; Titus 3:1

Grace

G race is one of the more beautiful words in all of language. Grace is not only not getting a punishment you deserve but also getting a treasure you do not deserve. Of all of the big ideas in God's Word, grace is possibly the most powerful.

Where sin exists, grace will exist all the more (Romans 5:20). Where works of the law and flesh exist, grace will be there outshining them both. Where there is conflict and uncertainty, grace will be present and will overwhelm all competitors. God's grace, which He extends to us and which we are to extend to others, is the most dramatic and powerful force in the world.

Key Verses

For the Lord God is a sun and shield; the Lord will give grace and glory; no good thing will He withhold from those who walk uprightly.

Psalm 84:11 NKJV

But God, being rich in mercy, because of the great love with which he loved us, even when we were dead in our trespasses, made us alive together with Christ—by grace you have been saved.

Ephesians 2:4–5 ESV

But He said to me, My grace (My favor and loving-kindness and mercy) is enough for you [sufficient against any danger and enables you to bear the trouble manfully]; for My strength and power are made perfect (fulfilled and completed) and show themselves most effective in [your] weakness. Therefore, I will all the more gladly glory in my weaknesses and infirmities, that the strength and power of Christ (the Messiah) may rest (yes, may pitch a tent over and dwell) upon me!

2 Corinthians 12:9–10 AMP

Additional Notable Verses Concerning Grace

Psalm 45:2; Proverbs 3:34; Zechariah 4:7; 12:10; Luke 2:40; 4:22; John 1:14–18; Acts 4:33; 15:11; 20:24; Romans 3:24; 5:12–21; 6:14; 1 Corinthians 15:10; 2 Corinthians 6:1; 9:8; Galatians 1:15; 5:4; Ephesians 1:3–10; 2:1–10; 4:29; Colossians 4:6; 2 Thessalonians 2:16; Titus 3:7; Hebrews 4:16; 10:29; 12:28; James 4:6; 1 Peter 1:3–12; 4:10; 5:10; 2 Peter 3:18

Grandparents

umor writer Dave Barry showed an awful lot of wisdom about grandparents when he wrote, "The best baby-sitters, of course, are the baby's grandparents. You feel completely comfortable entrusting your baby to them for long periods, which is why most grandparents flee to Florida."* No doubt many parents, grandparents, and infants can sympathize.

Biblically grandparents have a far greater responsibility, however, than just the occasional (or frequent) baby-sitting gig. They are the keepers of the family's spiritual heritage, and though they may not have the energy they once did, they are to strive to continue to honor and glorify God. The heritage and legacy of godly grandparents is one that will leave an indelible mark on their children, their grandchildren, and generations to come.

Key Verses

Only give heed to yourself and keep your soul diligently, so that you do not forget the things which your eyes have seen and they do not depart from your heart all the days of your life; but make them known to your sons and your grandsons.

Deuteronomy 4:9 NASB

Grandchildren are the crowning glory of the aged; parents are the pride of their children.

Proverbs 17:6 NLT

A good person leaves an inheritance for their children's children, but a sinner's wealth is stored up for the righteous.

Proverbs 13:22 NIV

I remember your true faith. That faith first lived in your grandmother Lois and in your mother Eunice, and I know you now have that same faith.

2 Timothy 1:5 NCV

Additional Notable Verses Concerning Grandparents

Exodus 34:5–7; Psalm 103:17–18; Proverbs 16:31; Isaiah 46:4; Titus 2:1–5

*Quoted in Bonnie Louise Kuchler, *Just Grandparents* (Minocqua, WI: Willow Creek Press, 2004).

Greed

Greed is one of the most tricky of sins because its appetite cannot be quenched. Are you greedy for money? Then no matter how much money you obtain you will still be greedy for money. Are you greedy for fame? Then no matter how famous you become you will never be quite famous enough. No matter what you are greedy for, the more of it that you obtain the more of it you will desire.

The counter to greed in the Scriptures is generosity. Rather than being greedy and constantly seeking to get more and more, we should passionately and proactively seek to give. This can be a hard lesson to learn, and an even harder one to implement, but we must realize that in Christ we already have all that we need. Greed leaves you wanting more; Christ leaves you wanting nothing.

Key Verses

Give freely and become more wealthy; be stingy and lose everything.

Proverbs 11:24 NLT

What will you gain, if you own the whole world but destroy yourself? What could you give to get back your soul?

Mark 8:36–37 CEV

For the love of money is a root of all kinds of evil. Some people, eager for money, have wandered from the faith and pierced themselves with many griefs.

1 Timothy 6:10 NIV

Let your conduct be without covetousness; be content with such things as you have. For He Himself has said, "I will never leave you nor forsake you."

Hebrews 13:5 NKJV

Additional Notable Verses Concerning Greed

Psalm 119:36; Proverbs 15:27; 20:21; 23:6; 28:22, 25; 29:4; Isaiah 57:17; Jeremiah 8:10; Ezekiel 33:31; Matthew 6:19–34; 23:25; Mark 7:21–23; Luke 11:39; 12:13–21; Romans 1:29; 1 Corinthians 5:10–11; Ephesians 5:3–5; Colossians 3:5; 1 Thessalonians 2:5; 1 Timothy 6:9; James 3:14–16; 1 Peter 5:2; 2 Peter 2:3, 12–15

Hatred

Hate is a very strong term. When a word like *hate* is used in the Bible, we should stand up and take notice. An expression like this is not used lightly by the human writers of the Bible, and it is certainly not by happenstance that the Holy Spirit inspired those writers to use such strong confrontational language.

Because of how strong the word *hatred* is, we should pay special attention to the things that God hates. We should also pay particular attention to the things that God's Word tells us to hate, and the things that it tells us not to hate. Every time you see the word *hate* on the Bible's pages, pay close attention. What you hate is almost as important as what you love.

Key Verses

You shall not hate your brother in your heart, but you shall reason frankly with your neighbor, lest you incur sin because of him.

Leviticus 19:17 ESV

You will be hated by all because of My name, but it is the one who has endured to the end who will be saved.

Matthew 10:22 NASB

Whosoever hateth his brother is a murderer: and ye know that no murderer hath eternal life abiding in him.

1 John 3:15 KJV

Additional Notable Verses Concerning Hatred

Genesis 27:41; 37:4; Esther 9:1–5; Psalm 34:21; 35:19; 44:7; 97:10; 101:3; 119:104, 128; 139:21–22; Proverbs 8:13; 10:12, 18; 15:17; 26:24–28; 29:10; Matthew 5:43–48; John 7:7; 15:18–27; Romans 1:28–32; Galatians 5:19–23; Colossians 3:8; Titus 3:3; 1 John 2:7–11; 3:13; 4:20

Healing

Healings are one of the most frequent miracles to occur in the Bible. From Genesis to Revelation healings occur repeatedly. In fact, when John the Baptist sent messengers to ask Jesus if He was the Christ, the messengers were given the response, "The blind receive sight and the lame walk, the lepers are cleansed and the deaf hear, the dead are raised up, and the poor have the gospel preached to them" (Matthew 11:5 NASB).

Healing was an authentication of the identity of Jesus. Later on, after Jesus' ascension into heaven, the apostles healed people as an authentication of their message as followers of Christ. Healings were about more than just a sick person getting well; they were about God showing His power along with His compassion. Whenever God heals someone today, it also shows His power and His compassion.

Key Verses

Have mercy on me, O Lord, for I am weak; O Lord, heal me, for my bones are troubled.

Psalm 6:2 NKJV

A cheerful heart is good medicine, but a crushed spirit dries up the bones.

Proverbs 17:22 NIV

Are you hurting? Pray. Do you feel great? Sing. Are you sick? Call the church leaders together to pray and anoint you with oil in the name of the Master. Believing-prayer will heal you, and Jesus will put you on your feet. And if you've sinned, you'll be forgiven—healed inside and out.

James 5:13–15 THE MESSAGE

Additional Notable Verses Concerning Healing

Numbers 12:1–16; Deuteronomy 32:39; 2 Kings 20:1–11; 2 Chronicles 7:14; Job 5:18; Psalm 6:2; 41:4; 60:2; 103:2–4; 147:3; Proverbs 16:24; Ecclesiastes 3:3; Isaiah 19:22; 53:5; 57:15–19; Jeremiah 3:22; 17:14; Hosea 6:1; Zechariah 11:16; Matthew 10:1; 12:10–13; 13:15; Luke 14:1–4; John 4:43–54; 1 Peter 2:24

Health/Healthcare

The Bible is not a self-help book about how to take care of your body. If you are looking for something to tell you what your caloric intake should be, your ideal cholesterol levels, or how much exercise you need, the Bible is not your book. That is not to say that the Bible has nothing to say about your health; it actually has plenty to say.

The Bible lays down many principles for the best ways to take care of our bodies and to stay in good health. Prescriptions for good health from the Bible include placing God first, getting bodily exercise, and even laughing. No, God's Word is not a health book, but it is definitely the first stop on the way to a healthy lifestyle.

Key Verses

A man's spirit will endure sickness, but a crushed spirit who can bear?
Proverbs 18:14 ESV

And so, dear brothers and sisters, I plead with you to give your bodies to God because of all he has done for you. Let them be a living and holy sacrifice—the kind he will find acceptable. This is truly the way to worship him.
Romans 12:1 NLT

For bodily exercise profits a little, but godliness is profitable for all things, having promise of the life that now is and of that which is to come.
1 Timothy 4:8 NKJV

Additional Notable Verses Concerning Health/Healthcare
Exodus 15:26; 23:25; Job 12:10; Psalm 38:3–8; 63:5; 103:1–5; 119:93; 145:15–16; Proverbs 3:7–8; 4:20–22; 12:25; 13:12; 14:30; 17:22; Isaiah 40:29–31; 58:11; Matthew 6:27; 9:12; 11:28–29; 1 Corinthians 6:19–20; 1 Timothy 4:3–5; 3 John 1:2

Heaven

Imagine for a moment that life here on earth was as good as it ever got. Think of how depressing it would be sitting for hours in a doctor's waiting room watching the time tick by and knowing that this was the high point for you. Your good days would seem okay, but there are far too few of them, and on the worst days you would be near suicide knowing that there was nothing better to come.

Fortunately, life here on earth is not as good as it gets for the Christian. For the believer in Jesus Christ there is something far better waiting for all of eternity. Heaven, and being forever in the presence of Christ, awaits Christians after death. Not only is there more than life here on earth, but what there is after this life is more wonderful than we can even begin to imagine.

Key Verses

However, do not rejoice that the spirits submit to you, but rejoice that your names are written in heaven.

Luke 10:20 NIV

Do not store up for yourselves treasures on earth, where moth and rust destroy, and where thieves break in and steal. But store up for yourselves treasures in heaven, where neither moth nor rust destroys, and where thieves do not break in or steal; for where your treasure is, there your heart will be also.

Matthew 6:19–21 NASB

No eye has seen, no ear has heard, and no mind has imagined what God has prepared for those who love him.

1 Corinthians 2:9 NLT *

Additional Notable Verses Concerning Heaven

Genesis 1:1; Deuteronomy 26:15; 1 Kings 8:26–61; Psalm 20:6; 89:29; 103:11; Isaiah 66:1; Jeremiah 23:24; 31:37; Daniel 4:35; Matthew 5:12; 6:9; 11:25; 18:10; Luke 12:33; 15:7; 23:39–43; John 14:2; Acts 7:49; 1 Corinthians 15:50; 2 Corinthians 5:1; 12:1–6; Hebrews 11:16; 12:23; 1 Peter 1:4; Revelation 10:6

Hell

As difficult as it may be to accept, the Bible clearly teaches that hell is a very real place. The existence of hell is confirmed repeatedly in the Scriptures and is a frequent topic of Jesus himself. Let us live and speak in such a way that we will have done our part to keep it empty.

Key Verses

> Then He will also say to those on His left, "Depart from Me, accursed ones, into the eternal fire which has been prepared for the devil and his angels; for I was hungry, and you gave Me nothing to eat; I was thirsty, and you gave Me nothing to drink; I was a stranger, and you did not invite Me in; naked, and you did not clothe Me; sick, and in prison, and you did not visit Me." Then they themselves also will answer, "Lord, when did we see You hungry, or thirsty, or a stranger, or naked, or sick, or in prison, and did not take care of You?" Then He will answer them, "Truly I say to you, to the extent that you did not do it to one of the least of these, you did not do it to Me." These will go away into eternal punishment, but the righteous into eternal life.
>
> Matthew 25:41–46 NASB

> The sea gave up the dead that were in it, and death and Hades gave up the dead that were in them, and each person was judged according to what they had done. Then death and Hades were thrown into the lake of fire. The lake of fire is the second death. Anyone whose name was not found written in the book of life was thrown into the lake of fire.
>
> Revelation 20:13–15 NIV

Additional Notable Verses Concerning Hell

Matthew 5:27–30; 10:26–28; 13:36–43, 47–50; Mark 9:42–48; Luke 16:19–31; Acts 2:29–31; 1 Peter 3:13–22; 2 Peter 2:4–9; Jude 1:6; Revelation 19:19–21; 20:1–7

History

istory may not have been your favorite subject in school. Some people love studying days gone by, while others find it boring, tedious, and dry. If you are one of those people who disdained history, you probably hoped that when you received your last diploma, you had seen the last of history lessons as well. Then you opened your Bible and found the first twelve books were books of history.

What sets the Bible apart with regard to history is that it is not *just* history. History in God's Word is not just a reciting of facts from long ago, but rather the story of God, His redemption, and His people. The history that the Scriptures tell is not always exciting in and of itself. Genesis 4:18, for example, is far from exciting: "And unto Enoch was born Irad: and Irad begat Mehujael: and Mehujael begat Methusael: and Methusael begat Lamech" (KJV). Yet the story that is woven together throughout a biblical view of history shows us life as it really happened, and it gives us examples from which to learn how to live.

Key Verses

For inquire, please, of bygone ages, and consider what the fathers have searched out. For we are but of yesterday and know nothing, for our days on earth are a shadow. Will they not teach you and tell you and utter words out of their understanding?

Job 8:8–10 ESV

For whatever things were written before were written for our learning, that we through the patience and comfort of the Scriptures might have hope.

Romans 15:4 NKJV

The things that happened to those people are examples. They were written down to teach us, because we live in a time when all these things of the past have reached their goal.

1 Corinthians 10:11 NCV

Additional Notable Verses Concerning History
Joshua 24:1–15; 1 Corinthians 10:1–13

Holiness

Holiness is one of those words so important and integral to our understanding of God that before we can even think about it we must make sure that we know exactly what it means. When we use the term *holiness*, we are referring to someone being sinless, or existing separate from sin.

Holiness is as much a part of who God is as love, grace, and mercy. It is only through the power of the Holy Spirit that we can be holy.

Key Verses

For I am the Lord your God. Consecrate yourselves therefore, and be holy, for I am holy. And you shall not make yourselves unclean with any of the swarming things that swarm on the earth.

Leviticus 11:44 NASB

Therefore, I urge you, brothers and sisters, in view of God's mercy, to offer your bodies as a living sacrifice, holy and pleasing to God—this is your true and proper worship. Do not conform to the pattern of this world, but be transformed by the renewing of your mind. Then you will be able to test and approve what God's will is—his good, pleasing and perfect will.

Romans 12:1–2 NIV

Now that you are obedient children of God do not live as you did in the past. You did not understand, so you did the evil things you wanted. But be holy in all you do, just as God, the One who called you, is holy. It is written in the Scriptures: "You must be holy, because I am holy."

1 Peter 1:14–16 NCV

Additional Notable Verses Concerning Holiness

Leviticus 19:2; 20:7; 21:6; 1 Chronicles 16:29; Psalm 24:3–4; 29:2; 86:2; 93:5; Isaiah 35:8; 52:11; Jeremiah 2:3; Zechariah 14:20–21; Romans 6:22; 12:1–2; Mark 6:20; 1 Corinthians 3:17; 2 Corinthians 7:1; Ephesians 1:4; 4:24; 1 Thessalonians 2:10; 3:13; 4:7; Titus 1:8; 2:3; 1 Timothy 4:12; 2 Timothy 1:9; 3:2; Hebrews 7:26; 12:4–17; 1 Peter 2:21–22; 3:5; 2 Peter 3:11; Revelation 22:11

Holy Spirit

The Holy Spirit is the member of the Trinity who is often the most overlooked and in some ways the most mysterious. To many who have not taken the time to dutifully study the Scriptures, He is an unseen force similar to something you would find in a science fiction summer blockbuster.

The Holy Spirit is just as much God as the Father and the Son. He carried an equal load in the acts of creation and the resurrection of Jesus (Romans 8:11). We will never fully discover the depths of the person of the Holy Spirit, but without Him we would be forever lost.

Key Verses

God's Spirit makes us loving, happy, peaceful, patient, kind, good, faithful, gentle, and self-controlled. There is no law against behaving in any of these ways. And because we belong to Christ Jesus, we have killed our selfish feelings and desires. God's Spirit has given us life, and so we should follow the Spirit.

Galatians 5:22–25 CEV

And we have the prophetic word more fully confirmed, to which you will do well to pay attention as to a lamp shining in a dark place, until the day dawns and the morning star rises in your hearts, knowing this first of all, that no prophecy of Scripture comes from someone's own interpretation. For no prophecy was ever produced by the will of man, but men spoke from God as they were carried along by the Holy Spirit.

2 Peter 1:19–21 ESV

Additional Notable Verses Concerning the Holy Spirit

Job 33:4; Proverbs 1:23; Isaiah 11:2; 40:13–14; 48:16; Matthew 28:19; Mark 13:11; Luke 12:12; John 14:15–31; 15:26; 16:4–15; Acts 1:4–5, 16; 2; 5:9; 7:51; 9:31; 13:2; 15:23–28; 16:6–7; 20:28; 21:11; Romans 5:3–5; 8:26; 14:17; 15:13–21; 1 Corinthians 2:10–16; 6:11; 12:1–11; 2 Corinthians 13:14; Galatians 5:5, Ephesians 4:30; 1 Thessalonians 1:6; Hebrews 9:14; 1 Peter 1:11–12

Homemaking

Homemakers are responsible for much of the training and education of a society. These women, and some men, sacrifice a lot to be there with and for their children. Yet the sacrifices are all worth it for those who believe that God has called them to remain primarily in the home and to focus on raising their children and running a household.

The Scriptures are very positive toward the homemaker. Many today make this decision, and in the biblical era it was the dominant, though not only, role for women. Many of the giants of the faith who leap from the pages of Scripture have the homemaking of their mothers to thank for it.

Key Verses

Therefore, I want younger widows to get married, bear children, keep house, and give the enemy no occasion for reproach.

1 Timothy 5:14 NASB

Older women likewise are to be reverent in behavior, not slanderers or slaves to much wine. They are to teach what is good, and so train the young women to love their husbands and children, to be self-controlled, pure, working at home, kind, and submissive to their own husbands, that the word of God may not be reviled.

Titus 2:3–5 ESV

Additional Notable Verses Concerning Homemaking
Proverbs 31:10–31

Hope

There are several essential facets of the Christian life. Christianity without any one of these gives you a faith that is incomplete and lacking in some way. One of the most joyous of these is hope.

Hope plays such an important role in our lives that it is all but indispensable. Hope is what allows us to persevere through persecution, to endure through tribulations, and to overcome trials. Hope takes the worst that life has to offer and believes that there is something on the other side. Little wonder that Charles Spurgeon once advised, "Hope as much as ever a man can hope; for when your hope is in God you cannot hope too much."*

Key Verses

The hope of the righteous is gladness, but the expectation of the wicked perishes.

Proverbs 10:28 NASB

And so, Lord, where do I put my hope? My only hope is in you.

Psalm 39:7 NLT

I pray that the God who gives hope will fill you with much joy and peace while you trust in him. Then your hope will overflow by the power of the Holy Spirit.

Romans 15:13 NCV

Additional Notable Verses Concerning Hope

Job 27:8; 31:24–28; Psalm 33:18; 39:7; 71:14; 119:16; 146:5; Proverbs 14:32; Ecclesiastes 9:4; Acts 26:6–7; Romans 4:18; 5:1–5; 8:25; 12:12; 15:13; 1 Corinthians 15:12–19; Galatians 5:5; Ephesians 4:4; Colossians 1:3–7; 1 Thessalonians 1:3; 2 Thessalonians 2:16; 1 Timothy 1:1; Titus 1:2; 2:13; 3:7; Hebrews 3:6; 6:19; 7:19; 1 Peter 1:3–25; 1 John 3:3

---

*Charles Haddon Spurgeon, *Words of Wisdom for Daily Living* (New Kensington, PA: Whitaker House, 1993), 187.

Hospitality

There are some people who live to entertain. They are such social creatures that they constantly desire their home to be filled with guests. These people want to throw the Christmas party, offer up their spare room to visiting missionaries, and use their living room to host Bible study. God has given them one of the most instrumental gifts that He ever gave to the church: the gift of hospitality.

The gift of hospitality is important for many reasons in the Bible. Not the least of these reasons is given in Hebrews 13:1–2: "Let love of the brethren continue. Do not neglect to show hospitality to strangers, for by this some have entertained angels without knowing it" (NASB). Not only is hospitality important to the earthly family of God, but believers must persist in hospitality in case angels happen to be in need of a place to stay. Now there is a reason to leave the front porch light on.

Key Verses

When a stranger resides with you in your land, you shall not do him wrong. The stranger who resides with you shall be to you as the native among you, and you shall love him as yourself, for you were aliens in the land of Egypt; I am the Lord your God.

Leviticus 19:33–34 NASB

Be ready with a meal or a bed when it's needed. Why, some have extended hospitality to angels without ever knowing it!

Hebrews 13:2 THE MESSAGE

Offer hospitality to one another without grumbling.

1 Peter 4:9 NIV

Additional Notable Verses Concerning Hospitality
Exodus 23:9; Job 31:32; Matthew 25:34–40; Mark 9:38–41; Luke 14:7–14; Romans 12:10–13; 1 Timothy 3:2; 5:9–10; Titus 1:8; 3 John 1:5–8

Humility

True humility was just as much of a rarity in biblical times as it is in our own. The ancient Greeks listed hubris as one of their most offensive crimes. Hubris was an extreme form of arrogance that far exceeded mere confidence. Stories were told of mortal men in a position of power who became so enamored with their own abilities that they thought themselves to be equal to Zeus, Apollo, and the other Greek deities. In these stories, anytime one of these mere mortals showed hubris, they were severely punished by the gods. Thus no one wanted to show hubris, so an entire culture feigned humility.

This is why the Scriptures say that real, genuine humility is so important. God desires that His children be honest and sincere people who are submissive to Him and to human authorities, and who understand that their fellow human beings are important to Him, and should be to them. True humility is understanding where you fit in God's world and proceeding accordingly.

Key Verses

Though you are above us all, you care for humble people, and you keep a close watch on everyone who is proud.

Psalm 138:6 CEV

No, O people, the Lord has told you what is good, and this is what he requires of you: to do what is right, to love mercy, and to walk humbly with your God.

Micah 6:8 NLT

Humble yourselves [feeling very insignificant] in the presence of the Lord, and He will exalt you [He will lift you up and make your lives significant].

James 4:10 AMP

Additional Notable Verses Concerning Humility

2 Chronicles 7:14; 33:23; 36:12; Job 22:29; Psalm 9:12; 34:2; Proverbs 3:34; 15:33; 16:19; 18:12; 22:4; 29:23; Isaiah 57:15; Jeremiah 44:10; Matthew 18:1–4; Luke 14:7–11; 18:9–14; John 13:1–17; Colossians 3:12; 1 Peter 5:5

Husbands

In the time when the New Testament was written, husbands were in charge in a family. They had all the authority and all the power in a marriage relationship. But God revealed a plan for marriage that was very different. Husbands are to love their wives as Christ loved the church—to lay down their lives for them.

Key Verses

Husbands, go all out in your love for your wives, exactly as Christ did for the church—a love marked by giving, not getting. Christ's love makes the church whole. His words evoke her beauty. Everything he does and says is designed to bring the best out of her, dressing her in dazzling white silk, radiant with holiness. And that is how husbands ought to love their wives. They're really doing themselves a favor—since they're already "one" in marriage.

Ephesians 5:25–28 THE MESSAGE

Husbands, love your wives and do not be harsh with them.

Colossians 3:19 NIV

You husbands in the same way, live with your wives in an understanding way, as with someone weaker, since she is a woman; and show her honor as a fellow heir of the grace of life, so that your prayers will not be hindered.

1 Peter 3:7 NASB

Additional Notable Verses Concerning Husbands
Genesis 2:24; Malachi 2:14–15; Mark 10:6–8; 1 Corinthians 7; 11:3

Hygiene

There is a good chance that the ancient world was a fairly stinky one. For those who love to burn candles, decorate tables with flowers, and use air fresheners in every room of the house, it would be quite a shock. The world without running water, deodorant, and antibacterial wipes was certainly a different world.

Good hygiene, without modern conveniences, was very much on the mind of God as He handed down the Law to the nation of Israel. Because of the lack of understanding of things like germs and contagious diseases, God gave the Israelites a plan to implement proper hygiene in their camps and their cities. The old saying that cleanliness is next to godliness is not in the Bible, but maybe God's focus on taking care of hygiene is where the idea comes from.

Key Verses

Command the people of Israel to remove from the camp anyone who has a skin disease or a discharge, or who has become ceremonially unclean by touching a dead person. This command applies to men and women alike. Remove them so they will not defile the camp in which I live among them.

Numbers 5:2–3 NLT

Also you shall have a place outside the camp, where you may go out; and you shall have an implement among your equipment, and when you sit down outside, you shall dig with it and turn and cover your refuse. For the Lord your God walks in the midst of your camp, to deliver you and give your enemies over to you; therefore your camp shall be holy, that He may see no unclean thing among you, and turn away from you.

Deuteronomy 23:12–14 NKJV

Additional Notable Verses Concerning Hygiene
Leviticus 11; 13; 15; Numbers 19:11–22

Hypocrisy

n the Greek theater, one who wore a mask in order to portray someone else was referred to as a hypocrite. Only the hypocrite knew their true identity, for it was hidden from everyone else on and off stage by the mask they wore.

The hypocrite who is roundly condemned in Scripture is not on stage, but is pretending to be someone who they are not in real life. On stage at the end of the play, the hypocrite would pull off the mask and everyone knew who was playing that role. But in real life discernment is necessary to unmask those who say and do things contrary to their true identity.

Key Verses

The hypocrite with his mouth destroys his neighbor, but through knowledge the righteous will be delivered.

Proverbs 11:9 NKJV

For the vile person will speak villany, and his heart will work iniquity, to practise hypocrisy, and to utter error against the Lord, to make empty the soul of the hungry, and he will cause the drink of the thirsty to fail.

Isaiah 32:6 KJV

Now when He had spoken, a Pharisee asked Him to have lunch with him; and He went in, and reclined at the table. When the Pharisee saw it, he was surprised that He had not first ceremonially washed before the meal. But the Lord said to him, "Now you Pharisees clean the outside of the cup and of the platter; but inside of you, you are full of robbery and wickedness. You foolish ones, did not He who made the outside make the inside also? But give that which is within as charity, and then all things are clean for you."

Luke 11:37–41 NASB

Additional Notable Verses Concerning Hypocrisy
Job 8:13; 20:5; 34:30; 36:13; Isaiah 9:17; 29:13–15; Matthew 7:1–5; 15:1–11; 22:18; 23:1–36; Luke 12:1; 18:1–14; 1 Timothy 4:1–5; 1 Peter 2:1

Idolatry

Human beings have not really changed all that much throughout history. We drive cars instead of walking, but we are very similar to those who followed God in the Old and New Testaments. If you doubt this, take a moment to study what the Bible has to say about idolatry.

The Israelites struggled with idolatry so much that even when God used something to save them, that thing had to be destroyed lest they turn it into an idol (2 Kings 18:4). Today idolatry takes a much more subtle form. We may not worship golden calves or brass serpents, but we can very quickly allow other things or people to take over God's place of priority in our lives.

Key Verses

I am the Lord your God, who brought you out of the land of Egypt, out of the house of slavery. You shall have no other gods before me.

Exodus 20:2–3 ESV

Our God is in heaven doing whatever he wants to do. Their gods are metal and wood, handmade in a basement shop: carved mouths that can't talk, painted eyes that can't see, tin ears that can't hear, molded noses that can't smell, hands that can't grasp, feet that can't walk or run, throats that never utter a sound. Those who make them have become just like them, have become just like the gods they trust.

Psalm 115:3–8 THE MESSAGE

For of this you can be sure: No immoral, impure or greedy person—such a person is an idolater—has any inheritance in the kingdom of Christ and of God.

Ephesians 5:5 NIV

Additional Notable Verses Concerning Idolatry

Genesis 35:1–5; Exodus 20:4–6; 22:20; 23:13; 32; Deuteronomy 4:15–31; 5:8–10; 7:4; 8:19; 18:20; 30:15–20; 2 Kings 17:35; Ezekiel 14:1–11; Daniel 3; Psalm 81:9; 106; Acts 15:20; 19:21–41; Romans 2:21–22; 1 Corinthians 5:11; 6:9–10; 8:4; 12:2; Colossians 3:5; 1 Thessalonians 1:9

Immigration/Immigrants

Unless you live in the Garden of Eden, which would be newsworthy, you are the product of some form of immigration. Many of us are actually products of multiple immigrations and the blending of several different ethnicities and nationalities. Though we may not have been the ones who moved our families to where we live now, we are all the result of immigration at one time or another.

Immigrants were important in the Bible for a variety of reasons. First, God placed a high priority on how the ancient Israelites treated immigrants and those traveling through Israel. Second, in the New Testament the life of the immigrant is an example of what life is like for the Christian. All believers are now living life in a temporary home (earth) as we make our way to our permanent home (heaven). For the believer, immigration is a way of life.

Key Verses

Do not cheat or hurt a foreigner, because you were foreigners in the land of Egypt.

Exodus 22:21 NCV

When a stranger resides with you in your land, you shall not do him wrong. The stranger who resides with you shall be to you as the native among you, and you shall love him as yourself, for you were aliens in the land of Egypt; I am the Lord your God.

Leviticus 19:33–34 NASB

Then I will draw near to you for judgment. I will be a swift witness against the sorcerers, against the adulterers, against those who swear falsely, against those who oppress the hired worker in his wages, the widow and the fatherless, against those who thrust aside the sojourner, and do not fear me, says the Lord of hosts.

Malachi 3:5 ESV

Additional Notable Verses Concerning Immigration/Immigrants

Deuteronomy 10:18–19; 16:9–15; 23:1–5; 24:14–22; 26:10–13; Jeremiah 7:5–7; Ezekiel 47:22; Zechariah 7:9–10; Romans 13:1–7

Incest

All sins are violations of God's law, but sins differ in the consequences that result from them. The sexual contact between family members is a sin that bears serious consequences for the perpetrator. It is one of the few crimes about which many of the world's governments actually agree—with each other and with the Bible.

Today incest is not, at least openly, committed as often as it was in the pagan religions that surrounded Israel and later the church. Yet we do ourselves and others a disservice if we neglect to search out what the Scriptures say about an issue, even if it is one that has never impacted our lives personally—particularly with a sin that hides in the dark like incest.

Key Verses

No one is to approach any close relative to have sexual relations. I am the Lord.

Leviticus 18:6 NIV

It is actually reported that there is sexual immorality among you, and such sexual immorality as is not even named among the Gentiles—that a man has his father's wife!

1 Corinthians 5:1 NKJV

Additional Notable Verses Concerning Incest

Genesis 19:30–38; 35:22; 38; Leviticus 18:6–18; 20:11–23; Deuteronomy 22:30; 2 Samuel 13:1–22; Mark 6:14–29

Infertility

According to the Centers for Disease Control, 6.1 million women in the United States alone are dealing with infertility. That is roughly 10 percent of the women ages 15–44 in this country.* If it is not you or someone you love struggling with this issue, 10 percent can seem like a small number, but once it affects you personally, you start to realize just how staggering those statistics are.

Infertility was a common problem in biblical times. Many women, such as Hannah the mother of Samuel, Sarah the mother of Isaac, and Elizabeth the mother of John the Baptist, petitioned God to open their wombs. Others, such as King David's wife Michal, were made infertile as a punishment for sin. Infertility is not a problem too big for God to handle. God will not open every womb that is closed, but He will open His ears to every cry.

Key Verses

Abraham and Sarah were old by this time, very old. Sarah was far past the age for having babies. Sarah laughed within herself, "An old woman like me? Get pregnant? With this old man of a husband?" God said to Abraham, "Why did Sarah laugh saying, 'Me? Have a baby? An old woman like me?' Is anything too hard for God? I'll be back about this time next year and Sarah will have a baby."

Genesis 18:11–14 THE MESSAGE

He gives the childless woman a family, making her a happy mother. Praise the Lord!

Psalm 113:9 NLT

Additional Notable Verses Concerning Infertility
Genesis 16–21; 25:21; 30:1–24; Judges 13:2–24; 1 Samuel 1; 2 Samuel 6:16–23; 2 Kings 4:8–17; Luke 1:5–25

*"Infertility FAQs," Centers for Disease Control and Prevention, www.cdc.gov/reproductivehealth/Infertility/.

Ingratitude

Gratitude is not something that comes naturally. That is why if you spend any time around the parents of a toddler you might hear them say to their child, "Now, what do you say?" as they prompt their offspring to say "Thank you." Sometimes the child will catch on quickly, and sometimes children have a very difficult time expressing gratitude when they just want to take what they were given and go play with it.

In truth, adults are not much better at overcoming ingratitude than their toddler counterparts. Luke 17:11–19 tells the story of ten men who were healed from leprosy by Jesus. Of the ten who were healed, only one expressed thanks at having been brought back from the depths of such a horrible disease. Most of us have seen God work in our lives, and if we are as ungrateful as those men, God may be feeling underappreciated.

Key Verses

Thus they have repaid me evil for good and hatred for my love.

Psalm 109:5 NASB

There was a small town with only a few people in it. A strong king came and mounted an attack, building trenches and attack posts around it. There was a poor but wise man in that town whose wisdom saved the town, but he was promptly forgotten. (He was only a poor man, after all.)

Ecclesiastes 9:14–15 The Message

They knew God, but they did not give glory to God or thank him. Their thinking became useless. Their foolish minds were filled with darkness. They said they were wise, but they became fools.

Romans 1:21–22 NCV

Additional Notable Verses Concerning Ingratitude

Genesis 31:38–42; 40; Deuteronomy 8:11–14; 32:6; Psalm 35:12; 106; Proverbs 17:13; Luke 17:11–19; 2 Timothy 3:2

Injustice

Justice is actually one of the characteristics of God. We are right to say that God is love, but we are equally right to say that God is just. This is the quality of God that cannot and will not allow sin to go unpunished. As a result, this is the quality of God that required His Son to die for us on the cross. God could not merely look away from sin; His justice required it be paid for.

With justice so closely related to who God is, we can see that as God looks around our planet He finds much that violates His character. The prevalence of injustice in the world is not and never has been okay with God. At times it may seem as if God is no longer interested in righting the wrongs that we endure, but we must remember and believe that with justice, it is God's very reputation that is at stake.

Key Verses

Do not pervert justice; do not show partiality to the poor or favoritism to the great, but judge your neighbor fairly.

Leviticus 19:15 NIV

Acquitting the guilty and condemning the innocent—both are detestable to the Lord.

Proverbs 17:15 NLT

An unjust man is an abomination to the righteous, and he who is upright in the way is an abomination to the wicked.

Proverbs 29:27 NKJV

Additional Notable Verses Concerning Injustice

Exodus 23:1–8; Leviticus 19:35; Deuteronomy 27:17–19; 1 Samuel 8:1–3; Psalm 12:5; 58:1–2; 82:2; Proverbs 20:10; 22:16; 28:8; 31:5; Ecclesiastes 3:16; 5:8; Isaiah 26:10; 59:14; Jeremiah 6:11–18; Lamentations 3:35–36; Ezekiel 22:12; Daniel 6; Micah 2:1–2; Habakkuk 1:4; Luke 16:10; James 5:4; 1 Thessalonians 4:4–6

Inspiration of Scripture

I f the Bible were just another book ,we would do well to visit its pages occasionally. At times we would glean something from its wisdom, and at others we would chuckle at the antiquated notions it contains. But the Bible is not just another book; it is in fact God's inspired words to mankind. The Bible was not just written by human authors. Human authors wrote as they were inspired by God, leading to a document that is "God-breathed" and is also alive. The Bible is no mere collection of ancient sayings and wisdom; it is God's revelation of himself, His will, and His plan to us.

Key Verses

Joyful are people of integrity, who follow the instructions of the Lord. Joyful are those who obey his laws and search for him with all their hearts. They do not compromise with evil, and they walk only in his paths. You have charged us to keep your commandments carefully. Oh, that my actions would consistently reflect your decrees!

Psalm 119:1–5 NLT

All Scripture is breathed out by God and profitable for teaching, for reproof, for correction, and for training in righteousness, that the man of God may be complete, equipped for every good work.

2 Timothy 3:16–17 ESV

So we have the prophetic word made more sure, to which you do well to pay attention as to a lamp shining in a dark place, until the day dawns and the morning star arises in your hearts. But know this first of all, that no prophecy of Scripture is a matter of one's own interpretation, for no prophecy was ever made by an act of human will, but men moved by the Holy Spirit spoke from God.

2 Peter 1:19–21 NASB

Additional Notable Verses Concerning the Inspiration of Scripture
Psalm 119; Amos 3:7; Matthew 22:29; Luke 24:45; John 17:17; Acts 1:16; 1 Corinthians 2:12–13; Hebrews 1:1; 2 Peter 3:15–16; Revelation 1:1–11

Jesus

Summarizing what the Bible says about Jesus is difficult because the entirety of the Scriptures revolves around Him. The Old Testament looks forward to His coming, and the New Testament tells of His coming and its continuing effects.

At various times in God's Word He is referred to as the Alpha and Omega, the Bread of Life, the Cornerstone, the Image of God, the Just One, the Lamb of God, the Light of the World, and the Prince of Peace. Those are just a few of the literally dozens of names and titles given to Jesus in the Bible. All of these are just scratching the surface of exactly who Jesus is and what He did.

Key Verses

Therefore the Lord himself will give you a sign: The virgin will conceive and give birth to a son, and will call him Immanuel.

Isaiah 7:14 NIV

"I am the way, the truth, and the life!" Jesus answered. "Without me, no one can go to the Father."

John 14:6 CEV

But we do see Him who was made for a little while lower than the angels, namely, Jesus, because of the suffering of death crowned with glory and honor, so that by the grace of God He might taste death for everyone.

Hebrews 2:9 NASB

Additional Notable Verses Concerning Jesus
Isaiah 9:6; Jeremiah 23:5; Matthew 1–2; 14:22–33; Luke 1:26–56; 2; John 1:1–34; 4:31–38; 6:22–59; 8:21–30; 9:35–41; 10:1–21; 2 Corinthians 5:16–21; 8:9; Romans 5:1–11; Galatians 3:10–14; 4:4; Hebrews 4:14–6:20; 1 John 4:10; Revelation 1

Jesus' Deity

One of the most difficult things to understand about Jesus is that He was 100 percent God and 100 percent man. It can be challenging to grasp how in one human body both God and man resided. This is why many throughout history have concluded that Christ was one or the other—that He was just a man or that He was God and His human form was some sort of a mirage.

The picture that the Bible paints of Jesus, however, makes Jesus' nature and deity very clear. He is specifically referred to as God on a number of occasions. He is described as being preexistent. He is seen as being a rightful recipient of worship. He even forgives sins. The deity of Jesus may be something that our finite minds have a hard time comprehending, but nothing about an infinite God becoming man should be easy.

Key Verses

In the beginning was the Word, and the Word was with God, and the Word was God.

John 1:1 ESV

Have this attitude in yourselves which was also in Christ Jesus, who, although He existed in the form of God, did not regard equality with God a thing to be grasped, but emptied Himself, taking the form of a bond-servant, and being made in the likeness of men.

Philippians 2:5–7 NASB

Beware lest anyone cheat you through philosophy and empty deceit, according to the tradition of men, according to the basic principles of the world, and not according to Christ. For in Him dwells all the fullness of the Godhead bodily; and you are complete in Him, who is the head of all principality and power.

Colossians 2:8–10 NKJV

Additional Notable Verses Concerning Jesus' Deity

Isaiah 9:6; Matthew 1:22–23; Mark 2:1–12; John 8:58; 10:30–33; 20:28; Colossians 1:15–20; 1 Timothy 6:13–16; Hebrews 1:1–4; Revelation 1:4–8; 17:14

Joy

Joy is not dependent upon circumstances. If joy is subject to what happens, it will only exist in spurts and sputters.

True joy, the kind that will endure, can only come from God. The Scriptures speak of a joy that is able to survive imprisonment, opposition, and persecution. This joy finds hope and is anchored in the person of God, and since God never changes, that joy can continue and even thrive in circumstances that may ordinarily cause one to lose hope. A joy that comes from God can stay bright even in the darkest of days.

Key Verses

You have put more joy in my heart than they have when their grain and wine abound.

Psalm 4:7 ESV

Though the fig tree may not blossom, nor fruit be on the vines; though the labor of the olive may fail, and the fields yield no food; though the flock may be cut off from the fold, and there be no herd in the stalls—yet I will rejoice in the Lord, I will joy in the God of my salvation.

Habakkuk 3:17–18 NKJV

God's kingdom isn't a matter of what you put in your stomach, for goodness' sake. It's what God does with your life as he sets it right, puts it together, and completes it with joy.

Romans 14:17 THE MESSAGE

Be happy [in your faith] and rejoice and be glad-hearted continually (always).

1 Thessalonians 5:16 AMP

Additional Notable Verses Concerning Joy

Psalm 5:11; 16:11; 21:1–6; 32:11; 68:3; 89:16; 97:11; 105:43; 126:5; Proverbs 12:20; 21:15; 23:24; Ecclesiastes 2:26; Isaiah 29:19; 35:10; 55:12; 56:7; 61:10; Jeremiah 15:16; Zechariah 9:9; Matthew 5:11–12; Luke 2:10–11; 24:52; John 15:10–11; Acts 15:3; Romans 5:1–11; 2 Corinthians 8:1–4; Galatians 5:22; Philippians 1:20; 3:1–3; 4:4; 1 Thessalonians 1:6; Hebrews 13:17; James 1:2; 1 Peter 1:3–9; 4:13; 3 John 1:4

Judging Others

Do not judge." These words of Jesus are often quoted by people, many of whom seem to know little of the Bible, or even of the context of these words. Jesus' talk about judging is really about hypocrisy. Frequently in God's Word people are told to be discerning and to judge the words and actions of others. The apostles judged the doctrine and theology of false teachers, and in the epistles they continually urge churches and individual believers to do the same. Where our judging of others goes awry is when we try to judge others by our own standards. As Christians we are called to judge people by God's standards, but never by our own.

Key Verses

Do not judge so that you will not be judged. For in the way you judge, you will be judged; and by your standard of measure, it will be measured to you. Why do you look at the speck that is in your brother's eye, but do not notice the log that is in your own eye? Or how can you say to your brother, "Let me take the speck out of your eye," and behold, the log is in your own eye? You hypocrite, first take the log out of your own eye, and then you will see clearly to take the speck out of your brother's eye.

Matthew 7:1–5 NASB

Look beneath the surface so you can judge correctly.

John 7:24 NLT

The person with the Spirit makes judgments about all things, but such a person is not subject to merely human judgments, for, "Who has known the mind of the Lord so as to instruct him?" But we have the mind of Christ.

1 Corinthians 2:15–16 NIV

Additional Notable Verses Concerning Judging Others
Luke 6:37; Romans 14:12–13; 1 Corinthians 2:1–16; 4:5; 2 Timothy 4:1–5; James 4:11–12; 1 John 4:1–13

Judgment of God

There are those who have accepted Christ as Savior, and those who are lost without Him. The first group relates to God as their heavenly Father. Though they will at times incur their Father's discipline, Jesus took on the judgment for their sins on the cross.

The judgment of God that the Bible describes for those without Christ is a fearsome one. But Christians must also be prepared to face Christ.

Key Verses

For God so loved the world, that he gave his only Son, that whoever believes in him should not perish but have eternal life. For God did not send his Son into the world to condemn the world, but in order that the world might be saved through him. Whoever believes in him is not condemned, but whoever does not believe is condemned already, because he has not believed in the name of the only Son of God. And this is the judgment: the light has come into the world, and people loved the darkness rather than the light because their works were evil.

John 3:16–19 ESV

Therefore we make it our aim, whether present or absent, to be well pleasing to Him. For we must all appear before the judgment seat of Christ, that each one may receive the things done in the body, according to what he has done, whether good or bad. Knowing, therefore, the terror of the Lord, we persuade men; but we are well known to God, and I also trust are well known in your consciences.

2 Corinthians 5:9–11 NKJV

And just as each person is destined to die once and after that comes judgment.

Hebrews 9:27 NLT

Additional Notable Verses Concerning the Judgment of God

Genesis 19:1–29; Exodus 9:14–16; 22:21–24; Deuteronomy 28:15–68; 29:20; Job 12:23; Psalm 34:16; 37:28; Proverbs 2:22; Jeremiah 19; Ezekiel 39:21–24; Amos 4; Matthew 25; Luke 13:1–3, 22–30; Romans 2:1–16; 1 Corinthians 4:1–5; 2 Peter 2:4–11; Jude 1:5–7; Revelation 20:1–15; 21:1–8

Justice

J ustice is a very fleeting thing here on planet earth. The people who are entrusted to ensure justice and fairness are regularly involved in scandals, even in cultures that are allegedly decent and civilized. Sports judges and referees rig competitions in favor of particular teams. Legal judges take bribes and rule in favor of the defense or prosecution for many reasons other than the law. Election officials turn the other way while political parties stuff ballot boxes or intimidate opposition voters.

The state of justice can be quite depressing, particularly when you consider that there are other places in our world that are much worse off. Yet, there is hope. The only way to truly have justice on the earth is for the world to be ruled by God himself. Thankfully that day is coming. There is a day in the future when Jesus Christ will reign on the earth. He will rule from His throne and there will finally be justice.

Key Verses

You shall do no injustice in judgment. You shall not be partial to the poor, nor honor the person of the mighty. In righteousness you shall judge your neighbor.
Leviticus 19:15 NKJV

When justice is done, it brings joy to the righteous but terror to evildoers.
Proverbs 21:15 NIV

But let justice roll down like waters, and righteousness like an ever-flowing stream.
Amos 5:24 ESV

The Lord God has told us what is right and what he demands: "See that justice is done, let mercy be your first concern, and humbly obey your God."
Micah 6:8 CEV

Additional Notable Verses Concerning Justice

Deuteronomy 16:20; 27:19; 2 Samuel 8:15; 1 Kings 3:16–27; Job 37:23; Psalm 33:5; 106:3; 119:121; 140:12; Proverbs 1:3; 28:5; 29:7; Ecclesiastes 5:8; Isaiah 1:17; 10:1–2; 30:18; 51:4–5; 56:1; 61:8; Jeremiah 22:15; 23:5; Ezekiel 34:15–16; 45:9; Zechariah 7:9; Matthew 12:18; 23:23; Luke 11:42; Acts 17:30–32

Kindness

Kindness is something that God values. It is not something that the world at large values. The world is so far from valuing what God values that now the expression "No good deed goes unpunished" is a common one. It has even become so prevalent to sue people who attempt to come to the aid of those involved in accidents that states have had to enact "Good Samaritan Laws" to prevent those lawsuits.

The world may not value kindness, but it is something that God not only values but demands from His creation. Kindness calls us to live lives that are benevolent, considerate, and helpful. We are to model those characteristics that are reflective of our heavenly Father to everyone we encounter.

Key Verses

Kindness is rewarded—but if you are cruel, you hurt yourself.

Proverbs 11:17 CEV

Therefore, return to your God, observe kindness and justice, and wait for your God continually.

Hosea 12:6 NASB

Instead, be kind to each other, tenderhearted, forgiving one another, just as God through Christ has forgiven you.

Ephesians 4:32 NLT

Additional Notable Verses Concerning Kindness

Genesis 39:21; Ruth 3:10; 2 Samuel 9; Psalm 141:5; Proverbs 3:3; 12:25; 14:22; 19:17; 31:26; Jeremiah 9:23–24; Hosea 10:12; Zechariah 7:9; Acts 9:36; 14:17; Romans 2:4; 11:22; 1 Corinthians 13:4; 2 Corinthians 6:6; Galatians 5:22–23; Ephesians 2:7; Colossians 3:12; Titus 3:4–6; 2 Peter 1:1–7

Knowledge

The Latin phrase *scientia potentia est* is translated as the common phrase "knowledge is power." The phrase is often quoted by people urging others to stay in school or to pursue a degree in higher education. The underlying philosophy behind the phrase is that knowledge is the key that opens all of the locks in life.

Knowledge is very important, but the Bible does not agree with the assertion that knowledge is power. The Scriptures actually teach the opposite. First Corinthians 8:1 says, "Knowledge makes arrogant, but love edifies" (NASB). The Bible has much to say in favor of knowledge, but on its own, knowledge is not enough.

Key Verses

The mind of the prudent acquires knowledge, and the ear of the wise seeks knowledge.

Proverbs 18:15 NASB

Wisdom is a shelter as money is a shelter, but the advantage of knowledge is this: Wisdom preserves those who have it.

Ecclesiastes 7:12 NIV

My people will be destroyed, because they have no knowledge. You have refused to learn, so I will refuse to let you be priests to me. You have forgotten the teachings of your God, so I will forget your children.

Hosea 4:6 NCV

Oh, the depth of the riches and wisdom and knowledge of God! How unsearchable are his judgments and how inscrutable his ways!

Romans 11:33 ESV

Additional Notable Verses Concerning Knowledge

Genesis 2:9; Job 36:3; Psalm 119:66; Proverbs 1:7, 22; 2:10–11; 3:20; 8:10; 11:14; 12:1; 13:16; 15:14; 24:5; Isaiah 11:9; Daniel 12:4; Hosea 6:6; Malachi 2:7; Luke 1:77; John 17:3; 1 Timothy 2:4

Law

Many of the laws of Western civilization were derived from the laws that God gave to Moses on Mount Sinai. The entirety of the Law of Moses contains 613 commandments, ten of which are the famous Ten Commandments in Exodus 20. This group of laws formed the basis for Israelite civilization.

The Law of Moses was imposing for the ancient Israelites, and its shadow hangs over the rest of the Bible. Jesus himself said that He came to fulfill the law (Matthew 5:17). Jesus removed the need to keep the law, and much of the New Testament contains instructions on how to live by grace. The time for attempting to relate to God by the law is done.

Key Verses

And He said to them, "You are those who justify yourselves before men, but God knows your hearts. For what is highly esteemed among men is an abomination in the sight of God. The law and the prophets were until John. Since that time the kingdom of God has been preached, and everyone is pressing into it. And it is easier for heaven and earth to pass away than for one tittle of the law to fail."

Luke 16:15–17 NKJV

For the Law was given through Moses; grace and truth were realized through Jesus Christ.

John 1:17 NASB

For we hold that one is justified by faith apart from works of the law.

Romans 3:28 ESV

Additional Notable Verses Concerning the Law

Exodus 20:2–17; 31:18; Ezra 7:10; Psalm 19:7–9; 78:5; 119:1–8; Proverbs 28:4; Ecclesiastes 12:13; Isaiah 33:22; Malachi 4:4; Matthew 5:17–45; Mark 12:29–33; John 7:19; Acts 7:53; 15:1–29; Romans 2:12–29; 7:1–13; 13:8–10; Galatians 3:15–29; 1 Timothy 1:3–11; Hebrews 2:2; James 2:10; 1 John 3:4; 5:3

Lawsuits

Lawsuits have existed for thousands of years. The need for there to be some type of system whereby people's legal disputes could be resolved has been around almost as long as sin.

Though lawsuits became a necessary evil for humanity, God has a different plan for His children. The Scriptures detail God's desire, particularly for His children, to settle their disputes with wisdom.

Key Verses

Come to terms quickly with your accuser while you are going with him to court, lest your accuser hand you over to the judge, and the judge to the guard, and you be put in prison.

Matthew 5:25 ESV

And how dare you take each other to court! When you think you have been wronged, does it make any sense to go before a court that knows nothing of God's ways instead of a family of Christians? The day is coming when the world is going to stand before a jury made up of followers of Jesus. If someday you are going to rule on the world's fate, wouldn't it be a good idea to practice on some of these smaller cases? Why, we're even going to judge angels! So why not these everyday affairs? As these disagreements and wrongs surface, why would you ever entrust them to the judgment of people you don't trust in any other way? I say this as bluntly as I can to wake you up to the stupidity of what you're doing. Is it possible that there isn't one levelheaded person among you who can make fair decisions when disagreements and disputes come up? I don't believe it. And here you are taking each other to court before people who don't even believe in God! How can they render justice if they don't believe in the God of justice? These court cases are an ugly blot on your community. Wouldn't it be far better to just take it, to let yourselves be wronged and forget it?

1 Corinthians 6:1–7 THE MESSAGE

Additional Notable Verses Concerning Lawsuits
Matthew 5:38–48; 18:15–17

138

Laziness

No matter what type of government or society is implemented, there will always be people trying to get something for nothing. These people seek to live and exist by the work of others rather than by their own efforts.

Laziness exists because sin exists. It is not a by-product of a particular form of government or culture, but it is just as much a sin as adultery and lying. Laziness is nothing short of dishonesty. It is expecting a day's wages for less than a day's work. Laziness costs all involved, and it pays no one.

Key Verses

Take a lesson from the ants, you lazybones. Learn from their ways and become wise! Though they have no prince or governor or ruler to make them work, they labor hard all summer, gathering food for the winter. But you, lazybones, how long will you sleep? When will you wake up? A little extra sleep, a little more slumber, a little folding of the hands to rest—then poverty will pounce on you like a bandit; scarcity will attack you like an armed robber.

Proverbs 6:6–11 NLT

The desire of the lazy man kills him, for his hands refuse to labor. He covets greedily all day long, but the righteous gives and does not spare.

Proverbs 21:25–26 NKJV

For even when we were with you, we would give you this command: If anyone is not willing to work, let him not eat.

2 Thessalonians 3:10 ESV

Anyone who does not provide for their relatives, and especially for their own household, has denied the faith and is worse than an unbeliever.

1 Timothy 5:8 NIV

Additional Notable Verses Concerning Laziness

Proverbs 10:4–5; 12:24; 13:4; 14:23; 18:9; 19:15; 20:4, 13; 24:30–34; 26:13–16; Ecclesiastes 9:10; Romans 12:11; Colossians 3:23; 2 Thessalonians 3:11–12

Leadership

Some of the greatest leadership examples in history are located on the Bible's pages. But the Bible tells of some of history's biggest leadership disasters as well. All of these examples, both good and bad, show us that leadership is nothing more than influence. Put simply, quality leadership is influencing people to move in the right direction in the right way.

Though much can be said for the leadership of King David, Joseph, Moses, and Elijah, there is no greater example of leadership in the Bible than Jesus Christ. The leadership of Christ can be seen in how far people were willing to go to follow Him (to death) and how long His influence has lasted (going on 2,000 years).

Key Verses

And David shepherded them with integrity of heart; with skillful hands he led them.

Psalm 78:72 NIV

Without wise leadership, a nation falls; there is safety in having many advisers.

Proverbs 11:14 NLT

So Jesus got them together to settle things down. He said, "You've observed how godless rulers throw their weight around, how quickly a little power goes to their heads. It's not going to be that way with you. Whoever wants to be great must become a servant. Whoever wants to be first among you must be your slave. That is what the Son of Man has done: He came to serve, not be served—and then to give away his life in exchange for the many who are held hostage."

Matthew 20:25–28 THE MESSAGE

Additional Notable Verses Concerning Leadership
Exodus 18:21; 1 Kings 3:1–15; Proverbs 15:22; 16:12; 20:18; 24:3–4; 28:16; 29:2–4, 14; Isaiah 16:5; Jeremiah 23:1–4; Matthew 25:45–47; Luke 6:39; 22:25–28; Acts 20:28; Romans 2:17–24; 12:8; Philippians 2:3–7; 1 Timothy 3:1–16; 4:12; 5:17–18; 2 Timothy 2:24–26; Titus 1:5–16; Hebrews 13:7, 17

Legalism

Legalism is one of the most dangerous diseases that a Christian can contract. Legalism is thinking that we are to relate to God based upon a list of regulations. It takes a beautiful relationship and turns it into a giant to-do list, and most of the list ends up being human rules rather than God's.

The Bible very stringently warns against this philosophy. It is a popular one today—just as it was two thousand years ago—because living by rules is so much more natural than living by grace. Yet this leads to hypocrisy, and eventually you may begin to equate human rules with God's rules. The Pharisees of Jesus' day were the first legalists. The church of the first century struggled with legalism just as the church does today.

Key Verses

"For you ignore God's law and substitute your own tradition." Then he said, "You skillfully sidestep God's law in order to hold on to your own tradition."

Mark 7:8–9 NLT

Accept the one whose faith is weak, without quarreling over disputable matters. One person's faith allows them to eat anything, but another, whose faith is weak, eats only vegetables. The one who eats everything must not treat with contempt the one who does not, and the one who does not eat everything must not judge the one who does, for God has accepted them. Who are you to judge someone else's servant? To their own master, servants stand or fall. And they will stand, for the Lord is able to make them stand.

Romans 14:1–4 NIV

We have freedom now, because Christ made us free. So stand strong. Do not change and go back into the slavery of the law.

Galatians 5:1 NCV

Additional Notable Verses Concerning Legalism
Matthew 5:17–48; 6:1–15; 11:19; Mark 7:1–13; Luke 18:1–14; Romans 14; 1 Corinthians 6:12–20; 8; Galatians 4; 5

Leisure

Recess. Who didn't love the part of the day when you could put the books, papers, and pencils away and go do what you wanted to do? You could play hide-and-go-seek, climb on the monkey bars, use the teeter-totter, join in a nice game of kickball, or jump from the swings.

Leisure time is very important to maintaining a sense of balance and sanity in life. Though we shouldn't be legalistic about keeping the Sabbath, the Bible emphasizes the importance of taking time to honor God and to rest.

Key Verses

Remember the sabbath day, to keep it holy. Six days you shall labor and do all your work, but the seventh day is a sabbath of the Lord your God; in it you shall not do any work, you or your son or your daughter, your male or your female servant or your cattle or your sojourner who stays with you. For in six days the Lord made the heavens and the earth, the sea and all that is in them, and rested on the seventh day; therefore the Lord blessed the sabbath day and made it holy.

Exodus 20:8–11 NASB

It is no use for you to get up early and stay up late, working for a living. The Lord gives sleep to those he loves.

Psalm 127:2 NCV

And he said to them, "Come away by yourselves to a desolate place and rest a while." For many were coming and going, and they had no leisure even to eat.

Mark 6:31 ESV

Additional Notable Verses Concerning Leisure
Proverbs 3:24; Mark 2:23–27; Hebrews 4:9–11

Love

A s one might expect, the Bible has much to say on the topic of love. The Bible defines love, gives examples of true love, tells of false love, and shows what love is willing to do.

The greatest example of love in the Scriptures has to be God the Father sending His only Son to die for the sins of humanity. If God loved us so much, how much more should we love one another?

Key Verses

Hang my locket around your neck, wear my ring on your finger. Love is invincible facing danger and death. Passion laughs at the terrors of hell. The fire of love stops at nothing—it sweeps everything before it. Flood waters can't drown love, torrents of rain can't put it out. Love can't be bought, love can't be sold—it's not to be found in the marketplace.

Song of Solomon 8:6–7 THE MESSAGE

No, in all these things we are more than conquerors through him who loved us. For I am convinced that neither death nor life, neither angels nor demons, neither the present nor the future, nor any powers, neither height nor depth, nor anything else in all creation, will be able to separate us from the love of God that is in Christ Jesus our Lord.

Romans 8:37–39 NIV

Behold what manner of love the Father has bestowed on us, that we should be called children of God! Therefore the world does not know us, because it did not know Him.

1 John 3:1 NKJV

Additional Notable Verses Concerning Love

Psalm 31:16; 63:3; Proverbs 10:12; 17:17; Matthew 5:43–48; 6:24–25; Mark 12:28–30; John 3:16; 14:21–24; 15:9–10; Romans 5:8; 13:8; 1 Corinthians 13:1–13; Galatians 2:20; 5:13; 1 Peter 1:22; 1 John 3:8; 4:7–21

Loyalty

There are many theories as to the origin of the phrase "true blue." The expression refers to someone who is loyal or unwavering in support of a cause or of a friend. One suggestion has been that the saying derives from an English town that used to dye clothes blue. The clothes that were dyed in this town were very resistant to fading, and thus that particular color became known as "true blue."

Whatever the origin of the expression, the idea of "true blue" is very much in keeping with what the Scriptures have in mind with regard to loyalty. In the Bible, loyalty is a very highly sought after virtue. A person should seek to be a man or woman of loyalty. A friend who is loyal is not just there for others when it's convenient; that friend is as good as family and can make all the difference in the world.

Key Verses

A friend loves at all times, and a brother is born for adversity.
Proverbs 17:17 ESV

A man of too many friends comes to ruin, but there is a friend who sticks closer than a brother.
Proverbs 18:24 NASB

Many claim to have unfailing love, but a faithful person who can find?
Proverbs 20:6 NIV

Additional Notable Verses Concerning Loyalty

1 Chronicles 29:18–19; Esther 2:21–23; Psalm 78:8, 36–38; Proverbs 20:28; 21:21; Hosea 6:4–6

Lust

The big danger with shooting fireworks in dry areas is that, should a spark land in the wrong place, you will have a wildfire on your hands. Instead of a beautiful celebration, you have the potential for disaster—all caused by a spark that was not where it belonged.

Lust is like that spark. Within the bonds of marriage between a man and a woman, physical fireworks are not only acceptable, they glorify God. But when those sparks go outside of the bonds of that marriage relationship, they can start a wildfire that will destroy all in its path. The damage done by this wildfire may never be repaired. To prevent such a tragedy, avoid lust and keep the focus on your own marital fireworks.

Key Verses

You have heard the commandment that says, "You must not commit adultery." But I say, anyone who even looks at a woman with lust has already committed adultery with her in his heart.

Matthew 5:27–28 NLT

Let no one say when he is tempted, "I am being tempted by God"; for God cannot be tempted by evil, and He Himself does not tempt anyone. But each one is tempted when he is carried away and enticed by his own lust. Then when lust has conceived, it gives birth to sin; and when sin is accomplished, it brings forth death.

James 1:13–15 NASB

For all that is in the world—the lust of the flesh, the lust of the eyes, and the pride of life—is not of the Father but is of the world.

1 John 2:16 NKJV

Additional Notable Verses Concerning Lust
1 Corinthians 6:18; Galatians 5:16; Colossians 3:5; 1 Thessalonians 4:3–5; James 4:2; 2 Peter 1:4

Lying

The concept of absolute truth is so very lost on people today that the term *truthiness* has been coined to describe something that we wish to be true rather than something that we know to be true.* In ages gone by they too had a term for these things; they called them lies. Our struggle with believing in absolute truth has taken lying and turned it into "truthiness," or "bending the truth," or even "stretching the truth."

Where we imagine gray areas to accommodate our own sins and weaknesses the Bible gives no such cushion. When the Bible speaks of truth, it is something that is black and white. There is speaking the truth, and there is lying. There is no middle ground of truth-like speech that allows the speaker to lie, but without admitting it. Given that biblically there are only two options for our speech, we should be careful about what comes out of our mouths.

Key Verses

You shall not bear false witness against your neighbor.
Exodus 20:16 NASB

I hate and despise lies, but I love your teachings.
Psalm 119:163 NCV

God can't stomach liars; he loves the company of those who keep their word.
Proverbs 12:22 THE MESSAGE

Additional Notable Verses Concerning Lying

Genesis 3; 27; Leviticus 19:11; Joshua 9; 2 Kings 5:1–27; 2 Kings 5; Psalm 40:4; 52:3; 101:7; 119:29; Proverbs 6:16–19; 10:18; 12:19; 13:5; 14:5, 25; 17:4; 21:6; 26:28; 29:12; 30:8; Isaiah 59:2–3; Jeremiah 23:14; Zephaniah 3:13; John 8:44; Acts 5:1–11; Colossians 3:9; 1 Timothy 4:1–5

*"Word of the Year 2006," Merriam-Webster, www.merriam-webster.com/info/06words.htm.

Manslaughter

Legally there is a difference between manslaughter and murder. Murder is generally an act perpetrated with the intent to kill, whereas manslaughter is an act that ends with an accidental or unintentional death. Both acts are a crime, but they carry with them far different consequences.

The distinction between willful murder and manslaughter is maintained in the Scriptures as well. Though manslaughter was certainly not something condoned in the Bible, consideration was given to the circumstances under which it was committed and who was affected by the offense.

Key Verses

Anyone who strikes a person with a fatal blow is to be put to death. However, if it is not done intentionally, but God lets it happen, they are to flee to a place I will designate.

Exodus 21:12–13 NIV

If men struggle with each other and strike a woman with child so that she gives birth prematurely, yet there is no injury, he shall surely be fined as the woman's husband may demand of him, and he shall pay as the judges decide. But if there is any further injury, then you shall appoint as a penalty life for life, eye for eye, tooth for tooth, hand for hand, foot for foot, burn for burn, wound for wound, bruise for bruise.

Exodus 21:22–25 NASB

Additional Notable Verses Concerning Manslaughter
Exodus 22:2–4; Numbers 35:6–34

Maturity

There are different types of maturity: physical maturity, emotional maturity, mental maturity, social maturity, spiritual maturity, and many other types. It is amazing that a person can be very mature in one area while at the same time very immature in another area, or even multiple areas. And just because people come across as mature in a particular area does not mean that they are genuinely mature. They may have just learned how to fake it well.

The Bible is concerned with all sorts of maturity, particularly spiritual maturity. A person's spiritual maturity is the most important because it will in turn affect all of the others. The more mature a person is spiritually, the closer he or she will be to God, and the closer a person is to God the more he or she will seek to serve others. The Scriptures encourage everyone to invest in growing up, and to do so quickly.

Key Verses

Brethren, do not be children in understanding; however, in malice be babes, but in understanding be mature.

1 Corinthians 14:20 NKJV

And he gave the apostles, the prophets, the evangelists, the shepherds and teachers, to equip the saints for the work of ministry, for building up the body of Christ, until we all attain to the unity of the faith and of the knowledge of the Son of God, to mature manhood, to the measure of the stature of the fullness of Christ.

Ephesians 4:11–13 ESV

Therefore leaving the elementary teaching about the Christ, let us press on to maturity, not laying again a foundation of repentance from dead works and of faith toward God.

Hebrews 6:1 NASB

Additional Notable Verses Concerning Maturity

Romans 5:1–5; 1 Corinthians 2:6; Hebrews 5:14

Meaning and Purpose

There are two things that everyone wants to know about life, but not everyone looks in the right place. Everybody wants to know that life has a meaning and a purpose, and everybody wants to know what they are.

All we need to know is in the Bible. But people either do not see it there, or they do not like the Bible's answers to their questions, so they keep searching. The Bible's answers are wrapped up in the person of God. Life is not about our getting what we want; meaning and purpose in life revolve around God and His glory. That may not be the answer that people want, but it is the answer just the same.

Key Verses

The Lord has made everything for its own purpose, even the wicked for the day of evil.

Proverbs 16:4 THE MESSAGE

Here is the conclusion of the matter: Fear God and keep his commandments, for this is the duty of all mankind. For God will bring every deed into judgment, including every hidden thing, whether it is good or evil.

Ecclesiastes 12:13–14 NIV

He has shown you, O man, what is good; and what does the Lord require of you but to do justly, to love mercy, and to walk humbly with your God?

Micah 6:8 NKJV

Is there any encouragement from belonging to Christ? Any comfort from his love? Any fellowship together in the Spirit? Are your hearts tender and compassionate? Then make me truly happy by agreeing wholeheartedly with each other, loving one another, and working together with one mind and purpose.

Philippians 2:1–2 NLT

Additional Notable Verses Concerning Meaning and Purpose

Job 42:1–2; Proverbs 19:21; Ecclesiastes 3:1; Isaiah 46:10–11; Luke 7:30; John 12:27; Romans 9:6–29; 2 Corinthians 5:5; Ephesians 1:5–14; 3:8–11; Colossians 1:28–29; 1 Thessalonians 4:7; 1 Timothy 4:7–10; 2 Timothy 1:8–11; 1 Peter 2:21–25; 3:8–9; 4:1–7

Mercy

Mercy is one of the rare concepts that are timeless and universal. Most people understand that to show mercy is to withhold judgment or punishment when it is due to someone. Everyone wants mercy, but few people seem to want to show it to others.

Human beings often make terrible mercy conductors. The Bible teaches that as recipients of God's mercy we should also show others mercy. Even though the passages about mercy are not difficult to understand, they are rarely followed because mercy is costly. To show mercy you must give up your rights to revenge and punishment. We do not want to show mercy because of what it will cost us, but imagine what it cost God to show us mercy.

Key Verses

Mercy and truth preserve the king: and his throne is upholden by mercy.
Proverbs 20:28 KJV

Thus has the Lord of hosts spoken: Execute true judgment and show mercy and kindness and tender compassion, every man to his brother.
Zechariah 7:9 AMP

Show mercy, just as your Father shows mercy.
Luke 6:36 NCV

For judgment will be merciless to one who has shown no mercy; mercy triumphs over judgment.
James 2:13 NASB

Additional Notable Verses Concerning Mercy
Psalm 37:26; 136; Proverbs 3:3; 12:10; 11:17; 14:21, 31; Daniel 4:27; Hosea 4:1–3; 6:6; 12:6; Matthew 5:7; 18:21–35; 23:23; Luke 10:25–37; Romans 12:20–21; Colossians 3:12; Hebrews 4:16; 1 Peter 1:3; Jude 1:20–23

Military

The Bible is full of wars, and some of its greatest heroes are soldiers (Joshua, David, Deborah). But God also calls us to live in peace (Romans 12:18). The subject of the military is obviously very complicated, and we can't summarize what God has to say about it by referring to any single verse of Scripture. We must study how the entire Bible treats the topic before drawing any conclusions. You might be surprised at what you find.

Jesus told us to turn the other cheek and to love our enemies (Matthew 5:39; Luke 6:27). Yet He didn't rebuke Roman soldiers who conquered nations for a living, including Israel. Instead, He healed their sick relatives and servants. In the book of Acts when a centurion comes to Christ through the ministry of Peter, he is not even told to quit his job.

One other surprise in the Bible with regard to the military is that the life of a soldier is used as a metaphor for the Christian life. Though the Christian's weapons are different, we are very much soldiers in the Lord's army.

Key Verses

I will see that your borders reach from the Red Sea to the Euphrates River and from the Mediterranean Sea to the desert. I will let you defeat the people who live there, and you will force them out of the land.

Exodus 23:31 CEV

Surely you need guidance to wage war, and victory is won through many advisers.

Proverbs 24:6 NIV

"What should we do?" asked some soldiers.

John replied, "Don't extort money or make false accusations. And be content with your pay."

Luke 3:14 NLT

Additional Notable Verses Concerning the Military

Genesis 14; Exodus 15:3; 1 Samuel 13:2; 1 Kings 10:26; Isaiah 2:4; Matthew 8:5–13; 27:54; Mark 15:39–45; Luke 23:47; Acts 10; Ephesians 6:10–20; Philippians 2:25; 1 Corinthians 9:7; 2 Timothy 2:3–4; Philemon 1:2

Minorities

No matter how much we might desire it to be, the world is not populated by people who are blind to skin color and race. Until that happens, there will be groups who are minorities in a particular country, state, or locale. Sometimes minorities are treated well, and at other times minorities are abused and taken advantage of.

The Scriptures give us unique teachings regarding minorities. The Bible paints an interesting picture of the topic because in the Old Testament the Israelites experienced being the minority and also the majority. As slaves in Egypt and later as exiles, the descendants of Abraham were frequently treated poorly as a minority. That is why God was so emphatic that when they possessed the Promised Land, they remember their experience and show minorities grace because of it.

Key Verses

Thou shalt neither vex a stranger, nor oppress him: for ye were strangers in the land of Egypt.

Exodus 22:21 KJV

Now in case a countryman of yours becomes poor and his means with regard to you falter, then you are to sustain him, like a stranger or a sojourner, that he may live with you.

Leviticus 25:35 NASB

Additional Notable Verses Concerning Minorities

Genesis 12; 23; Exodus 2:15–24; 23:9; Leviticus 19:32–34; Ruth 1–4; Isaiah 56:1–3; Ezekiel 22:29; Matthew 15:21–28; John 4:4–42; Hebrews 13:2

Miracles

The existence of miracles is one of many people's biggest objections to the authority and truthfulness of Scripture. Thomas Jefferson, for example, found the teaching of Jesus to be profound, but he did not believe in the Bible's miracles.*

Peter (2 Peter 1:16–21) and John (1 John 1:1–4) both stressed that the epistles they wrote were based on their own eyewitness experiences. Those who disbelieve the miracles in the Bible disbelieve eyewitness accounts of men who were willing to die for what they saw.

Key Verses

Then Jesus began to denounce the towns where he had done so many of his miracles, because they hadn't repented of their sins and turned to God. "What sorrow awaits you, Korazin and Bethsaida! For if the miracles I did in you had been done in wicked Tyre and Sidon, their people would have repented of their sins long ago, clothing themselves in burlap and throwing ashes on their heads to show their remorse. I tell you, Tyre and Sidon will be better off on judgment day than you."

Matthew 11:20–22 NLT

Now there was a man of the Pharisees named Nicodemus, a ruler of the Jews. This man came to Jesus by night and said to him, "Rabbi, we know that you are a teacher come from God, for no one can do these signs that you do unless God is with him."

John 3:1–2 ESV

And truly Jesus did many other signs in the presence of His disciples, which are not written in this book; but these are written that you may believe that Jesus is the Christ, the Son of God, and that believing you may have life in His name.

John 20:30–31 NKJV

Additional Notable Verses Concerning Miracles

Exodus 4:1–9; 10:2; Numbers 14:21–23; Psalm 78:12; 105:5; Jeremiah 32:20–21; Matthew 4:23–25; 10:1; 11:2–6; 13:54–58; 17:20; John 2:1–12; 9; 11:1–44; Acts 2:22–24; 6:8; 19:11–12; Romans 15:18–20; 2 Corinthians 12:12; Hebrews 2:1–4

---

*Louis Sahagun, "A Founding Father's View of God," *Los Angeles Times,* July 5, 2008, http://articles.latimes.com/2008/jul/05/local/me-beliefs5.

Money

Some churches talk about money so much that you would think that the Bible is a very large investment prospectus. Other churches talk about money so rarely that you might be led to believe that the topic is never discussed in the Scriptures. As hard as it is to strike a balance, the Bible does frequently speak about money. Jesus himself actually spends a lot of time speaking on the subject.

Though it may be uncomfortable for us at times, the teaching that the Scriptures give regarding finances is full of wisdom. Human beings are destined to struggle with allowing money to become too important to them. Rather than viewing money as a tool, there is a constant temptation to give money too high a place in our lives. When this happens, people have a choice to make. We cannot serve God and money.

Key Verses

The rich rules over the poor, and the borrower becomes the lender's slave.

Proverbs 22:7 NASB

You can't worship two gods at once. Loving one god, you'll end up hating the other. Adoration of one feeds contempt for the other. You can't worship God and Money both.

Matthew 6:24 THE MESSAGE

The love of money causes all kinds of evil. Some people have left the faith, because they wanted to get more money, but they have caused themselves much sorrow.

1 Timothy 6:10 NCV

Additional Notable Verses Concerning Money

Leviticus 25:35–46; Proverbs 13:11, 22; 21:20; Ecclesiastes 5:10; 7:12; Isaiah 55:2; Matthew 6:19–21, 31–33; 22:15–21; Luke 12:22–34; 16:10–13; John 2:13–22; Acts 5:1–11; 8:14–24; Hebrews 13:5

Mothers

There is something about a mother that touches the heart of her children like no one else. The kind words and loving touch of a mother will stay with her children for decades, even after she is dead and gone. By the same token, a mother's derogatory words or harsh actions will also stay with her children as a sad legacy. Mothers have a unique relationship with their children, and that relationship can be one of tremendous blessing with a godly mother.

From what we see in Scripture, mothers are due all of the love and respect that their children can give. Even Christ, while dying on the cross to pay the price for the sins of humanity, saw to it that His mother was taken care of and provided for. A child can never repay his or her mother for all that she has done, but the Word of God tells us that we should live life in such a way that will honor our mothers.

Key Verses

You must respect your mother and father, and you must keep my Sabbaths. I am the Lord your God.

Leviticus 19:3 NCV

Her children rise up and bless her; her husband also, and he praises her, saying: "Many daughters have done nobly, but you excel them all."

Proverbs 31:28–29 NASB

Additional Notable Verses Concerning Mothers

Genesis 3:20; Exodus 20:12; Deuteronomy 5:16; Proverbs 1:8–9; 10:1; 15:20; 20:20; 23:25; 29:15; 30:11; Isaiah 66:13; Ezekiel 16:44; Matthew 10:37–38; Mark 10:29–30; John 19:26–27; 2 Timothy 1:5; Titus 2:3–5

Mourning

The Bible tells us that Christ has defeated death and that death is not an end, but rather the beginning of eternal life.

Knowing what the Bible says about death, however, does not always help us to know how best to mourn. Exactly what form that mourning should take and how long it should last are topics that the Bible does not cover in detail. It does teach that it is okay to mourn (1 Thessalonians 4:13–18), so long as we know that mourning is temporary.

Key Verses

Three of Job's friends heard of all the trouble that had fallen on him. Each traveled from his own country—Eliphaz from Teman, Bildad from Shuhah, Zophar from Naamath—and went together to Job to keep him company and comfort him. When they first caught sight of him, they couldn't believe what they saw—they hardly recognized him! They cried out in lament, ripped their robes, and dumped dirt on their heads as a sign of their grief. Then they sat with him on the ground. Seven days and nights they sat there without saying a word. They could see how rotten he felt, how deeply he was suffering.

Job 2:11–13 THE MESSAGE

The Lord is near to the brokenhearted and saves those who are crushed in spirit.

Psalm 34:18 NASB

Jesus wept.
John 11:35 KJV

He will wipe every tear from their eyes. There will be no more death or mourning or crying or pain, for the old order of things has passed away.

Revelation 21:4 NIV

Additional Notable Verses Concerning Mourning

Numbers 20:27–29; 1 Samuel 30:1–6; 2 Samuel 1:1–12; 12:11–23; Psalm 10:14; 22:24; 30:5; 147:3; Ecclesiastes 3:4; Isaiah 49:13; Jeremiah 31:13; Lamentations 3:32–33; Matthew 2:16–18; 5:4; Luke 6:21; John 11:1–44; 1 Thessalonians 4:13–18

Murder

Murder shows just how far our thoughts are from God. We attempt to justify our wickedness, but according to Jesus we are almost all murderers. The standard that Christ sets—that of murder in the heart—places the bar fairly low to be a murderer. Maybe you never killed Colonel Mustard in the library with a candlestick, but if you've ever referred to someone as an idiot in your own head you are just as guilty in God's eyes as someone on death row (Matthew 5:21–22). We have all committed the worst offense that we can think of.

Key Verses

I will demand blood for life. I will demand the life of any animal that kills a person, and I will demand the life of anyone who takes another person's life. Whoever kills a human being will be killed by a human being, because God made humans in his own image.

Genesis 9:5–6 NCV

You shall not murder.
Exodus 20:13 NASB

You have heard that it was said to the people long ago, "You shall not murder, and anyone who murders will be subject to judgment." But I tell you that anyone who is angry with a brother or sister will be subject to judgment. Again, anyone who says to a brother or sister, "Raca," is answerable to the court. And anyone who says, "You fool!" will be in danger of the fire of hell.

Matthew 5:21–22 NIV

Everyone who hates his brother is a murderer, and you know that no murderer has eternal life abiding in him.

1 John 3:15 ESV

Additional Notable Verses Concerning Murder

Genesis 4:2–15; Exodus 21:14; Numbers 35; Deuteronomy 5:17; 19; 2 Samuel 11:14–27; 1 Kings 21; Proverbs 6:16–17; Matthew 15:19; Romans 13:9; Galatians 5:19–21; 1 Timothy 1:9; 1 Peter 4:15

Music

Music was one of God's greatest gifts to mankind and He is glorified by it, particularly when music is used to worship Him.

Bach said regarding music, "The aim and final end of all music should be none other than the glory of God and the refreshment of the soul."* It was for this purpose that many of the psalms and songs in the Scripture were created: for God's glory and the soul's refreshment.

Key Verses

Lamech and Adah had two sons, Jabal and Jubal. Their son Jabal was the first to live in tents and raise sheep and goats. Jubal was the first to play harps and flutes.

Genesis 4:20–21 CEV

Hallelujah! Praise God in his holy house of worship, praise him under the open skies; praise him for his acts of power, praise him for his magnificent greatness; praise with a blast on the trumpet, praise by strumming soft strings; praise him with castanets and dance, praise him with banjo and flute; praise him with cymbals and a big bass drum, praise him with fiddles and mandolin. Let every living, breathing creature praise God! Hallelujah!

Psalm 150:1–6 THE MESSAGE

And do not get drunk with wine, for that is dissipation, but be filled with the Spirit, speaking to one another in psalms and hymns and spiritual songs, singing and making melody with your heart to the Lord; always giving thanks for all things in the name of our Lord Jesus Christ to God, even the Father.

Ephesians 5:18–20 NASB

Additional Notable Verses Concerning Music

Exodus 15:1–18; 1 Samuel 16:14–23; 2 Samuel 6:1–5; 1 Chronicles 15:25–28; 16:1–7; 23:1–6; 25; 2 Chronicles 5:11–13; 29:25–28; Ezra 3:9–10; Nehemiah 12:27–28; Psalm 33:2; 71:22; 98:6; Acts 16:25; Revelation 5:8–9

---

*Gregory Wilbur, *Glory and Honor: The Musical and Artistic Legacy of Johann Sebastian Bach* (Nashville: Cumberland House, 2005), 1.

Natural Disasters

For insurance purposes natural disasters are often referred to as "acts of God." This can be a little confusing when it is applied theologically because that seems to make tornadoes, earthquakes, tsunamis, and hurricanes all things that were caused by God. So what does cause natural disasters? Does God take action to initiate dangerous and deadly natural disasters?

The Bible tells us that death and disasters occur as a result of sin entering into the world. When sin came, the earth was thrown into a fallen state just as humanity was. Because of sin's effect on the planet, the world exists in an ever-increasing state of chaos. God knows of every disaster that will occur, and for His purposes He allows them to happen, but natural disasters should not be referred to as "acts of God," but rather "acts of sin."

Key Verses

I am the Lord, and there is no other. I form light and create darkness, I make well-being and create calamity, I am the Lord, who does all these things.

Isaiah 45:6–7 ESV

For nation will rise against nation, and kingdom against kingdom, and in various places there will be famines and earthquakes. But all these things are merely the beginning of birth pangs.

Matthew 24:7–8 NASB

Pilate had murdered some people from Galilee as they were offering sacrifices at the Temple. "Do you think those Galileans were worse sinners than all the other people from Galilee?" Jesus asked. "Is that why they suffered? Not at all! And you will perish, too, unless you repent of your sins and turn to God. And what about the eighteen people who died when the tower in Siloam fell on them? Were they the worst sinners in Jerusalem? No, and I tell you again that unless you repent, you will perish, too."

Luke 13:1–5 NLT

Additional Notable Verses Concerning Natural Disasters
Genesis 6–8; Proverbs 17:5; Amos 3:6; Luke 21:25–28; John 9:1–3

Nature

Today, the idea of a literal Mother Nature may not be widely accepted, but there are definitely those who seek to elevate nature and natural objects to a place of deity.

The Bible tells us that nature has a very valuable place in the world that God has created, but that place is as a resource. The most notable thing about nature is who its Creator is. Creation is not valuable because it is divine, it is valuable because it is the handiwork of The Divine.

Key Verses

I look up at your macro-skies, dark and enormous, your handmade sky-jewelry, moon and stars mounted in their settings. Then I look at my micro-self and wonder, Why do you bother with us? Why take a second look our way? Yet we've so narrowly missed being gods, bright with Eden's dawn light. You put us in charge of your handcrafted world, repeated to us your Genesis-charge, made us lords of sheep and cattle, even animals out in the wild, birds flying and fish swimming, whales singing in the ocean deeps. God, brilliant Lord, your name echoes around the world.

Psalm 8:3–9 THE MESSAGE

Let the heavens rejoice, and let the earth be glad; let the sea roar, and all its fullness; let the field be joyful, and all that is in it. Then all the trees of the woods will rejoice before the Lord. For He is coming, for He is coming to judge the earth. He shall judge the world with righteousness, and the peoples with His truth.

Psalm 96:11–13 NKJV

For he makes his sun rise on the evil and on the good, and sends rain on the just and on the unjust.

Matthew 5:45 ESV

Additional Notable Verses Concerning Nature

Job 12:7–10; Psalm 24:1–2; 104:4; 145:5; 147:7–11; 148; Song of Solomon 2:12; Isaiah 17:11; Luke 12:22–31; Acts 14:17; Romans 1:20–23

Obedience

Obedience is valued in almost every walk of life. Employers want obedient employees, parents want obedient children, and governments want obedient citizens. Even though obedience is required in almost every aspect of life, it is an increasingly rare quality.

All of the areas where we are to exhibit obedience are important, but there is one that trumps them all: obedience to God. Obedience to God dictates that we will be obedient in other areas of our lives. When these other areas ask us to disobey God, we know it's time to disobey them. In truth, obedience to God is the simplest and most basic function of the Christian life.

Key Verses

You shall walk after the Lord your God and [reverently] fear Him, and keep His commandments and obey His voice, and you shall serve Him and cling to Him.

Deuteronomy 13:4 AMP

But Samuel replied, "What is more pleasing to the Lord: your burnt offerings and sacrifices or your obedience to his voice? Listen! Obedience is better than sacrifice, and submission is better than offering the fat of rams."

1 Samuel 15:22 NLT

Now all has been heard; here is the conclusion of the matter: Fear God and keep his commandments, for this is the duty of all mankind.

Ecclesiastes 12:13 NIV

Behave like obedient children. Don't let your lives be controlled by your desires, as they used to be. Always live as God's holy people should, because God is the one who chose you, and he is holy.

1 Peter 1:14–15 CEV

Additional Notable Verses Concerning Obedience

Genesis 6:22; 22:1–19; Exodus 19:5; 23:21–22; 24:7; Deuteronomy 11; 28; 1 Samuel 7:3; Psalm 119:35; 143:10; Isaiah 1:19; Jeremiah 7:23; Luke 11:28; Acts 4:18–22; 5:17–31; Romans 1:5; 6:17; 10:16–17; 16:19; 2 Corinthians 10:5; Philippians 2:12; Hebrews 5:8; 11:8; James 1:25

Occult

I n the late twentieth century zero-tolerance policies became popular with law enforcement agencies. The idea was that there are certain crimes and offenses that people should be punished for without being given a second chance. The hope behind a zero-tolerance policy is that with severe punishment coming so swiftly, people will reconsider committing those crimes.

While the phrase "zero tolerance" was a twentieth-century invention, the idea behind it is much older and biblical. In the Scriptures those involved with occult practices felt the power of the zero-tolerance policy. Being involved with the occult was something deadly, and it would spread like wildfire throughout the Israelite tribes if not dealt with severely and swiftly. The same attitude, if not the same punishments, must be ours when dealing with occult practices today.

Key Verses

Do not allow a sorceress to live.
Exodus 22:18 NIV

Do not turn to mediums or necromancers; do not seek them out, and so make yourselves unclean by them: I am the Lord your God.
Leviticus 19:31 ESV

And He said to me, "It is done! I am the Alpha and the Omega, the Beginning and the End. I will give of the fountain of the water of life freely to him who thirsts. He who overcomes shall inherit all things, and I will be his God and he shall be My son. But the cowardly, unbelieving, abominable, murderers, sexually immoral, sorcerers, idolaters, and all liars shall have their part in the lake which burns with fire and brimstone, which is the second death."
Revelation 21:6–8 NKJV

Additional Notable Verses Concerning the Occult

Leviticus 20:1–6, 27; Deuteronomy 4:19; 18:9–14; 1 Samuel 28:3–25; 2 Kings 21:6; 23:24–25; 2 Chronicles 33:6; Isaiah 8:19–22; Micah 5:12–15; Acts 8:9–24; 13:6–12; 16:16–18; 19:11–20; Galatians 5:19–21; Revelation 21:8; 22:15

Old Age

S ome people grow old gracefully. They look at old age and decide to face the changes that life brings them with as much humor and humility as they can muster. As a result, they are a joy to be around. Other people do not take growing old so gracefully. All of the changes that come upon them make them bitter and angry. They buckle at the loss of independence and their inability to continue life as they once had. They can be quite difficult to be around.

The picture that the Bible paints of old age should be encouraging for those who are there, or headed there quickly. Many of the characters in the Bible were active and serving God well into their senior years. There is no expiration date on usefulness in God's plan. God can and will use people so long as they are willing to be used by Him. Seniors have the same responsibility as their younger counterparts—they must make sure that they are useful vessels.

Key Verses

Show respect to the aged; honor the presence of an elder; fear your God. I am God.

Leviticus 19:32 THE MESSAGE

Gray hair is a crown of glory; it is gained by living a godly life.

Proverbs 16:31 NLT

Even to your old age I will be the same, and even to your graying years I will bear you! I have done it, and I will carry you; and I will bear you and I will deliver you.

Isaiah 46:4 NASB

Additional Notable Verses Concerning Old Age
Job 12:12; 32:7; Psalm 37:25; 71:9, 17–18; 90:10; 92:12–15; Proverbs 13:22; 17:6; Ecclesiastes 9:10; 12:1–7; Titus 2:1–5

Orphans

I f the story of an orphan does not touch your heart, there may be something wrong with you. One of the things that everyone has in common is that they are someone's son or daughter. No matter your relationship with your parents, the idea of having no parents at all is a very powerful one. Orphans live in such a state of need, who are without God's intended protectors and providers, that you cannot help but want to put your arms around them.

The emotion that we feel when we see or hear about an orphan is experienced by our heavenly Father as well. God's compassion is aroused by the plight of orphans, without the love and advantages that most children possess. God will not allow them to be taken advantage of. God has promised to do more than merely feel compassion for orphans; He has promised to come to their aid.

Key Verses

Do not mistreat widows or orphans. If you do, they will beg for my help, and I will come to their rescue. In fact, I will get so angry that I will kill your men and make widows of their wives and orphans of their children.

Exodus 22:22–24 CEV

A father of the fatherless, a defender of widows, is God in His holy habitation.

Psalm 68:5 NKJV

External religious worship [religion as it is expressed in outward acts] that is pure and unblemished in the sight of God the Father is this: to visit and help and care for the orphans and widows in their affliction and need, and to keep oneself unspotted and uncontaminated from the world.

James 1:27 AMP

Additional Notable Verses Concerning Orphans

Deuteronomy 24:17–21; Job 29:12; Psalm 10:14–18; 68:5; 82:3; 146:7–9; Proverbs 23:10; Isaiah 1:10–23; Jeremiah 5:28; 7:6–7; 22:3; Hosea 14:3; Malachi 3:5

Ownership

ndividuals and nations own land in the Scriptures. Frequently in the Bible there is fighting and struggle over exactly who owns what.

But there is an important point underlying all ownership in the Bible: Ultimately everything is owned by God. As Creator, it is God's divine right to allow someone to own something, and if He sees fit they may end up losing their property to someone else. Today when we own something, we must always remember and remain cognizant of the true owner. We really own nothing; God just allows us to be stewards.

Key Verses

When you enter the land the Lord your God is giving you, be very careful not to imitate the detestable customs of the nations living there. For example, never sacrifice your son or daughter as a burnt offering. And do not let your people practice fortune-telling, or use sorcery, or interpret omens, or engage in witchcraft, or cast spells, or function as mediums or psychics, or call forth the spirits of the dead. Anyone who does these things is detestable to the Lord. It is because the other nations have done these detestable things that the Lord your God will drive them out ahead of you. But you must be blameless before the Lord your God. The nations you are about to displace consult sorcerers and fortune-tellers, but the Lord your God forbids you to do such things.

Deuteronomy 18:9–14 NLT

The earth is the Lord's, and everything in it, the world, and all who live in it; for he founded it on the seas and established it on the waters.

Psalm 24:1–2 NIV

Additional Notable Verses Concerning Ownership
Exodus 21:1–6; Deuteronomy 11:31; Matthew 19:21; Luke 16:10–12; John 10:28–30

Parenthood

Parenthood is one of the highest callings in the Scriptures. The role of parents in raising up the next generation is of the utmost importance in the Bible. It is also the role in the Bible with perhaps the most responsibility. Yet God's Word is faithful to remind us that despite all of the toil and work of parenthood, children are ultimately a blessing from God.

Key Verses

Children are a blessing and a gift from the Lord. Having a lot of children to take care of you in your old age is like a warrior with a lot of arrows. The more you have, the better off you will be, because they will protect you when your enemies attack with arguments.

Psalm 127:3–5 CEV

Train up a child in the way he should go [and in keeping with his individual gift or bent], and when he is old he will not depart from it.

Proverbs 22:6 AMP

So don't feel sorry for yourselves. Or have you forgotten how good parents treat children, and that God regards you as his children? My dear child, don't shrug off God's discipline, but don't be crushed by it either. It's the child he loves that he disciplines; the child he embraces, he also corrects. God is educating you; that's why you must never drop out. He's treating you as dear children. This trouble you're in isn't punishment; it's training, the normal experience of children. Only irresponsible parents leave children to fend for themselves. Would you prefer an irresponsible God? We respect our own parents for training and not spoiling us, so why not embrace God's training so we can truly live?

Hebrews 12:5–9 THE MESSAGE

Additional Notable Verses Concerning Parenthood

Deuteronomy 6:6–9; Proverbs 1:8–9; 10:1; 13:24; 19:18; 22:15; 23:13–14; 29:15–17; Ephesians 6:4; Colossians 3:21

Patience

Most people have patience; they just do not have it for very long. Patience requires waiting, and waiting is not something that we are born willing to do. Our culture doesn't believe in doing much waiting either. We have instant everything, drive-throughs, and speed passes for anything humanly possible. With our hatred for waiting, is it any wonder that we struggle to be patient?

The Bible teaches us that patience is not only a good thing, it is necessary for our maturity as believers. The process of developing patience is not always an enjoyable one, but there is a purpose to it. Trials teach us patience, and developing patience makes us become more like Christ, which is our heavenly Father's ultimate goal for us as His children. Patience is not fun to get, but it is great to have.

Key Verses

Be still in the presence of the Lord, and wait patiently for him to act. Don't worry about evil people who prosper or fret about their wicked schemes.

Psalm 37:7 NLT

But if we hope for what we do not yet have, we wait for it patiently.

Romans 8:25 NIV

My brethren, count it all joy when you fall into various trials, knowing that the testing of your faith produces patience. But let patience have its perfect work, that you may be perfect and complete, lacking nothing.

James 1:2–4 NKJV

Additional Notable Verses Concerning Patience

Psalm 40:1; Ecclesiastes 7:8; Romans 5:3–5; 12:12; 15:4–5; 2 Corinthians 6:4; Colossians 1:11; 2 Thessalonians 3:5; 1 Timothy 6:11; Titus 2:2; Hebrews 6:12; 10:36; 12:1; James 5:7; 1 Peter 2:20; Revelation 2:2–3

Peace

Typically we think of peace as the state of being that is the opposite of war. That is one aspect of peace, but it is not the whole picture. Peace is also full reliance and dependence on God. This is why we can have peace when the world seems to be crumbling around us. Peace is a gift from God that allows us to remain steady and secure in any circumstance.

The peace that the Bible describes is not one that is experienced by the world at large. The ability to have this peace is only derived from faith in the God of the Bible. If God is who the Scriptures say He is, then He is someone who can be trusted and on whom we can rely. If we can trust and rely on God, then we can truly know His peace.

Key Verses

Depart from evil and do good; seek peace and pursue it.

Psalm 34:14 NKJV

When a man's ways please the Lord, he makes even his enemies to be at peace with him.

Proverbs 16:7 ESV

Blessed are the peacemakers, for they shall be called sons of God.

Matthew 5:9 NASB

Peace I leave with you; my peace I give you. I do not give to you as the world gives. Do not let your hearts be troubled and do not be afraid.

John 14:27 NIV

Additional Notable Verses Concerning Peace

Psalm 120:6–7; 122:6–8; Isaiah 26:3; 45:7; Mark 9:50; John 16:33; Romans 12:18; 14:19; 1 Corinthians 14:33; 2 Corinthians 13:11; Ephesians 4:3; 1 Thessalonians 5:13; 2 Timothy 2:22; Hebrews 12:14; James 3:17–18; 1 Peter 3:10–11

Perfection

When the Bible speaks of perfection, it is quite different from what is exhibited by those of us with perfectionist personalities. Perfectionists cannot stand mistakes or for things to be out of order. The Scriptures speak of perfection in different ways. At times, when the Bible speaks of God, for example, perfection refers to His being morally without flaw. Other times, such as when we are told to be perfect, the term refers to being mature and complete. It is not sinlessness, but a quality of living the Christian faith that is without glaring weaknesses and flaws.

Key Verses

Therefore you shall be perfect, just as your Father in heaven is perfect.

Matthew 5:48 NKJV

Not that I have already obtained it or have already become perfect, but I press on so that I may lay hold of that for which also I was laid hold of by Christ Jesus. Brethren, I do not regard myself as having laid hold of it yet; but one thing I do: forgetting what lies behind and reaching forward to what lies ahead, I press on toward the goal for the prize of the upward call of God in Christ Jesus. Let us therefore, as many as are perfect, have this attitude; and if in anything you have a different attitude, God will reveal that also to you; however, let us keep living by that same standard to which we have attained.

Philippians 3:12–16 NASB

Indeed, we all make many mistakes. For if we could control our tongues, we would be perfect and could also control ourselves in every other way.

James 3:2 NLT

Additional Notable Verses Concerning Perfection

Psalm 18:32; 37:37; 119:96; Proverbs 2:21; John 17:23; 2 Corinthians 7:1; 13:11; Colossians 1:28; 3:14; 2 Timothy 3:16–17; James 1:4, 25

Persecution

Though many American Christians have never experienced persecution, it's still common in the rest of the world. The Bible gives no magic spell for making persecution go away. Rather, it teaches two main facts regarding persecution. First, persecution will come to all who sincerely attempt to serve God. Second, enduring persecution will be worth it if the Christian perseveres. The Christian being persecuted must cling to God's promise that He will personally repay the sinner for his actions, and the saint for his faithfulness.

Key Verses

Peter began to say to Him, "Behold, we have left everything and followed You." Jesus said, "Truly I say to you, there is no one who has left house or brothers or sisters or mother or father or children or farms, for My sake and for the gospel's sake, but that he will receive a hundred times as much now in the present age, houses and brothers and sisters and mothers and children and farms, along with persecutions; and in the age to come, eternal life. But many who are first will be last, and the last, first."

Mark 10:28–31 NASB

But we have this treasure in jars of clay to show that this all-surpassing power is from God and not from us. We are hard pressed on every side, but not crushed; perplexed, but not in despair; persecuted, but not abandoned; struck down, but not destroyed.

2 Corinthians 4:7–9 NIV

Everyone who wants to live as God desires, in Christ Jesus, will be persecuted.

2 Timothy 3:12 NCV

Additional Notable Verses Concerning Persecution

Psalm 7:1; 10:2; 119:86; 143:3; Jeremiah 15:15; Matthew 5:10–12, 43–48; 10:16–42; Luke 21:10–18; John 5:16; 15:18–27; Acts 9:1–9; 13:43–52; Romans 8:35; 12:14; 1 Corinthians 4:12; 1 Peter 4:12–19

Perseverance

Perseverance can be a difficult quality to develop. Life has a way of beating us down, and we learn very young that sometimes the rules that apply to us do not apply to everyone else. As we get older we see more and more ways in which the world is unfair, but hopefully we also see that perseverance can and will pay off too. If you are not the person blessed with connections or other advantages, then you just may realize that perseverance is your only hope.

In God's Word we see great people of faith whom God used to do some amazing things. If we are not careful we can forget that those people did not just have faith, they had to persevere in their faith. Faith must continually be exercised, and we must with great effort persevere in it, or it is useless.

Key Verses

The steps of a man are established by the Lord, and He delights in his way. When he falls, he will not be hurled headlong, because the Lord is the One who holds his hand.

Psalm 37:23–24 NASB

But as for you, brethren, do not grow weary in doing good.

2 Thessalonians 3:13 NKJV

Look well to yourself [to your own personality] and to [your] teaching; persevere in these things [hold to them], for by so doing you will save both yourself and those who hear you.

1 Timothy 4:16 AMP

Additional Notable Verses Concerning Perseverance

1 Chronicles 16:11; Hosea 12:6; Matthew 10:22; John 8:31; 10:28; Romans 2:6–7; 5:1–5; 8:25; 15:1–7; 2 Corinthians 12:12; Galatians 6:9; Ephesians 6:18; Philippians 1:6; 2 Thessalonians 1:4; 1 Timothy 6:11; 2 Timothy 3:10; 4:7; Titus 2:2; Hebrews 3:6; 12:2–3; 2 Peter 1:5–9; Revelation 1:9; 2:2–3, 19, 26–28; 3:10; 13:10; 14:12

Pleasure

To hear some people tell it, God is very much against pleasure. You would almost think that pleasure was a tool of the devil designed to destroy the church and capture wayward souls. If you know these people or have been subjected to this type of thinking, it can be very hard to imagine that God is fun, or that He would ever do anything like enjoy himself.

The idea that pleasure equals sin is not a terribly new one, but it is not a terribly biblical one either. The Bible certainly tells us that loving pleasure too much or letting pleasure seeking become an obsession are wasteful and sinful attitudes. At the same time, it was God who told the Israelites to celebrate Him and to have festivals and feasts in His honor. It is hard to believe that God would be anti-pleasure and at the same time plan a party.

Key Verses

You make known to me the path of life; you will fill me with joy in your presence, with eternal pleasures at your right hand.

Psalm 16:11 NIV

Those who love pleasure become poor; those who love wine and luxury will never be rich.

Proverbs 21:17 NLT

I said to myself, "Come now, I will test you with pleasure. So enjoy yourself." And behold, it too was futility. I said of laughter, "It is madness," and of pleasure, "What does it accomplish?"

Ecclesiastes 2:1–2 NASB

Additional Notable Verses Concerning Pleasure

Ecclesiastes 2:10; 4:8; 7:4; 8:15; Isaiah 25:6; 58:13; Ezekiel 18:23, 32; 33:11; 2 Thessalonians 2:11–12; 1 Timothy 5:6; 2 Timothy 2:22; 3:1–5; James 5:1–6; 2 Peter 2:10–16

Polygamy

I n Scripture people lied, murdered, worshiped golden calves, and listened to talking snakes in gardens. Just because people in the Bible took particular actions does not mean that they were right.

One of the great things about the Scriptures is that they relate events as they happened without whitewashing them or attempting to paint characters in a more positive light than was justified. Polygamy is the perfect example. Though it wasn't part of God's plan, He chose to tolerate it. Every time we see multiple marriages in the Bible they are full of strife and anger. It is almost as if the punishment for polygamy was polygamy. Sometimes our sins are their own consequences.

Key Verses

Lamech married two women, one named Adah and the other Zillah.

Genesis 4:19 NIV

The king must not have many wives, or his heart will be led away from God. He must not have too much silver and gold.

Deuteronomy 17:17 NCV

King Solomon was obsessed with women. Pharaoh's daughter was only the first of the many foreign women he loved—Moabite, Ammonite, Edomite, Sidonian, and Hittite. He took them from the surrounding pagan nations of which God had clearly warned Israel, "You must not marry them; they'll seduce you into infatuations with their gods." Solomon fell in love with them anyway, refusing to give them up. He had seven hundred royal wives and three hundred concubines—a thousand women in all! And they did seduce him away from God. As Solomon grew older, his wives beguiled him with their alien gods and he became unfaithful—he didn't stay true to his God as his father David had done.

1 Kings 11:1–4 THE MESSAGE

Additional Notable Verses Concerning Polygamy
Exodus 21:10; Deuteronomy 21:15–17; 1 Chronicles 3:1–9; 2 Chronicles 11:21; 13:21; 1 Corinthians 7:2; 1 Timothy 3:2, 12

Pornography

Pornography is one of the greatest lies in history. It promises everything you ever wanted and desired without any of the work and for no cost. Yet the ugly truth behind pornography is that it enslaves those who partake in it, it ruins the perception of reality, it destroys marriages, and everyone who comes in contact with it will struggle to overcome its influence.

The Bible is very clear when it comes to the issue of pornography. Though there were no convenience stores with magazines behind the counter or XXX bookstores in biblical times, the urge and desire to take in and view that which is perverse was just as real. The writer of Proverbs puts his warning in the form of a question, "Can a man scoop fire into his lap without his clothes being burned?" (6:27 NIV).

Key Verses

I will set no worthless thing before my eyes; I hate the work of those who fall away; it shall not fasten its grip on me. A perverse heart shall depart from me; I will know no evil.

Psalm 101:3–4 NASB

You know the next commandment pretty well, too: "Don't go to bed with another's spouse." But don't think you've preserved your virtue simply by staying out of bed. Your heart can be corrupted by lust even quicker than your body. Those leering looks you think nobody notices—they also corrupt.

Matthew 5:27–28 THE MESSAGE

No temptation has overtaken you except such as is common to man; but God is faithful, who will not allow you to be tempted beyond what you are able, but with the temptation will also make the way of escape, that you may be able to bear it.

1 Corinthians 10:13 NKJV

Additional Notable Verses Concerning Pornography

Psalm 119:37; Job 31:1–4; Romans 6:14; 2 Timothy 2:22; James 4:7; 1 Peter 5:8–10; 2 Peter 2:9; 1 John 2:15–17

Poverty

No one wants to be in poverty. God tells us numerous times in His Word that He has great compassion on the poor. Judging by the words of Jesus, poverty is constantly on God's mind. Whether or not we help those who are in poverty and how we help them are very important to God. In fact, the Scriptures tell us that God views every bit of assistance to the poor as assistance to Him personally. The poor may never repay you for your kindness, but God certainly will.

Key Verses

If one of your brethren becomes poor, and falls into poverty among you, then you shall help him, like a stranger or a sojourner, that he may live with you. Take no usury or interest from him; but fear your God, that your brother may live with you. You shall not lend him your money for usury, nor lend him your food at a profit. I am the Lord your God, who brought you out of the land of Egypt, to give you the land of Canaan and to be your God.

Leviticus 25:35–38 NKJV

Open your mouth, judge righteously, defend the rights of the poor and needy.

Proverbs 31:9 ESV

Then Jesus turned to his disciples and said, "God blesses you who are poor, for the Kingdom of God is yours. God blesses you who are hungry now, for you will be satisfied. God blesses you who weep now, for in due time you will laugh.

Luke 6:20–21 NLT

Additional Notable Verses Concerning Poverty

Leviticus 19:9–10; Job 34:17–19; Psalm 12:5; 140:12; Proverbs 10:15; 20:13; 24:33–34; Ecclesiastes 9:16; Isaiah 25:4; 41:17; Matthew 25:34–40; 2 Corinthians 8:9; James 2:5, 14–17

Power

ere on earth power seems to be an incredibly corrupting force. One minute a politician seems like a good and honest person, and then after he or she has gotten a little bit of power the scandals begin to break and we realize that the person could not handle the power. This type of thing isn't limited to the field of politics. It is rampant anywhere there are people.

The Scriptures teach that there is only one who has not been and will not be corrupted by power: God. As an all-powerful being, He has no need to seek more power—He already has it all. The more we rely on God's power and the less we rely on ours, the better off we will be.

Key Verses

God's power is unlimited. He needs no teachers to guide or correct him.

Job 36:22–23 CEV

God hath spoken once; twice have I heard this; that power belongeth unto God.

Psalm 62:11 KJV

For he was crucified in weakness, but lives by the power of God. For we also are weak in him, but in dealing with you we will live with him by the power of God.

2 Corinthians 13:4 ESV

In conclusion, be strong in the Lord [be empowered through your union with Him]; draw your strength from Him [that strength which His boundless might provides].

Ephesians 6:10 AMP

Additional Notable Verses Concerning Power

Exodus 9:16; 15:6; 1 Chronicles 29:12; 2 Chronicles 16:9; Nehemiah 1:10; Job 26:14; 40:9; Psalm 21:13; 63:1–2; 66:7; 68:35; 79:11; 89:13; 106:8; 136:12; Isaiah 26:4; Jeremiah 10:12; Nahum 1:3–5; Matthew 6:13; Romans 1:16–20; 9:19–24; 1 Corinthians 1:18–31; 2:5; 6:14; Ephesians 1:18–23; 3:7, 20; Colossians 1:11; 2 Timothy 1:8; 1 Peter 1:5; Revelation 4:11; 5:13; 11:17

Praise

Praise is one concept that our world gets. We hear people praise their favorite athlete, musician, or movie star on a regular basis. Often the praise that is heaped on these finite people is beyond belief. Crowds flock to see these famous people, tussle for their autographs, and break into an all-out brawl for a piece of their clothing.

What our world gets wrong about praise is its object. It is fine to have a favorite athlete or musician, but God is really the only one worthy of humanity's praises. Everything that has ever been done by humans on earth pales in comparison to His mighty works. Creation alone was a more magnificent feat than anything humanity could ever dream up. There is nothing wrong with a standing ovation, just make sure the recipient of your praise is truly worthy.

Key Verses

I will call upon the Lord, who is worthy to be praised; so shall I be saved from my enemies.

2 Samuel 22:4 NKJV

I will exalt you, my God and King, and praise your name forever and ever. I will praise you every day; yes, I will praise you forever. Great is the Lord! He is most worthy of praise! No one can measure his greatness.

Psalm 145:1–3 NLT

Lord, you are my God; I will exalt you and praise your name, for in perfect faithfulness you have done wonderful things, things planned long ago.

Isaiah 25:1 NIV

Through Him then, let us continually offer up a sacrifice of praise to God, that is, the fruit of lips that give thanks to His name.

Hebrews 13:15 NASB

Additional Notable Verses Concerning Praise

Exodus 15:11; 1 Chronicles 16:25; 2 Chronicles 20:21; Psalm 42:5; 50:23; 89:5; 107:8; 138:2; 145; 148–150; Isaiah 12:1; Jeremiah 33:11; Matthew 21:16; Acts 16:25; Romans 15:11; Revelation 4:9–11; 5:12; 19:5

Prayer

Many people struggle to pray because it does not feel like they are actually doing anything. Prayer can very often feel like talking to the ceiling.

But the Bible tells us that prayer is one of the mightiest acts in all of the world. Jesus told His disciples that they could tell a mountain to move, and it would move (Matthew 17:20). Prayer is important because it changes things, and also because it changes us. Sometimes the answer to our prayers will be yes, and the mountain will move. Sometimes the answer to our prayers will be no, and instead we will be the ones to move. Prayer changes things, even cold-hearted Christians.

Key Verses

But you should ask God for help and pray to the Almighty for mercy.

Job 8:5 NCV

In the same way, the Spirit helps us in our weakness. We do not know what we ought to pray for, but the Spirit himself intercedes for us through wordless groans. And he who searches our hearts knows the mind of the Spirit, because the Spirit intercedes for God's people in accordance with the will of God.

Romans 8:26–27 NIV

Be anxious for nothing, but in everything by prayer and supplication with thanksgiving let your requests be made known to God.

Philippians 4:6 NASB

Be unceasing in prayer [praying perseveringly].

1 Thessalonians 5:17 AMP

Additional Notable Verses Concerning Prayer

1 Samuel 1:1–20; 2 Chronicles 7:14; 32:20–33; Nehemiah 1; Psalm 5:1–3; 17:1; 55:1; 61:1; 62:8; 65:2; 86:7; 143:1; Proverbs 15:8; Isaiah 55:6; Daniel 6; 9:3–23; Matthew 6:5–15; 7:7; 21:22; Mark 11:25; Luke 18:1–14; Romans 12:10–12; 1 Corinthians 14:15; Ephesians 3:14; 6:18; Colossians 4:2; 1 Timothy 2:8; 5:5; James 1:6; 5:13–18; 1 Peter 3:7; 1 John 5:14; Jude 1:20; Revelation 5:8

Predestination

redestination is a hotly debated topic. So much so that some Christians declare that they simply do not believe in it. The problem with not believing in it is that it is in the Bible.

The Bible definitely teaches such a thing as predestination. Exactly what that means has been argued by theologians for hundreds of years. Does predestination mean that God selected the destinies of His children for them, or does it simply mean that God knew in advance who would choose Him? It may mean one or the other, or maybe even a combination of the two, but it most certainly is something to believe in.

Key Verses

And we know that God causes all things to work together for good to those who love God, to those who are called according to His purpose. For those whom He foreknew, He also predestined to become conformed to the image of His Son, so that He would be the firstborn among many brethren; and these whom He predestined, He also called; and these whom He called, He also justified; and these whom He justified, He also glorified.

Romans 8:28–30 NASB

Blessed be the God and Father of our Lord Jesus Christ, who has blessed us in Christ with every spiritual blessing in the heavenly places, even as he chose us in him before the foundation of the world, that we should be holy and blameless before him. In love he predestined us for adoption as sons through Jesus Christ, according to the purpose of his will, to the praise of his glorious grace, with which he has blessed us in the Beloved.

Ephesians 1:3–6 ESV

Additional Notable Verses Concerning Predestination

John 6:44; Acts 2:23; 4:26–28; 13:48; 1 Corinthians 2:7; Ephesians 1:11–14; 2 Timothy 1:9; 1 Peter 1:2, 20

Pride

I t has been suggested by some that pride is the oldest of sins. This idea does have some biblical validity since it was the sin shown by Lucifer. It was for this sin that Lucifer and those fallen angels who followed him were thrown out of heaven (Isaiah 14:12–15).

The Bible condemns pride, and not just that of Lucifer, as outright rebellion against God. Pride makes us feel good about ourselves, but that is because pride is self-centeredness run amok. God's Word describes pride as an attitude and way of thinking that places oneself on the throne and refuses to accept anything other than what is best for oneself right now. Pride caused Lucifer to fall from heaven. How far will it cause you to fall?

Key Verses

The wicked, through the pride of his countenance, will not seek after God: God is not in all his thoughts.

Psalm 10:4 KJV

Everyone proud and arrogant in heart is disgusting, hateful, and exceedingly offensive to the Lord; be assured [I pledge it] they will not go unpunished.

Proverbs 16:5 AMP

And what he gives in love is far better than anything else you'll find. It's common knowledge that "God goes against the willful proud; God gives grace to the willing humble."

James 4:6 THE MESSAGE

Additional Notable Verses Concerning Pride

Exodus 18:11; 1 Samuel 2:3; 2 Kings 20:12–21; Psalm 10:2; 31:23; 40:4; 73:6; 101:5; 131:1; Proverbs 8:12–13; 11:2; 13:10; 21:4; 26:12; 28:25; 29:23; Isaiah 2:12; Jeremiah 13:15; Daniel 4; Hosea 7:10; Habakkuk 2:4–5; Zephaniah 2:10–11; Matthew 23:12; Mark 7:21–23; Luke 18:9–14; Romans 12:3; 1 Timothy 3:6; 1 John 2:16

Priorities

Everyone has priorities. Pay attention the next time you are in a building when the fire alarm goes off. Some people grab a purse, some people grab a laptop computer, some people grab a wallet, and some people grab a couple of photographs. It is when we think that our lives might be in danger, or at the very least our stuff may burn up, that our priorities truly become evident.

God has a list of priorities for our lives as well. His are pretty easy to keep track of. At number one on His priority list is God. At number two on His priority list is everything else. That list may seem a little abbreviated, but from the Bible's perspective that is how things should work. If we put God at number one and keep Him there, He will help us sort out everything that comes thereafter.

Key Verses

You shall have no other gods before me.
Exodus 20:3 NIV

Seek the Kingdom of God above all else, and live righteously, and he will give you everything you need.

Matthew 6:33 NLT

Do not love the world nor the things in the world. If anyone loves the world, the love of the Father is not in him. For all that is in the world, the lust of the flesh and the lust of the eyes and the boastful pride of life, is not from the Father, but is from the world. The world is passing away, and also its lusts; but the one who does the will of God lives forever.

1 John 2:15–17 NASB

Additional Notable Verses Concerning Priorities

Jeremiah 9:23–24; Matthew 6:19–34; 16:24–28; Luke 12:13–21; Colossians 3:1–4; James 1:5–8; Philippians 3:12–16

Prophecy

Today's modern work world loves long job descriptions. Some descriptions are so long that by the time you have read the whole thing you cannot remember what the job was.

For a prophet in biblical times the job description was easy. Speak for God, and do so infallibly every time. Make just one mistake and they are going to stone you for being a false prophet. No pressure, just make sure that when you speak for God you are relaying to the people what God actually said. It was a high-pressure job, but at least the job description was not complicated.

Key Verses

"But any prophet who fakes it, who claims to speak in my name something I haven't commanded him to say, or speaks in the name of other gods, that prophet must die." You may be wondering among yourselves, "How can we tell the difference, whether it was God who spoke or not?" Here's how: If what the prophet spoke in God's name doesn't happen, then obviously God wasn't behind it; the prophet made it up. Forget about him.

Deuteronomy 18:20–22 THE MESSAGE

Do not despise prophecies.
1 Thessalonians 5:20 NKJV

So we have the prophetic word made more sure, to which you do well to pay attention as to a lamp shining in a dark place, until the day dawns and the morning star arises in your hearts. But know this first of all, that no prophecy of Scripture is a matter of one's own interpretation, for no prophecy was ever made by an act of human will, but men moved by the Holy Spirit spoke from God.

2 Peter 1:19–21 NASB

Additional Notable Verses Concerning Prophecy

Deuteronomy 13:1–3; 1 Samuel 19:18–24; Jeremiah 1:5; 7:25; 14:14; Joel 2:28–32; Matthew 1:22–23; 23:34; Luke 24:13–27; 1 Corinthians 12:10; Ephesians 4:11; 1 Peter 1:10–11; Revelation 1:1–3; 22:7

Prostitution

I t did not take humanity long to turn sex from a beautiful gift of God between a married man and woman, to something that existed for pleasure and for profit. We like to think that the modern world is sex-crazed, and it is, but it is almost shocking how quickly and how frequently we see prostitution in the biblical story line.

The Bible is uniform in its condemnation of prostitution. It is a practice that makes a mockery of God's design for sex and is harmful to all involved. There is something to be said, however, for how often God forgives and shows grace to prostitutes. They appear in the bloodline of Christ. Prostitution violates God's moral standards, but God's grace and forgiveness extend further than His standards.

Key Verses

No Israelite man or woman must ever become a temple prostitute. Do not bring a male or female prostitute's pay to the Temple of the Lord your God to pay what you have promised to the Lord, because the Lord your God hates prostitution.

Deuteronomy 23:17–18 NCV

For on account of a harlot one is reduced to a loaf of bread, and an adulteress hunts for the precious life.

Proverbs 6:26 NASB

Run from sexual sin! No other sin so clearly affects the body as this one does. For sexual immorality is a sin against your own body. Don't you realize that your body is the temple of the Holy Spirit, who lives in you and was given to you by God? You do not belong to yourself, for God bought you with a high price. So you must honor God with your body.

1 Corinthians 6:18–20 NLT

Additional Notable Verses Concerning Prostitution

Genesis 38; Leviticus 19:29; Deuteronomy 22:13–21; Proverbs 23:27–28; Hosea 1–14; Matthew 21:31–32; Luke 7:36–50; 1 Corinthians 6:15–17; James 2:25

Public Opinion

One constant throughout history has been that there are few things more unreliable than public opinion. People are fickle creatures, and when you put them in large groups the proclivity for erratic thinking and behavior only gets worse. It is almost enough to make you feel sorry for politicians who base just about everything they say on public opinion polls. What people think today may be completely different by tomorrow.

People's opinions may not be consistent, but the Bible's message about them certainly is. Because public opinion is so fickle, it cannot and should not have a place of prominence in our lives. We are to find our bearings in life through God and His Word. Public opinion is useful insomuch as it lines up with what the Bible teaches. Where opinion differs from Scripture is where it is no longer useful.

Key Verses

I have concealed my transgressions as others do by hiding my iniquity in my heart, because I stood in great fear of the multitude, and the contempt of families terrified me, so that I kept silence, and did not go out of doors.

Job 31:33–34 ESV

Do not pay attention to every word people say, or you may hear your servant cursing you—for you know in your heart that many times you yourself have cursed others.

Ecclesiastes 7:21–22 NIV

My dear friends, don't let public opinion influence how you live out our glorious, Christ-originated faith.

James 2:1 THE MESSAGE

Additional Notable Verses Concerning Public Opinion

Numbers 13:21–14:10; Deuteronomy 1:19–40; 5:28–29; Joshua 24:19–24; 1 Samuel 8:4–9; 14:24–48; 15:24; Jeremiah 26:7–16; Matthew 21:8–11; 27:20–26; Acts 12:1–4

Racism

There is much hand-wringing by scholars and academics as to why the problem of racism still exists in the enlightened twenty-first century. They thought that by this point in human history—with all of our educational programs and incentives—that racism would be extinct. There is one important factor that is missed by these people. Racism is not a skin problem, it is a sin problem.

The Bible teaches us that all humans are sinners. As such, people will sin against one another. They will sin against others because they are taller, or smarter, or darker—it does not matter. So long as the root problem of our sin nature is not dealt with, racism will not only exist, it will thrive. The only answer to racism (or greed or lust or any other sin) is for our sins to be nailed to the cross and our lives given over to the power of the Holy Spirit.

Key Verses

Stop judging by the way things look, but judge by what is really right.
John 7:24 NCV

Jew and Gentile are the same in this respect. They have the same Lord, who gives generously to all who call on him.
Romans 10:12 NLT

Whoever says he is in the light and hates his brother is still in darkness. Whoever loves his brother abides in the light, and in him there is no cause for stumbling. But whoever hates his brother is in the darkness and walks in the darkness, and does not know where he is going, because the darkness has blinded his eyes.
1 John 2:9–11 ESV

Additional Notable Verses Concerning Racism
Genesis 1:27; Acts 10:34–35; Romans 2:11; Galatians 3:28; Colossians 3:10–11; James 2:9

Rape

Rape is not about sex; it is about power. Rape is stealing something precious to someone else, and doing so by deadly force. It is one of the most cruel and heartless things that one human being can do to another.

There are a handful of references to rape in the Scripture, and most of us would react to the rape of someone we love as Jacob's sons did in Genesis 34. They responded to the rape of their sister with a cruel and devious plan for revenge that ended in the slaughter of all those involved, and a whole lot more. As horrible a crime as rape is, it is important to know that God held Jacob's sons as responsible for their actions as the rapists. Two wrongs do not make a right, even if the first wrong is as bad as it gets.

Key Verses

But if in the open country a man meets a young woman who is betrothed, and the man seizes her and lies with her, then only the man who lay with her shall die. But you shall do nothing to the young woman; she has committed no offense punishable by death. For this case is like that of a man attacking and murdering his neighbor, because he met her in the open country, and though the betrothed young woman cried for help there was no one to rescue her. If a man meets a virgin who is not betrothed, and seizes her and lies with her, and they are found, then the man who lay with her shall give to the father of the young woman fifty shekels of silver, and she shall be his wife, because he has violated her. He may not divorce her all his days.

Deuteronomy 22:25–29 ESV

Additional Notable Verses Concerning Rape
Genesis 19:1–38; 34; 2 Samuel 13:1–33

Reconciliation

Reconciliation is a rare joy. Reconciliation takes a tremendous amount of work, and even after all of the work the process may still fall short. Though it is certainly a more difficult option than remaining at odds with another, the Bible places a high value on reconciliation. Much of this is because reconciliation is at the core of the doctrine of salvation. We were estranged from God, but he did 100 percent of the work to reconcile us to himself. Even when humanity was not interested in being saved, God was willing to sacrifice Christ to reconcile us to Him.

Key Verses

All this is from God, who through Christ reconciled us to himself and gave us the ministry of reconciliation; that is, in Christ God was reconciling the world to himself, not counting their trespasses against them, and entrusting to us the message of reconciliation. Therefore, we are ambassadors for Christ, God making his appeal through us. We implore you on behalf of Christ, be reconciled to God. For our sake he made him to be sin who knew no sin, so that in him we might become the righteousness of God.

2 Corinthians 5:18–21 ESV

But now in Christ Jesus you who formerly were far off have been brought near by the blood of Christ. For He Himself is our peace, who made both groups into one and broke down the barrier of the dividing wall, by abolishing in His flesh the enmity, which is the Law of commandments contained in ordinances, so that in Himself He might make the two into one new man, thus establishing peace, and might reconcile them both in one body to God through the cross, by it having put to death the enmity.

Ephesians 2:13–16 NASB

Additional Notable Verses Concerning Reconciliation

Daniel 9:24; Isaiah 53:5; Matthew 5:21–26; Romans 5:1–11; Colossians 1:15–23; 2:8–15; Hebrews 2:17

Refugees

For most of the refugees in the Bible the Scriptures are the only record of their plight. There were no blogs or other social media for them to communicate their story. God's Word tells us of a few refugees, and more important, it gives us God's expectations for how people seeking refuge are to be treated. This is important today because God's perspective on all believers is that we are refugees from sin. Our home world has been overrun by sin, and we must run to Him for refuge.

Key Verses

When you beat the olives from your olive trees, don't go over the boughs twice. Leave the remaining olives for the foreigners, orphans, and widows. When you gather the grapes in your vineyard, don't glean the vines after they are picked. Leave the remaining grapes for the foreigners, orphans, and widows. Remember that you were slaves in the land of Egypt. That is why I am giving you this command.

Deuteronomy 24:20–22 NLT

That's plain enough, isn't it? You're no longer wandering exiles. This kingdom of faith is now your home country. You're no longer strangers or outsiders. You belong here, with as much right to the name Christian as anyone. God is building a home. He's using us all—irrespective of how we got here—in what he is building. He used the apostles and prophets for the foundation. Now he's using you, fitting you in brick by brick, stone by stone, with Christ Jesus as the cornerstone that holds all the parts together. We see it taking shape day after day—a holy temple built by God, all of us built into it, a temple in which God is quite at home.

Ephesians 2:19–22 THE MESSAGE

Additional Notable Verses Concerning Refugees

1 Samuel 23–24; 1 Chronicles 29:14–15; Psalm 105; 137; Matthew 2:13–21; 8:20; Luke 2:1–7; 10:25–37

Religion

Religion has been described as humanity's attempts to reach God, whereas Christianity is God reaching down to humanity. The Bible condemns man-made or self-imposed religion, which is often just our best efforts to look good enough to God.

That said, the Bible does not condemn good deeds. It is actually quite adamant that God's children should be people who live out their faith on a regular and consistent basis. It is only when our religion flows from the forgiveness of God that it is truly a good thing.

Key Verses

Therefore, if you died with Christ from the basic principles of the world, why, as though living in the world, do you subject yourselves to regulations— "Do not touch, do not taste, do not handle," which all concern things which perish with the using—according to the commandments and doctrines of men? These things indeed have an appearance of wisdom in self-imposed religion, false humility, and neglect of the body, but are of no value against the indulgence of the flesh.

Colossians 2:20–23 NKJV

As the end approaches, people are going to be self-absorbed, money-hungry, self-promoting, stuck-up, profane, contemptuous of parents, crude, coarse, dog-eat-dog, unbending, slanderers, impulsively wild, savage, cynical, treacherous, ruthless, bloated windbags, addicted to lust, and allergic to God. They'll make a show of religion, but behind the scenes they're animals. Stay clear of these people.

2 Timothy 3:2–5 THE MESSAGE

If you claim to be religious but don't control your tongue, you are fooling yourself, and your religion is worthless. Pure and genuine religion in the sight of God the Father means caring for orphans and widows in their distress and refusing to let the world corrupt you.

James 1:26–27 NLT

Additional Notable Verses Concerning Religion

Leviticus 26:27–33; Psalm 31:6; Isaiah 1:14; 17:8; Jeremiah 2:8; 10; Hosea 6:6; Malachi 1:6–14; Matthew 7:28–29; Acts 17:22–34; Galatians 1:11–24; 2:15–21; 5:6

Respect

People often want to receive more respect than they give out. We all desire to be respected by our families, those we work with, and those we know socially. To many people, respect is one of the most important things in life. Yet we often show a tremendous disrespect, not only to those we come in contact with during the day, but to those closest to us and even to God himself.

Respect is not just important to us. It is imperative to our relationship with God that we understand how and why to respect God and others. The Bible teaches that our ability to show respect to God is indicative of our understanding of exactly who He is (Almighty Maker of Heaven and Earth), and exactly who we are (sinners saved only by His grace). Once we understand this, it will also trickle down to how we respect our fellow sinners, saved by grace or not.

Key Verses

Ye shall do no unrighteousness in judgment: thou shalt not respect the person of the poor, nor honor the person of the mighty: but in righteousness shalt thou judge thy neighbour.

Leviticus 19:15 KJV

Then shall I not be put to shame [by failing to inherit Your promises] when I have respect to all Your commandments.

Psalm 119:6 AMP

Love each other with genuine affection, and take delight in honoring each other.

Romans 12:10 NLT

Do nothing from selfishness or empty conceit, but with humility of mind regard one another as more important than yourselves; do not merely look out for your own personal interests, but also for the interests of others.

Philippians 2:3–4 NASB

Additional Notable Verses Concerning Respect

Leviticus 19:32; Numbers 16:15; 2 Samuel 14:14; Psalm 40:4; 74:20; 119:117; Isaiah 17:7–8; Lamentations 4:16; 1 Peter 2:17

Responsibility

People try to escape responsibility for their actions all the time. This usually does not work, but many times if you have enough fame or fortune you can get away with a crime.

No matter how much people may try, the Scriptures tell us that we are all responsible for our actions. In this temporal world we may escape the consequences for a time, but God will not allow anyone to avoid ultimate responsibility.

Key Verses

Whoever conceals their sins does not prosper, but the one who confesses and renounces them finds mercy.

Proverbs 28:13 NIV

The person who sins will die. The son will not bear the punishment for the father's iniquity, nor will the father bear the punishment for the son's iniquity; the righteousness of the righteous will be upon himself, and the wickedness of the wicked will be upon himself.

Ezekiel 18:20 NASB

Brothers, if anyone is caught in any transgression, you who are spiritual should restore him in a spirit of gentleness. Keep watch on yourself, lest you too be tempted. Bear one another's burdens, and so fulfill the law of Christ. For if anyone thinks he is something, when he is nothing, he deceives himself. But let each one test his own work, and then his reason to boast will be in himself alone and not in his neighbor. For each will have to bear his own load.

Galatians 6:1–5 ESV

Additional Notable Verses Concerning Responsibility

Deuteronomy 28; Proverbs 6:20; Ecclesiastes 12:14; Matthew 12:36; 25:1–30; Luke 12:41–48; 1 Corinthians 13:11; 2 Corinthians 5:1–10; Colossians 3:22–25; 1 Timothy 5:8; 1 John 1:9

Rest

There is a good chance that when you were a child you did everything you could to avoid taking naps or going to bed. As you grew older you probably thought the perfect day was one in which you slept in, but it was also probably preceded by a late night. As you reached mature adulthood and things like a mortgage, a steady job, a spouse, and children entered the picture, you suddenly found yourself treasuring any moment that you could have your eyes closed.

Good rest is very valuable, and no one understands this more than our Creator. God created us to rest regularly, and He knows all too well our propensity for trying to do without rest.

Key Verses

Thus the heavens and the earth were finished, and all the host of them. And on the seventh day God finished his work that he had done, and he rested on the seventh day from all his work that he had done. So God blessed the seventh day and made it holy, because on it God rested from all his work that he had done in creation.

Genesis 2:1–3 ESV

Do your work in six days and rest on the seventh day, even during the seasons for plowing and harvesting.

Exodus 34:21 CEV

It is useless for you to work so hard from early morning until late at night, anxiously working for food to eat; for God gives rest to his loved ones.

Psalm 127:2 NLT

Come to me, all you who are weary and burdened, and I will give you rest. Take my yoke upon you and learn from me, for I am gentle and humble in heart, and you will find rest for your souls.

Matthew 11:28–29 NIV

Additional Notable Verses Concerning Rest

Exodus 20:8–10; 23:12; 33:14; Psalm 55:6; Proverbs 19:23; Ecclesiastes 2:24–25; Isaiah 14:3–4; 30:15; Matthew 8:24; Mark 6:31; Hebrews 4:1–11

Retirement

We do not see many people retire in the Bible. That does not make it wrong; it just means that it was not as much a part of their world as it is ours. Largely employed in an agricultural society, the ancient Israelites were pretty much locked in to work until they could no longer work anymore. If you did not farm, you did not only do without income, you did without food.

The Scriptures may be light on verses about retirement, but they are not silent on the subject of people reaching the end of their life's work. When we search the Bible's pages, we learn that from God's perspective it is a very good thing for people to leave an inheritance. We also learn that even though the prospect of no longer working and going into retirement can be quite scary, God promises to be present every step of the way with those entering that phase of life.

Key Verses

Do not reject me when I am old; do not leave me when my strength is gone.
Psalm 71:9 NCV

A good person leaves an inheritance for their children's children, but a sinner's wealth is stored up for the righteous.
Proverbs 13:22 NIV

Listen to me, family of Jacob, everyone that's left of the family of Israel. I've been carrying you on my back from the day you were born, and I'll keep on carrying you when you're old. I'll be there, bearing you when you're old and gray. I've done it and will keep on doing it, carrying you on my back, saving you.
Isaiah 46:3–4 THE MESSAGE

Additional Notable Verses Concerning Retirement
Numbers 8:23–26; Psalm 37:25; Proverbs 16:31; 17:6; Ecclesiastes 6:1–6; Acts 20:24

Revenge

Stories of revenge always seem to intrigue people. Tales such as *Hamlet* and *The Count of Monte Cristo* are amazing in their ability to get you rooting for those rotten people who did something wrong to get what they deserve. Maybe these stories are so intoxicating because we can all probably come up with at least one person on whom we would like to exact revenge.

It is so easy to seek revenge. It feels right. They wronged you, so shouldn't you make them pay for their transgression? On the surface that sounds just, but when we dig further into our own motivations, we know that they are not as pure as we would like to pretend. Revenge is not ours to take. If someone's offense is prosecutable, let them be prosecuted, but ultimately we must take our desire for revenge and give it to God. He is more than happy to repay those who harm us.

Key Verses

Do not seek revenge or bear a grudge against anyone among your people, but love your neighbor as yourself. I am the Lord.

Leviticus 19:18 NIV

Don't try to get even. Trust the Lord, and he will help you.

Proverbs 20:22 CEV

Beloved, never avenge yourselves, but leave it to the wrath of God, for it is written, "Vengeance is mine, I will repay, says the Lord."

Romans 12:19 ESV

Additional Notable Verses Concerning Revenge

Genesis 34; Judges 15; 2 Samuel 13:20–36; Proverbs 24:17, 29; 25:21–22; Ezekiel 25:15–17; Amos 1:11–12; Matthew 5:38–41; Luke 6:35; 9:53–55; Romans 12:14; 1 Peter 2:23

Rewards

Everyone likes getting rewards. From children in kindergarten to business executives, people like being rewarded for things like hard work and achievement. Rewards—from a little gold star to a hefty bonus in your paycheck—are things that people will put forth tremendous effort to obtain.

The Bible mentions rewards in the context of the Christian life. The amazing thing is that the only way we are able to do anything beneficial is if God does it through us. God allows us to earn rewards by simply being willing to let Him work in our lives.

Key Verses

The wicked earns deceptive wages, but he who sows righteousness gets a true reward.

Proverbs 11:18 NASB

Do your work willingly, as though you were serving the Lord himself, and not just your earthly master. In fact, the Lord Christ is the one you are really serving, and you know that he will reward you.

Colossians 3:23–24 CEV

And without faith it is impossible to please him, for whoever would draw near to God must believe that he exists and that he rewards those who seek him.

Hebrews 11:6 ESV

Additional Notable Verses Concerning Rewards

Matthew 5:11–12; 25; Luke 6:32–36; Romans 4:1–8; 1 Corinthians 9:25; 2 Corinthians 5:1–10; 1 Thessalonians 2:17–20; 2 Timothy 4:1–8; Hebrews 10:35–36; James 1:12; 1 Peter 5:1–5; 2 John 1:8; Revelation 2:10; 3:21; 22:12

Sabbath

The Sabbath originated as a one-day rest for the people of Israel, based on God's example of resting one day after working for six in creation. The idea behind the Sabbath was not to give everyone a day off work to go to the lake, or even to the tabernacle to worship. It was meant to be a day of rest for the people, for animals, and even for the land.

The Pharisees added to God's Sabbath regulations—going well beyond what God intended—and constantly battled with Christ over the true nature and meaning of the Sabbath. It is also interesting what the Bible does not say about the Sabbath; the command to keep the Sabbath is not repeated in the New Testament for the church.

Key Verses

Remember the Sabbath day by keeping it holy. Six days you shall labor and do all your work, but the seventh day is a sabbath to the Lord your God. On it you shall not do any work, neither you, nor your son or daughter, nor your male or female servant, nor your animals, nor any foreigner residing in your towns. For in six days the Lord made the heavens and the earth, the sea, and all that is in them, but he rested on the seventh day. Therefore the Lord blessed the Sabbath day and made it holy.

Exodus 20:8–11 NIV

And Jesus said to them, The Sabbath was made on account and for the sake of man, not man for the Sabbath; so the Son of Man is Lord even of the Sabbath.

Mark 2:27–28 AMP

Additional Notable Verses Concerning the Sabbath

Genesis 2:1–3; Exodus 16:22–30; 23:12; 31; Leviticus 19:3, 30; 23:3; Deuteronomy 5:14–15; Nehemiah 13; Isaiah 58:13–14; Jeremiah 17:21–27; Matthew 12:1–14; Mark 2:23–28; Luke 6:1–11; 13:10–17; 14:1–6; John 9:1–17; Hebrews 4:4

Sacrifice

The first sacrifice in the Bible comes very quickly. It occurs shortly after the first sin of Adam and Eve. Once you understand the theology of the Scriptures, that sin requires sacrifice, it makes sense that this sacrifice occurred when it did. God's holiness required that there be a payment for infraction of His laws.

In the Old Testament there were six different types of sacrifices: burnt offerings, fellowship or peace offerings, sin offerings, guilt offerings, drink offerings, and grain offerings. They each had different purposes and times to be offered, but they had one thing in common. Each of the offerings was intended to foreshadow the ultimate sacrifice of Christ on the cross, the last and final sacrifice required by God.

Key Verses

And Samuel said, "Has the Lord as great delight in burnt offerings and sacrifices, as in obeying the voice of the Lord? Behold, to obey is better than sacrifice, and to listen than the fat of rams."

1 Samuel 15:22 ESV

Get rid of the old yeast, so that you may be a new unleavened batch—as you really are. For Christ, our Passover lamb, has been sacrificed.

1 Corinthians 5:7 NIV

Imitate God, therefore, in everything you do, because you are his dear children. Live a life filled with love, following the example of Christ. He loved us and offered himself as a sacrifice for us, a pleasing aroma to God.

Ephesians 5:1–2 NLT

Additional Notable Verses Concerning Sacrifice

Genesis 4:1–16; 8:20–21; Exodus 22:20; Leviticus 1–7; Numbers 15:1–13; 28–29; Deuteronomy 15:19–23; 17:1; 1 Samuel 1:21–28; 2:12–17; 2 Kings 5:17; 17:36; Job 1:5; Psalm 27:6; 40:5–6; 51:16–19; 66:15; 116:17; Proverbs 21:3; Jonah 1:16; Malachi 1:6–14; Mark 12:33; Romans 12:1–2; Philippians 2:17; 4:18; Hebrews 9:15–10:39; 13:15

Salvation

S alvation is the end goal of many major religions, but a large percentage of the world today does not even believe that it needs saving. The idea that people are essentially good, or that a loving God would never send someone to hell is accepted by a large percentage of the public. It has been one of Satan's greatest lies to convince people who are drowning in their own sins that they do not need a life raft.

The Bible teaches that mankind needs help, and that it can do nothing to help itself. Salvation came the only way that it could: from God to man. The world may be ignorant of its own state, but its Creator is not.

Key Verses

Turn to Me and be saved, all the ends of the earth; for I am God, and there is no other.

Isaiah 45:22 NASB

This [Jesus] is the Stone which was despised and rejected by you, the builders, but which has become the Head of the corner [the Cornerstone]. And there is salvation in and through no one else, for there is no other name under heaven given among men by and in which we must be saved.

Acts 4:11–12 AMP

For God saved us and called us to live a holy life. He did this, not because we deserved it, but because that was his plan from before the beginning of time—to show us his grace through Christ Jesus.

2 Timothy 1:9 NLT

Additional Notable Verses Concerning Salvation

Psalm 3:8; 37:29; 85:7; Isaiah 45:14–25; 52:7; Jeremiah 3:23; Lamentations 3:26; Matthew 1:21; 18:10–14; Luke 1:68–69; John 3:1–21; Acts 5:31; Romans 1:16; 5:8; 10:9–10; 1 Corinthians 1:18; 2 Corinthians 6:2; Ephesians 1:11–14; 2:1–10; 1 Thessalonians 5:9; 2 Thessalonians 2:13–15; 1 Timothy 1:15; 2:3–6; 2 Timothy 1:8–10; Titus 2:11–14; 3:4–7; Hebrews 2:10; 5:9; 1 Peter 1:3–12; 1 John 4:9–10; Revelation 19:1

Sarcasm

Sarcasm can be difficult to identify on a written page. When we hear people say something like, "Well, of course, he is the smartest person in the room," we can hear in their voice how they emphasize the word *he* and we can see how they point their finger. We are able to conclude quite easily that they really do not believe that the person they are referencing is the smartest in the room. Sarcasm in the Bible is so difficult to understand because we are not there to hear the speaker's tone and to see his mannerisms.

There are many occasions in the Bible when speakers, and even God himself, use sarcasm. It is almost always used to make a point that someone was about to miss. Yet even though the Bible uses this device, it also warns against how it is used in speech. If sarcasm is intended to belittle people or to deride them, it is wholly inappropriate, but if it is a device simply used to make a point, it has its place.

Key Verses

Like a maniac shooting flaming arrows of death is one who deceives their neighbor and says, "I was only joking!"

Proverbs 26:18–19 NIV

Even so the tongue is a little member and boasts great things. See how great a forest a little fire kindles! . . . With it we bless our God and Father, and with it we curse men, who have been made in the similitude of God. Out of the same mouth proceed blessing and cursing. My brethren, these things ought not to be so.

James 3:5; 9–10 NKJV

Additional Notable Verses Concerning Sarcasm
Exodus 14:11; 1 Kings 18:27; Job 12:2; John 19:3; 2 Corinthians 11:1–33

Satan

Though Satan opposes God, it is very important to remember that Satan is not God's opposite. He is a force for evil, just as God is the very embodiment of truth and justice, but Satan is one of God's creations. He is a powerful fallen angel who rebelled against God and will one day pay the ultimate price for his rebellion.

The Scriptures tell us Satan was one of God's greatest creations until he chose to sin. Today he accuses Christians before God and seeks to keep the world in darkness. The good news is that Satan's activities will only be temporary. His end is sure, and God will be victorious.

Key Verses

Anyone whom you forgive, I also forgive. Indeed, what I have forgiven, if I have forgiven anything, has been for your sake in the presence of Christ, so that we would not be outwitted by Satan; for we are not ignorant of his designs.
2 Corinthians 2:10–11 ESV

But I am not surprised! Even Satan disguises himself as an angel of light.
2 Corinthians 11:14 NLT

Therefore submit to God. Resist the devil and he will flee from you.
James 4:7 NKJV

Be well balanced (temperate, sober of mind), be vigilant and cautious at all times; for that enemy of yours, the devil, roams around like a lion roaring [in fierce hunger], seeking someone to seize upon and devour.
1 Peter 5:8 AMP

Additional Notable Verses Concerning Satan

Genesis 3; Job 1:1–2:10; 1 Chronicles 21:1; Isaiah 14:12–17; Ezekiel 28:1–19; Zechariah 3:1; Matthew 4:1–11; 13:19; 25:41; Luke 10:18; 22:3; John 8:44; Acts 5:3; Romans 16:20; 2 Corinthians 4:3–4; Ephesians 6:11–16; 1 Thessalonians 2:18; 2 Thessalonians 2:1–12; 1 Timothy 5:15; 2 Timothy 2:26; 1 John 2:13; 3:8; Jude 1:9; Revelation 12:10–11; 16:14; 20:7–10

Secularism

Secularism is the idea that our lives should exist apart from religious influence and bias. Secularism has come to invade every area of society and life. It has even come to invade the church.

The term *secularism* does not appear in the Bible, but the concept is there frequently. It is typically referred to as "the world." The world is the system of unbelief that is under the sway of Satan and is opposed to Christianity. Though referred to by a different name, secularism was one of the New Testament church's biggest concerns.

Key Verses

You are the salt of the earth, but if salt has lost its taste, how shall its saltiness be restored? It is no longer good for anything except to be thrown out and trampled under people's feet. You are the light of the world. A city set on a hill cannot be hidden. Nor do people light a lamp and put it under a basket, but on a stand, and it gives light to all in the house. In the same way, let your light shine before others, so that they may see your good works and give glory to your Father who is in heaven.

Matthew 5:13–16 ESV

Don't let anyone capture you with empty philosophies and high-sounding nonsense that come from human thinking and from the spiritual powers of this world, rather than from Christ.

Colossians 2:8 NLT

You adulterous people, don't you know that friendship with the world means enmity against God? Therefore, anyone who chooses to be a friend of the world becomes an enemy of God.

James 4:4 NIV

Additional Notable Verses Concerning Secularism

Isaiah 13:11; Romans 1:18–32; 12:1–2; 1 Corinthians 1:18–31; 2; 5:9–11; 2 Corinthians 4:1–6; Ephesians 2:11–22; 6:12; 1 John 2:15–17; 3:1–13; 4:1–6

Self-Confidence

Much is made in the twenty-first century about the somewhat ambiguous concept of self-confidence. It is said that those who possess it are champions of industry, athletics, politics, and entertainment. The theory goes that if you have self-confidence you can accomplish anything, and that if you are lacking in it you have paved the way for your own failures.

But the word *self-confidence* is nowhere in Scripture. Self-confidence is at best a foreign concept to Scripture, and at worst it is actually the opposite of what the Bible teaches. God's Word says that confidence in anything other than God and His ability to move in our lives is misplaced. We will not necessarily fail if we have too little self-confidence, but we will definitely fail if we have too little God-confidence.

Key Verses

Though a host encamp against me, my heart will not fear; though war arise against me, in spite of this I shall be confident.

Psalm 27:3 NASB

I can do all things through him who strengthens me.

Philippians 4:13 ESV

For God has not given us a spirit of fear, but of power and of love and of a sound mind.

2 Timothy 1:7 NKJV

So do not throw away your confidence; it will be richly rewarded. You need to persevere so that when you have done the will of God, you will receive what he has promised.

Hebrews 10:35–36 NIV

Additional Notable Verses Concerning Self-Confidence

Psalm 91; 138:8; 1 Corinthians 2:3–5; 2 Corinthians 12:7–10; Galatians 2:20; Ephesians 2:8–9; Philippians 1:6; 1 Timothy 4:12; Hebrews 4:16; 13:6; 2 Peter 1:3

Self-Defense

When Christ was reviled and attacked, and eventually wrongly executed, He mounted very little in the way of self-defense. Should Christianity turn all of God's children into committed pacifists? Should we refuse to go to war, refuse to fight, and even refuse to defend ourselves?

The Bible doesn't always give us clear answers to all our questions. The actions of Jesus are certainly something to consider with regard to self-defense, but we must never forget that by refusing to defend himself Christ was fulfilling His mission and in the process securing salvation for all who would accept Him. Many others in both the Old and New Testaments defended themselves when the need arose. Sometimes we have to pray for God's wisdom and direction for our specific circumstances.

Key Verses

If the thief is caught while breaking in and is struck so that he dies, there will be no bloodguiltiness on his account. But if the sun has risen on him, there will be bloodguiltiness on his account. He shall surely make restitution; if he owns nothing, then he shall be sold for his theft.

Exodus 22:2–3 NASB

You have heard that it was said, "An eye for an eye, and a tooth for a tooth." But I tell you, don't stand up against an evil person. If someone slaps you on the right cheek, turn to him the other cheek also. If someone wants to sue you in court and take your shirt, let him have your coat also. If someone forces you to go with him one mile, go with him two miles. If a person asks you for something, give it to him. Don't refuse to give to someone who wants to borrow from you.

Matthew 5:38–42 NCV

Additional Notable Verses Concerning Self-Defense

Nehemiah 4:1–23; Proverbs 20:22; Luke 11:21; Romans 12:19–21

Selfishness

I t is a severe understatement to say that human beings are selfish. It is like saying that fish live in the water, or that giraffes are tall. It simply goes without saying. Human beings enter the world with a fully intact and active sin nature, and a large part of that sin nature is dedicated to selfishness. Selfishness seeks to obtain whatever it wants through whatever means necessary. It will push a person to say and do things that you would not expect, all in the name of self.

What the Bible has to say about selfishness should be of little surprise. Even sports teams have discovered that by implementing a philosophy of "There is no I in team," they can be more successful than if everyone participates as an individual. So it is no shock that the Scriptures are practically dripping with admonitions to put away selfishness and to do away with self-centered attitudes. We are urged to be like Christ, who though God incarnate, put aside what was best for Him for the good of us all.

Key Verses

Do not eat the bread of a selfish man, or desire his delicacies; for as he thinks within himself, so he is. He says to you, "Eat and drink!" but his heart is not with you. You will vomit up the morsel you have eaten, and waste your compliments.

Proverbs 23:6–8 NASB

We who are strong ought to bear with the failings of the weak and not to please ourselves.

Romans 15:1 NIV

This royal law is found in the Scriptures: "Love your neighbor as you love yourself." If you obey this law, you are doing right.

James 2:8 NCV

Additional Notable Verses Concerning Selfishness

Joshua 7; Isaiah 56:11; Matthew 22:39; 1 Corinthians 10:23–33; 12:12–27; 2 Corinthians 5:14–15; Philippians 2:1–11; 2:21; 2 Timothy 3:1–5; James 3:13–18; 1 John 3:16–18

Sex

The battle over sex rages in our culture today. The modern world has become so obsessed with self-gratification and pleasure that sex has been elevated to a place of utmost importance.

The Bible teaches that sex is great and wonderful, so long as it is done within God's parameters. God instituted sex for a man and a woman within the confines of marriage. Sex is not a bad thing; it is actually a very good thing. God has never wanted to deny humans sex, He just wants it done as He created it to be done.

Key Verses

Let your wife be a fountain of blessing for you. Rejoice in the wife of your youth. She is a loving deer, a graceful doe. Let her breasts satisfy you always. May you always be captivated by her love. Why be captivated, my son, by an immoral woman, or fondle the breasts of a promiscuous woman? For the Lord sees clearly what a man does, examining every path he takes. An evil man is held captive by his own sins; they are ropes that catch and hold him. He will die for lack of self-control; he will be lost because of his great foolishness.

Proverbs 5:18–23 NLT

Now for the matters you wrote about: "It is good for a man not to have sexual relations with a woman." But since sexual immorality is occurring, each man should have sexual relations with his own wife, and each woman with her own husband. The husband should fulfill his marital duty to his wife, and likewise the wife to her husband. The wife does not have authority over her own body but yields it to her husband. In the same way, the husband does not have authority over his own body but yields it to his wife.

1 Corinthians 7:1–4 NIV

Additional Notable Verses Concerning Sex
Genesis 1:28; 9:1; Song of Solomon 1–8

Sexual Purity

Sexual purity is something that has been a challenge since, well, since sex began. The sex drive is a God-given part of what it means to be a human being, so there is nothing wrong with the desire to have sex, but there is something very wrong with the desire to have it at the wrong time or with the wrong person.

The Scriptures tell us to keep our sex lives pure, but they also do much more than that. Repeatedly throughout the Bible we see people doing what is necessary to keep their sexual purity, and we also see people failing to do what is necessary and falling into sin. Whether it is Joseph literally running from the grasp of an impure relationship or King David refusing to be where he needed to be and giving in to temptation, the Bible shows us both the good and the bad of sexual purity.

Key Verses

You have heard that it was said, "You shall not commit adultery"; but I say to you that everyone who looks at a woman with lust for her has already committed adultery with her in his heart.

Matthew 5:27–28 NASB

Put to death, therefore, whatever belongs to your earthly nature: sexual immorality, impurity, lust, evil desires and greed, which is idolatry. Because of these, the wrath of God is coming.

Colossians 3:5–6 NIV

Marriage is honorable among all, and the bed undefiled; but fornicators and adulterers God will judge.

Hebrews 13:4 NKJV

Additional Notable Verses Concerning Sexual Purity

Exodus 20:14; Leviticus 18; Proverbs 5:18–23; 6:32; Mark 7:20–23; Romans 13:13; 1 Corinthians 6:9–20; Galatians 5:19–21; Ephesians 5:3–5; 1 Thessalonians 4:3–8; 1 Timothy 1:8–10; Revelation 21:8

Shame

Shame is a very powerful emotion. Just the thought of someone you greatly love or respect telling you that they are ashamed of you can be enough to make you sick. At the same time, shame does have a positive aspect. Hopefully the shame caused by some actions keeps us from doing them. Shame may be one of the best motivators for living a godly life.

The Bible has some interesting perspectives on shame. Our actions have consequences, and shame is one of those. But one thing we should never be ashamed of is our Lord.

Key Verses

If anyone is ashamed of me and my words in this adulterous and sinful generation, the Son of Man will be ashamed of them when he comes in his Father's glory with the holy angels.

Mark 8:38 NIV

Therefore, since we are surrounded by such a huge crowd of witnesses to the life of faith, let us strip off every weight that slows us down, especially the sin that so easily trips us up. And let us run with endurance the race God has set before us. We do this by keeping our eyes on Jesus, the champion who initiates and perfects our faith. Because of the joy awaiting him, he endured the cross, disregarding its shame. Now he is seated in the place of honor beside God's throne. Think of all the hostility he endured from sinful people; then you won't become weary and give up.

Hebrews 12:1–3 NLT

Additional Notable Verses Concerning Shame

Genesis 3:1–10; Ezra 9:7; Psalm 14:6; 31:17; 35:26; 40:15; 44:7; 109:29; 119:31; 129:5; Proverbs 13:18; 18:13; 29:15; Isaiah 42:17; 44:9–11; 49:23; 54:4; 61:7; Jeremiah 8:9; Daniel 9:7–8; Joel 2:26–27; Zephaniah 3; Luke 9:23–26; Acts 5:41; 1 Corinthians 1:27; 4:4; 6:5; 11:22; 15:34; Philippians 1:19–20; 3:18–19; 2 Thessalonians 3:14; 1 Peter 3:14–16; 1 John 2:28

Sickness

I t would be great if those who loved God and wanted to serve Him never got sick. But we live in a fallen world, and God allows His children to feel the effects of that fallenness just as much as those who oppose Him.

Many of those who followed God in the Bible became very ill. Some of them were healed, but many of them were not. The Scriptures show us that God is very powerful and He can and will heal people when He chooses to, but God also has purposes far beyond what we could ever understand (2 Corinthians 12:9). For the Christian, sickness is only a temporary thing; it cannot touch us in eternity. For the unbeliever, sickness may be as good as it ever gets.

Key Verses

Bless the Lord, O my soul, and forget none of His benefits; who pardons all your iniquities, who heals all your diseases.

Psalm 103:2–3 NASB

When evening came, many who were demon-possessed were brought to him, and he drove out the spirits with a word and healed all the sick. This was to fulfill what was spoken through the prophet Isaiah: "He took up our infirmities and bore our diseases."

Matthew 8:16–17 NIV

If you are sick, ask the church leaders to come and pray for you. Ask them to put olive oil on you in the name of the Lord. If you have faith when you pray for sick people, they will get well. The Lord will heal them, and if they have sinned, he will forgive them. If you have sinned, you should tell each other what you have done. Then you can pray for one another and be healed. The prayer of an innocent person is powerful, and it can help a lot.

James 5:14–16 CEV

Additional Notable Verses Concerning Sickness

Exodus 23:25; Deuteronomy 28:59–61; Psalm 30:2; 91:3–7; 107:18–20; Isaiah 38; Matthew 25:34–40; Luke 8:42–48; 17:11–19; Acts 3:1–10; 1 Corinthians 11:27–32; 2 Corinthians 12:7–10; Philippians 2:27

Sin

Sin. The word is ugly. Even in a world that does not seem to care about whether or not something is a sin, people still avoid using the word. Instead people will apologize for mistakes, inappropriate behavior, or even errors in judgment. Rarely does anyone actually come out and say that they sinned.

The Bible has none of the qualms that we do about calling something a sin. Anything that falls short of God's perfection is a sin. Murder is a sin, but so are gossip and deceitfulness. Any sin is enough to separate us from God. Sin required the death of God's Son.

Key Verses

Your word I have treasured in my heart, that I may not sin against You.
Psalm 119:11 NASB

Righteousness exalteth a nation: but sin is a reproach to any people.
Proverbs 14:34 KJV

Let no one say when he is tempted, "I am being tempted by God," for God cannot be tempted with evil, and he himself tempts no one. But each person is tempted when he is lured and enticed by his own desire. Then desire when it has conceived gives birth to sin, and sin when it is fully grown brings forth death.
James 1:13–15 ESV

Everyone who commits (practices) sin is guilty of lawlessness; for [that is what] sin is, lawlessness (the breaking, violating of God's law by transgression or neglect—being unrestrained and unregulated by His commands and His will).
1 John 3:4 AMP

Additional Notable Verses Concerning Sin

Genesis 3; Exodus 34:6–8; 1 Samuel 2:12–17; Psalm 4:4; 51; 66:18; 90:8; Proverbs 16:6; 24:9; 28:13; Ecclesiastes 7:20; Isaiah 1:18; Matthew 15:10–20; Mark 2:1–12; John 1:19–34; 8:34; Romans 3:19–26; 5:6–21; 6–7; 14:23; 1 Corinthians 15:54–58; 2 Corinthians 5:21; Ephesians 1:3–7; 1 Thessalonians 5:22; 1 Timothy 5:24; Hebrews 3:13; 4:15; James 2:10–11; 4:17; 1 Peter 2:21–25; 4:1–6; 1 John 1:5–10; 3:4–10; 5:13–21

Singles

How singles are viewed has undergone a major transformation in the last few decades. Today more and more people are waiting much later to get married, and many are not getting married at all.

While there is much to be said for marrying and starting a family, there are many good reasons to remain single as well. The apostle Paul felt that his singleness was a gift from God meant to help him serve his Lord.

Key Verses

For there are eunuchs who have been so from birth, and there are eunuchs who have been made eunuchs by men, and there are eunuchs who have made themselves eunuchs for the sake of the kingdom of heaven. Let the one who is able to receive this receive it.

Matthew 19:12 ESV

Yet I wish that all men were even as I myself am. However, each man has his own gift from God, one in this manner, and another in that. But I say to the unmarried and to widows that it is good for them if they remain even as I. But if they do not have self-control, let them marry; for it is better to marry than to burn with passion.

1 Corinthians 7:7–9 NASB

I am not telling you this because I need anything. I have learned to be satisfied with the things I have and with everything that happens. I know how to live when I am poor, and I know how to live when I have plenty. I have learned the secret of being happy at any time in everything that happens, when I have enough to eat and when I go hungry, when I have more than I need and when I do not have enough. I can do all things through Christ, because he gives me strength.

Philippians 4:11–13 NCV

Additional Notable Verses Concerning Singles
Hosea 2:19–20; 1 Corinthians 7:25–35

Slavery

The rationalization of slavery is not relegated only to those who are without God. Many Christians throughout the ages have owned slaves. Some of these slave owners even owned fellow Christians as slaves, and on top of it all they used the Scriptures to defend their wickedness.

To be sure, the biblical message about slavery is not as clear-cut as we would like it to be. God condoned specific types of slavery with very specific rules in the Old Testament. The New Testament does not condone slavery so much as it fails to condemn it in the way that we think it should. When we search the Scriptures we see that a society's laws are important, but how God's people treat others is the most important thing.

Key Verses

He who kidnaps a man and sells him, or if he is found in his hand, shall surely be put to death.

Exodus 21:16 NKJV

Slaves, obey your earthly masters in everything you do. Try to please them all the time, not just when they are watching you. Serve them sincerely because of your reverent fear of the Lord. Work willingly at whatever you do, as though you were working for the Lord rather than for people. Remember that the Lord will give you an inheritance as your reward, and that the Master you are serving is Christ. But if you do what is wrong, you will be paid back for the wrong you have done. For God has no favorites. Masters, be just and fair to your slaves. Remember that you also have a Master—in heaven.

Colossians 3:22–4:1 NLT

Additional Notable Verses Concerning Slavery
Exodus 21; Leviticus 25; Deuteronomy 23:15–16; 24:7; Titus 2:9–10; 1 Timothy 6:1–2

Social Services

I t can be very easy for Christians to focus on people merely as spiritual beings. But people are physical beings as well, and loving people does not mean just telling them about God's love and keeping your distance; loving people means caring for the whole person.

Key Verses

Is not this the kind of fasting I have chosen: to loose the chains of injustice and untie the cords of the yoke, to set the oppressed free and break every yoke? Is it not to share your food with the hungry and to provide the poor wanderer with shelter—when you see the naked, to clothe them, and not to turn away from your own flesh and blood? Then your light will break forth like the dawn, and your healing will quickly appear; then your righteousness will go before you, and the glory of the Lord will be your rear guard. Then you will call, and the Lord will answer; you will cry for help, and he will say: Here am I.

Isaiah 58:6–9 NIV

Are not two sparrows sold for a cent? And yet not one of them will fall to the ground apart from your Father. But the very hairs of your head are all numbered. So do not fear; you are more valuable than many sparrows.

Matthew 10:29–31 NASB

Jesus replied, "The most important commandment is this: 'Listen, O Israel! The Lord our God is the one and only Lord. And you must love the Lord your God with all your heart, all your soul, all your mind, and all your strength.' The second is equally important: 'Love your neighbor as yourself.' No other commandment is greater than these."

Mark 12:29–31 NLT

Additional Notable Verses Concerning Social Services

Genesis 1:26–27; Micah 6:7–8; Matthew 25:31–46; Luke 4:14–30; 10:25–37; John 4:1–42

Sorcery

Popular culture has done an excellent job of turning sorcery into something that is cute and harmless. This is not the picture of sorcery that the Bible presents. God's Word says that the attempt to work magic and cast spells is working with and through the power of the devil himself. Sorcery was not allowed and bore the strictest of penalties because to participate in sorcery was to align oneself with Satan and his power. There is nothing cute or harmless about working with the devil.

Key Verses

Do not allow a sorceress to live.
Exodus 22:18 NIV

And when they say to you, "Inquire of the mediums and the necromancers who chirp and mutter," should not a people inquire of their God? Should they inquire of the dead on behalf of the living?
Isaiah 8:19 ESV

Then a strong angel took up a stone like a great millstone and threw it into the sea, saying, "So will Babylon, the great city, be thrown down with violence, and will not be found any longer. And the sound of harpists and musicians and flute-players and trumpeters will not be heard in you any longer; and no craftsman of any craft will be found in you any longer; and the sound of a mill will not be heard in you any longer; and the light of a lamp will not shine in you any longer; and the voice of the bridegroom and bride will not be heard in you any longer; for your merchants were the great men of the earth, because all the nations were deceived by your sorcery."
Revelation 18:21–23 NASB

Additional Notable Verses Concerning Sorcery
Leviticus 19:31; 20:6; 20:27; 1 Samuel 28; 2 Kings 23:24; 1 Chronicles 10:13; 2 Chronicles 33:6; Isaiah 19:3; Micah 3:7; 5:10–15; Acts 8:9–25; 19:11–20; Galatians 5:19–21

Spiritual Gifts

The death, burial, and resurrection of Jesus Christ carries with it some very obvious implications. Christ paid the price for our sins and became the ultimate and final sacrifice that God would ever need to satisfy his holiness. But we often forget that when Christ defeated sin and redeemed believers, He also gave each person spiritual gifts. These gifts are made available through the person of the Holy Spirit, who comes to indwell every believer at the moment of their conversion.

Key Verses

A spiritual gift is given to each of us so we can help each other. To one person the Spirit gives the ability to give wise advice; to another the same Spirit gives a message of special knowledge. The same Spirit gives great faith to another, and to someone else the one Spirit gives the gift of healing. He gives one person the power to perform miracles, and another the ability to prophesy. He gives someone else the ability to discern whether a message is from the Spirit of God or from another spirit. Still another person is given the ability to speak in unknown languages, while another is given the ability to interpret what is being said. It is the one and only Spirit who distributes all these gifts. He alone decides which gift each person should have.

1 Corinthians 12:7–11 NLT

As each of you has received a gift (a particular spiritual talent, a gracious divine endowment), employ it for one another as [befits] good trustees of God's many-sided grace [faithful stewards of the extremely diverse powers and gifts granted to Christians by unmerited favor].

1 Peter 4:10 AMP

Additional Notable Verses Concerning Spiritual Gifts

Romans 12:6–8; 1 Corinthians 12:28–31; Ephesians 4:7–13

Spiritual Growth

Spiritual growth is not reliant on the number of years lived, or the experiences that one has had, although those certainly help. According to the Bible, spiritual growth has everything to do with things like Bible study, prayer, and involvement in Christian community. Even with all of those things, an individual believer has to make a conscious decision to allow the Holy Spirit to direct his or her life. Spiritual growth is a matter of maturity; it does not just arrive with gray hair.

Key Verses

Because of this, since the day we heard about you, we have continued praying for you, asking God that you will know fully what he wants. We pray that you will also have great wisdom and understanding in spiritual things so that you will live the kind of life that honors and pleases the Lord in every way. You will produce fruit in every good work and grow in the knowledge of God.

Colossians 1:9–10 NCV

Have nothing to do with irreverent, silly myths. Rather train yourself for godliness; for while bodily training is of some value, godliness is of value in every way, as it holds promise for the present life and also for the life to come.

1 Timothy 4:7–8 ESV

Therefore, putting aside all malice and all deceit and hypocrisy and envy and all slander, like newborn babies, long for the pure milk of the word, so that by it you may grow in respect to salvation, if you have tasted the kindness of the Lord.

1 Peter 2:1–3 NASB

Additional Notable Verses Concerning Spiritual Growth
Psalm 119:105; Luke 9:23–27; Galatians 5:22–23; Ephesians 4:14–16; Colossians 2:18–19; Hebrews 5:11–14; James 1:2–4; 2 Peter 3:17–18

Spiritual Warfare

Some people enter the army as volunteers. Others serve in the military because they are conscripted in what is usually called a draft. In modern Israel there is no volunteering. When you turn eighteen you take your turn in the military.

Spiritual warfare resembles the Israeli military. You do not volunteer for battle; everyone is in the battle. The Scriptures describe for us an enemy—Satan and his demons—who is evil, wicked, and intent on destroying God's people. God's Word also describes for us the role that God, our great Commanding Officer, plays in winning the battle and protecting His soldiers. The battle rages, and we are fighting whether we realize it or not.

Key Verses

For though we walk in the flesh, we are not waging war according to the flesh. For the weapons of our warfare are not of the flesh but have divine power to destroy strongholds. We destroy arguments and every lofty opinion raised against the knowledge of God, and take every thought captive to obey Christ, being ready to punish every disobedience, when your obedience is complete.

2 Corinthians 10:3–6 ESV

Keep a cool head. Stay alert. The Devil is poised to pounce, and would like nothing better than to catch you napping. Keep your guard up. You're not the only ones plunged into these hard times. It's the same with Christians all over the world. So keep a firm grip on the faith. The suffering won't last forever. It won't be long before this generous God who has great plans for us in Christ—eternal and glorious plans they are!—will have you put together and on your feet for good. He gets the last word; yes, he does.

1 Peter 5:8–11 THE MESSAGE

Additional Notable Verses Concerning Spiritual Warfare

Daniel 10; 2 Corinthians 11:12–15; Ephesians 6:10–20; James 4:7; 1 John 5:4–5; Revelation 12:7–9; 17:1–13; 20:1–10

Sports

In the last few decades sports have become an idol to many who are obsessed with how their favorite team fares. Now whenever a team loses a big game, and sometimes when it wins, there can be rioting and looting.

For a long time, however, sports were not viewed as an idol, but as an effective tool for teaching important life lessons like determination, teamwork, and humility. It is in this context that the Bible refers to sports. Sports can teach us a lot about life, God, and what it takes to persevere in the Christian faith.

Key Verses

Do you not know that those who run in a race all run, but only one receives the prize? Run in such a way that you may win. Everyone who competes in the games exercises self-control in all things. They then do it to receive a perishable wreath, but we an imperishable. Therefore I run in such a way, as not without aim; I box in such a way, as not beating the air; but I discipline my body and make it my slave, so that, after I have preached to others, I myself will not be disqualified.

1 Corinthians 9:24–27 NASB

Athletes cannot win the prize unless they follow the rules.
2 Timothy 2:5 NLT

Therefore we also, since we are surrounded by so great a cloud of witnesses, let us lay aside every weight, and the sin which so easily ensnares us, and let us run with endurance the race that is set before us, looking unto Jesus, the author and finisher of our faith, who for the joy that was set before Him endured the cross, despising the shame, and has sat down at the right hand of the throne of God.

Hebrews 12:1–2 NKJV

Additional Notable Verses Concerning Sports
Philippians 3:12–14

Stealing

Stealing is not just about taking something that does not belong to you. At its heart, the sin of stealing is truly an affront to the nature of God. If we were content with our lives and trusted God to take care of us, there would be no need to steal. Committing robbery exhibits a lack of trust in God.

In the Bible, stealing is a serious offense and one that is punished swiftly. The admonition not to steal is one of the Ten Commandments, and despite the fact that it is a common crime, it is not to be tolerated. God's Word prohibits stealing, no matter the motivation, and will not allow us to justify it. Stealing is sin whether it is from the offering plate or the Internal Revenue Service.

Key Verses

Do not steal.
Exodus 20:15 CEV

Otherwise, I may have too much and disown you and say, "Who is the Lord?" Or I may become poor and steal, and so dishonor the name of my God.
Proverbs 30:9 NIV

Don't store up treasures here on earth, where moths eat them and rust destroys them, and where thieves break in and steal. Store your treasures in heaven, where moths and rust cannot destroy, and thieves do not break in and steal. Wherever your treasure is, there the desires of your heart will also be.
Matthew 6:19–21 NLT

He who steals must steal no longer; but rather he must labor, performing with his own hands what is good, so that he will have something to share with one who has need.
Ephesians 4:28 NASB

Additional Notable Verses Concerning Stealing
Exodus 22:7; Leviticus 6:1–7; 19:11; Deuteronomy 5:19; Jeremiah 7:9–11; Psalm 62:10; John 10:10; Romans 2:21; 13:9; 1 Corinthians 6:9–11

Stewardship

The idea of being a steward is not as common today as it was in biblical times. Today we tend to think mostly in terms of owning or renting, neither of which truly captures the idea and spirit of being a steward. A steward is not the owner. He is a hired hand responsible for the caretaking and running of something for the owner.

The Scriptures repeatedly refer to Christians as stewards of God's work here on earth. We are not in the position of ownership, but we are responsible to God for what we do as stewards.

Key Verses

Give up trying so hard to get rich. Your money flies away before you know it, just like an eagle suddenly taking off.

Proverbs 23:4–5 CEV

As for the rich in this present age, charge them not to be haughty, nor to set their hopes on the uncertainty of riches, but on God, who richly provides us with everything to enjoy. They are to do good, to be rich in good works, to be generous and ready to share, thus storing up treasure for themselves as a good foundation for the future, so that they may take hold of that which is truly life.

1 Timothy 6:17–19 ESV

As each of you has received a gift (a particular spiritual talent, a gracious divine endowment), employ it for one another as [befits] good trustees of God's many-sided grace [faithful stewards of the extremely diverse powers and gifts granted to Christians by unmerited favor].

1 Peter 4:10 AMP

Additional Notable Verses Concerning Stewardship

Genesis 9:1–4; Proverbs 3:27–28; 13:22; 24:3–4; Malachi 3:10; Matthew 25:14–30; Luke 12:35–48; 16:1–13; 1 Corinthians 4:1–5; 6:19–20; 9:15–18; Ephesians 3:1–3; Colossians 1:24–26; Titus 1:7–9

Stubbornness

Sometimes our best traits are also our worst traits. Determination is one of the best qualities to possess. It will help you to persist when life is not going your way, and it can help you to become successful long after others have given up. The other side of the coin of determination, however, is stubbornness. Stubbornness can make you unyielding when you need to learn lessons and unwilling to consider other people and their ideas. Determination is good, but stubbornness is not.

As you might expect, God's Word is less than complimentary with regard to stubbornness. It links stubbornness to sin and tells us that God frequently must discipline those who exhibit stubbornness. We may stubbornly persist in thinking that we are right, but God values people who are willing and humble more than He values people who are successful in their own minds.

Key Verses

But my people did not listen to me; Israel did not want me. So I let them go their stubborn way and follow their own advice. I wish my people would listen to me; I wish Israel would live my way.

Psalm 81:11–13 NCV

Listen to me, you stubborn of heart, you who are far from righteousness: I bring near my righteousness; it is not far off, and my salvation will not delay; I will put salvation in Zion, for Israel my glory.

Isaiah 46:12–13 ESV

But because of your stubbornness and your unrepentant heart, you are storing up wrath against yourself for the day of God's wrath, when his righteous judgment will be revealed. God "will repay each person according to what they have done."

Romans 2:5–6 NIV

Additional Notable Verses Concerning Stubbornness

Exodus 7:14; 13:15, Deuteronomy 9:6, 13; 21:18–21; 31:27; Judges 2:16–19; Nehemiah 9:16–17, 29; Psalm 78:5–8; Jeremiah 5:23; 7:24; 9:13–15; 16:12; Ezekiel 3:7; Hosea 4:16; Zechariah 7:11

Study

There is a tremendous difference between simply reading something and studying it. Even though you may read with great care and comprehension, it is nothing like actually taking the time and putting forth the effort to study something. Study requires that you dissect something, that you take it apart, that you research and digest it. Study is reading something and taking it to a whole other level of interest and knowledge.

Often in the Bible people read the Scriptures, but precious few are said to actually study them. It was a requirement for kings that they study God's Word and that it be their constant companion. In the Bible people are commended for studying God's Word and scouring it for its meaning and application to their lives. Studying the Bible is one of the things we can do that we know will make our heavenly Father proud.

Key Verses

Ezra had set his heart to study the law of the Lord and to practice it, and to teach His statutes and ordinances in Israel.

Ezra 7:10 NASB

But, my child, let me give you some further advice: Be careful, for writing books is endless, and much study wears you out.

Ecclesiastes 12:12 NLT

Study to shew thyself approved unto God, a workman that needeth not to be ashamed, rightly dividing the word of truth.

2 Timothy 2:15 KJV

Additional Notable Verses Concerning Study
Deuteronomy 17:18–20; Nehemiah 8:13–18; Isaiah 8:20; Galatians 1:11–24

Submission

No one likes the idea of having to yield power or authority over themselves to someone else. People do not like having to cede control of their lives to a perfect and loving God, much less submitting to another human being such as a husband or an elder of the church.

Unpopular though it may be, the idea of submission is definitely one that the Scriptures teach. Wives are to submit to husbands, wives and husbands are both to submit to God, the church is to submit to the elders, and Christians are to submit to one another. Submission is not a dirty word. It is actually one of the main ways that the Scriptures teach us to show our love for God and one another.

Key Verses

Since you died with Christ to the elemental spiritual forces of this world, why, as though you still belonged to the world, do you submit to its rules: "Do not handle! Do not taste! Do not touch!"? These rules, which have to do with things that are all destined to perish with use, are based on merely human commands and teachings. Such regulations indeed have an appearance of wisdom, with their self-imposed worship, their false humility and their harsh treatment of the body, but they lack any value in restraining sensual indulgence.

Colossians 2:20–23 NIV

Obey your leaders and submit to them, for they keep watch over your souls as those who will give an account. Let them do this with joy and not with grief, for this would be unprofitable for you.

Hebrews 13:17 NASB

Likewise, you who are younger, be subject to the elders. Clothe yourselves, all of you, with humility toward one another, for "God opposes the proud but gives grace to the humble."

1 Peter 5:5 ESV

Additional Notable Verses Concerning Submission

Luke 22:42; 1 Corinthians 14:33–35; Ephesians 5:15–21, 22–24; 1 Timothy 2:11–15; James 4:7; 1 Peter 2:13–17

Success

What does it take to be a success? This question has spawned countless books and self-help speeches. Businesses, athletic teams, hospitals, armies, and even churches are concerned and possibly obsessed with the idea of success. Yet what defines success, and exactly who gets to make that definition, are anything but decided.

When one looks to the Bible for ways to be a success, there is much less there than you would hope. The Bible's teaching on success really boils down to one simple concept—serve God. In serving God you may end up wealthy, you may end up poor, you may end up healthy, you may end up sick, you may end up famous, or you may end up anonymous. Success in God's eyes is focused on eternity, and your eternity is impacted by how you define success here on earth.

Key Verses

My son, do not forget my teaching, but let your heart keep my commandments, for length of days and years of life and peace they will add to you. Let not steadfast love and faithfulness forsake you; bind them around your neck; write them on the tablet of your heart. So you will find favor and good success in the sight of God and man.

Proverbs 3:1–4 ESV

I can do all things through Christ which strengtheneth me.

Philippians 4:13 KJV

Humble yourselves [feeling very insignificant] in the presence of the Lord, and He will exalt you [He will lift you up and make your lives significant].

James 4:10 AMP

Additional Notable Verses Concerning Success

Genesis 39:3; Deuteronomy 29:9; 30:1–10; Joshua 1:7; 1 Kings 2:1–4; 1 Chronicles 22:13; Nehemiah 2:20; Job 5:8–12; Psalm 1; 37:4; 122:6; Proverbs 28:13, 25; Ecclesiastes 10:10; Isaiah 52:13; Matthew 6:25–33; 16:26; 3 John 1:2

Surrogate Mothers

The idea of surrogacy today is very different from the concept in biblical times. Modern technology has made it possible for a woman to actually physically carry another woman's child. In biblical times surrogacy usually meant a servant standing in for her mistress. The servant would have relations with the husband and bear a child in the wife's stead.

Through the years surrogacy has always been controversial. In biblical times, even though the act wasn't condemned outright, it never turned out well. Today, as with other medical practices, people must consider the ethics and theological implications of surrogacy.

Key Verses

And God blessed them. And God said to them, "Be fruitful and multiply and fill the earth and subdue it, and have dominion over the fish of the sea and over the birds of the heavens and over every living thing that moves on the earth."

Genesis 1:28 ESV

Now Sarai, Abram's wife, had borne him no children. And she had an Egyptian maidservant whose name was Hagar. So Sarai said to Abram, "See now, the Lord has restrained me from bearing children. Please, go in to my maid; perhaps I shall obtain children by her." And Abram heeded the voice of Sarai. Then Sarai, Abram's wife, took Hagar her maid, the Egyptian, and gave her to her husband Abram to be his wife, after Abram had dwelt ten years in the land of Canaan. So he went in to Hagar, and she conceived. And when she saw that she had conceived, her mistress became despised in her eyes.

Genesis 16:1–4 NKJV

Additional Notable Verses Concerning Surrogate Mothers
Genesis 16:1–15; 30:1–9; Psalm 139:13–16

Talent

When someone speaks of stewardship we tend to thing primarily of money, and secondarily of time. While it is true that we must be stewards of money and time, we must not forget that we are also called to be stewards of talent. Each person has been given unique talents and abilities by God that can be used for His glory. We must be good stewards of those, just as we are of things like finances and time.

There were many in the Bible who were faithful stewards of their talents, and there were many who wasted their talents. Those who were faithful stewards all had one basic principle in common: They recognized that talents were meant to glorify God. We can use our talents for a lot of purposes, but talents that are used to glorify God are never wasted.

Key Verses

All who are gifted artisans among you shall come and make all that the Lord has commanded.

Exodus 35:10 NKJV

In his grace, God has given us different gifts for doing certain things well. So if God has given you the ability to prophesy, speak out with as much faith as God has given you. If your gift is serving others, serve them well. If you are a teacher, teach well.

Romans 12:6–7 NLT

Whatever you do, work heartily, as for the Lord and not for men, knowing that from the Lord you will receive the inheritance as your reward. You are serving the Lord Christ.

Colossians 3:23–24 ESV

Additional Notable Verses Concerning Talent
1 Corinthians 10:31; 12; 2 Timothy 1:6–7; 1 Peter 4:10–11

Taxes

No one likes to pay taxes. Just about everyone believes that their taxes are too high, no matter how high or low they really are.

Tax collectors in Palestine during the New Testament collected taxes for the Romans from their Jewish brothers and sisters. In order to make money themselves, they would take the exorbitant tax rates of the Romans and raise them even more. Even with this as a background, Jesus commanded His followers to pay taxes.

Key Verses

That's when the Pharisees plotted a way to trap him into saying something damaging. They sent their disciples, with a few of Herod's followers mixed in, to ask, "Teacher, we know you have integrity, teach the way of God accurately, are indifferent to popular opinion, and don't pander to your students. So tell us honestly: Is it right to pay taxes to Caesar or not?"

Jesus knew they were up to no good. He said, "Why are you playing these games with me? Why are you trying to trap me? Do you have a coin? Let me see it." They handed him a silver piece.

"This engraving—who does it look like? And whose name is on it?"

They said, "Caesar."

"Then give Caesar what is his, and give God what is his."

The Pharisees were speechless. They went off shaking their heads.

Matthew 22:15–22 THE MESSAGE

Therefore it is necessary to be in subjection, not only because of wrath, but also for conscience' sake. For because of this you also pay taxes, for rulers are servants of God, devoting themselves to this very thing. Render to all what is due them: tax to whom tax is due; custom to whom custom; fear to whom fear; honor to whom honor.

Romans 13:5–7 NASB

Additional Notable Verses Concerning Taxes
2 Kings 23:35; Matthew 9:9–11; 11:19; 17:24–27; Mark 2:13–17; 12:13–17; Luke 18:9–14; 19:1–10; 23:2

Teaching

Matthew 28:19–20 is often looked at as the Christian's mission statement, referred to as the Great Commission: "Go therefore and make disciples of all the nations, baptizing them in the name of the Father and the Son and the Holy Spirit, teaching them to observe all that I commanded you; and lo, I am with you always, even to the end of the age" (NASB).

It is interesting that teaching plays an important role in the Great Commission. In the Christian faith, teaching is just as important as going to other nations, discipling, and baptizing.

Key Verses

Hear, O Israel: The Lord our God, the Lord is one. You shall love the Lord your God with all your heart and with all your soul and with all your might. And these words that I command you today shall be on your heart. You shall teach them diligently to your children, and shall talk of them when you sit in your house, and when you walk by the way, and when you lie down, and when you rise. You shall bind them as a sign on your hand, and they shall be as frontlets between your eyes. You shall write them on the doorposts of your house and on your gates.

Deuteronomy 6:4–9 ESV

Show me your ways, Lord, teach me your paths. Guide me in your truth and teach me, for you are God my Savior, and my hope is in you all day long.

Psalm 25:4–5 NIV

Additional Notable Verses Concerning Teaching

Exodus 18:13–20; Deuteronomy 4:1–14; 6:1–9; Job 21:22; Psalm 27:11; 32:8; 34:11; 86:11; 90:12; 119:66–68; Proverbs 1:8; 3:1; 4:2; Matthew 7:28–29; 28:20; Mark 11:18; John 7:16–17; Acts 2:42; 5:22–42; Romans 16:17; 1 Corinthians 14:26; Colossians 1:28; 1 Timothy 4:12–16; 2 Timothy 2:23–26; 3:16–17; 4:2; Titus 1:7–11; Hebrews 6:1; 2 John 1:9–10

Temptation

I n the Scriptures we have the ultimate example of defeating temptation: Jesus Christ himself. When tempted, Jesus responded with Scriptures that showed where the devil was wrong and expressed His faith in God. What a fantastic pattern for us to follow when we battle temptation.

Key Verses

Dear friend, if bad companions tempt you, don't go along with them. If they say—"Let's go out and raise some hell. Let's beat up some old man, mug some old woman. Let's pick them clean and get them ready for their funerals. We'll load up on top-quality loot. We'll haul it home by the truckload. Join us for the time of your life! With us, it's share and share alike!"—Oh, friend, don't give them a second look; don't listen to them for a minute. They're racing to a very bad end, hurrying to ruin everything they lay hands on. Nobody robs a bank with everyone watching, yet that's what these people are doing—they're doing themselves in.

Proverbs 1:10–18 THE MESSAGE

The only temptation that has come to you is that which everyone has. But you can trust God, who will not permit you to be tempted more than you can stand. But when you are tempted, he will also give you a way to escape so that you will be able to stand it.

1 Corinthians 10:13 NCV

Blessed is a man who perseveres under trial; for once he has been approved, he will receive the crown of life which the Lord has promised to those who love Him. Let no one say when he is tempted, "I am being tempted by God"; for God cannot be tempted by evil, and He Himself does not tempt anyone. But each one is tempted when he is carried away and enticed by his own lust. Then when lust has conceived, it gives birth to sin; and when sin is accomplished, it brings forth death.

James 1:12–15 NASB

Additional Notable Verses Concerning Temptation

Genesis 3; 39; Proverbs 16:29; Matthew 4:1–11; 6:13; 26:41; Mark 1:12–13; Luke 4:1–13; 1 Thessalonians 3:5; 1 Timothy 6:9–10; Hebrews 2:18; 4:15; James 1:2–3; 1 Peter 1:6; 2 Peter 2:9; Revelation 3:10

Thanksgiving

There are many recurring themes throughout Scripture, but most of them appear in less than half of the sixty-six books that compose the Bible. Thanksgiving is one of those rare ideas that appears in nearly every biblical book. Over and over again people give thanks and show gratitude to God for His mighty works.

The Scriptures' repeated instructions and examples of thanksgiving have a powerful message for believers today. The Bible shows us that giving thanks is not something to be done only around a holiday. We are to be thankful year-round, in good times and in bad. Thanksgiving is to be a part of everyday life.

Key Verses

It is good to give thanks to the Lord and to sing praises to Your name, O Most High.

Psalm 92:1 NASB

Do not be anxious about anything, but in every situation, by prayer and petition, with thanksgiving, present your requests to God.

Philippians 4:6 NIV

Be thankful in all circumstances, for this is God's will for you who belong to Christ Jesus.

1 Thessalonians 5:18 NLT

Additional Notable Verses Concerning Thanksgiving

Psalm 18:49; 30:4; 35:18; 50:14–15; 75:1; 92:1; 97:12; 106:1; 107:1; 136; 1 Chronicles 29:13–15; Nehemiah 12:27–47; Daniel 2:23; 6:10; Jonah 2:9; Matthew 11:25; 26:27; John 6:11; 11:41; Romans 1:8; 6:17; 14:6–7; 1 Corinthians 1:4; 15:57; 2 Corinthians 1:11; 2:14; 9:11–15; Ephesians 1:16; 5:20; Philippians 1:3–5; Colossians 1:3–6; 3:17; 1 Thessalonians 1:2; 2:13; 2 Thessalonians 1:3; 1 Timothy 1:12; 2:1; 4:3–4; Hebrews 13:15; Revelation 4:9; 11:16–17

Time

The passage of time is one of the great subjects of literature, music, and movies. All of these avenues tell stories of how people encounter and view time. The people in these stories may go back in time, they may go forward in time, and they even may find a way to make time stop. Despite all of the fanciful ideas, however, time does not stop, and once it is gone, it is gone for good.

It is no surprise that time is a recurrent topic in the Bible. The Scriptures have much to tell us about time and how we use it. All humanity is bound by time, but God exists out of time. God's Word teaches that time is a commodity of which we must be careful stewards. When a day is gone, we will never be able to get it back, and the only way to get to tomorrow is to live today. Time is precious.

Key Verses

To every thing there is a season, and a time to every purpose under the heaven.

Ecclesiastes 3:1 KJV

Therefore be careful how you walk, not as unwise men but as wise, making the most of your time, because the days are evil.

Ephesians 5:15–16 NASB

For God says, "At just the right time, I heard you. On the day of salvation, I helped you." Indeed, the "right time" is now. Today is the day of salvation.

2 Corinthians 6:2 NLT

Additional Notable Verses Concerning Time

Psalm 39:4–5; 90:12; Ecclesiastes 3:1–11; 9:15; Isaiah 49:8; Mark 1:15; Acts 17:26; Romans 13:11–14; Galatians 4:4; 6:9–10; Colossians 4:5–6; Hebrews 4:16; 1 Peter 1:17; 2 Peter 3:8

Tithing

n its most basic form the word *tithe* refers to a tenth of anything. The term did not originally refer specifically to giving to a church, synagogue, or religious institution. It could refer to giving a tenth of the spoils of war or a tenth of the harvest to a priest or king. The Old Testament Israelites were required to pay tithes that were not to be taken from leftovers but from the first and best of the crops and cattle. The New Testament speaks of tithing, but Christians are divided as to whether the practice should continue today.

Key Verses

Then after his return from the defeat of Chedorlaomer and the kings who were with him, the king of Sodom went out to meet him at the valley of Shaveh (that is, the King's Valley). And Melchizedek king of Salem brought out bread and wine; now he was a priest of God Most High. He blessed him and said, "Blessed be Abram of God Most High, possessor of heaven and earth; and blessed be God Most High, who has delivered your enemies into your hand." He gave him a tenth of all.

Genesis 14:17–20 NASB

Will man rob God? Yet you are robbing me. But you say, "How have we robbed you?" In your tithes and contributions. You are cursed with a curse, for you are robbing me, the whole nation of you. Bring the full tithe into the storehouse, that there may be food in my house. And thereby put me to the test, says the Lord of hosts, if I will not open the windows of heaven for you and pour down for you a blessing until there is no more need.

Malachi 3:8–10 ESV

Additional Notable Verses Concerning Tithing

Genesis 28:22; Leviticus 27; Numbers 18:21–32; Deuteronomy 12:1–19; 14:22–28; 26:12–15; 2 Chronicles 31:1–12; Nehemiah 10:37; 13:10–14; Matthew 23:23; Luke 11:42; Hebrews 7:6

Tongues

The Greek word *glossa* (pronounced gloce-sah') is translated "tongues" in the New Testament. The word can refer to the physical organ of the tongue. But most often the word actually refers to a language or dialect used by a particular group of people that is different from that of other people or nations.

When the Holy Spirit was given to believers on the day of Pentecost He enabled those believers to speak different languages to spread the gospel to the many different nationalities that were gathered in Jerusalem at that time. This gifting of the Holy Spirit happens numerous times in Acts and is discussed in detail in the book of 1 Corinthians.

Key Verses

When the day of Pentecost arrived, they were all together in one place. And suddenly there came from heaven a sound like a mighty rushing wind, and it filled the entire house where they were sitting. And divided tongues as of fire appeared to them and rested on each one of them. And they were all filled with the Holy Spirit and began to speak in other tongues as the Spirit gave them utterance.

Acts 2:1–4 ESV

Brethren, do not be children in understanding; however, in malice be babes, but in understanding be mature. In the law it is written: "With men of other tongues and other lips I will speak to this people; and yet, for all that, they will not hear Me," says the Lord. Therefore tongues are for a sign, not to those who believe but to unbelievers; but prophesying is not for unbelievers but for those who believe.

1 Corinthians 14:20–22 NKJV

Additional Notable Verses Concerning Tongues

Isaiah 28:11; Mark 16:17; Acts 2:1–13; 10:44–48; 19:1–7; 1 Corinthians 12:8–11, 28–30; 14

Traditions

Traditions can be a very good thing. Many families have traditions relating to Christmas, birthday celebrations, and even things like national holidays. Every July in Pamplona, Spain, for example, a group of bulls is let loose onto the streets, where they chase a group of young men. The men in that area able to outrun the bulls think that this is a fun tradition. Those who do not outrun the bulls do not seem to think it is as fun.

The Bible speaks of traditions as a good thing but cautions that they can become too important to us. When traditions become more important than people, or when they are equated with God's Word, they are no longer a good thing.

Key Verses

Then the Lord said, "Because this people draw near with their words and honor Me with their lip service, but they remove their hearts far from Me, and their reverence for Me consists of tradition learned by rote, therefore behold, I will once again deal marvelously with this people, wondrously marvelous; and the wisdom of their wise men will perish, and the discernment of their discerning men will be concealed."

Isaiah 29:13–14 NASB

See to it that no one carries you off as spoil or makes you yourselves captive by his so-called philosophy and intellectualism and vain deceit (idle fancies and plain nonsense), following human tradition (men's ideas of the material rather than the spiritual world), just crude notions following the rudimentary and elemental teachings of the universe and disregarding [the teachings of] Christ (the Messiah).

Colossians 2:8 AMP

And now, dear brothers and sisters, we give you this command in the name of our Lord Jesus Christ: Stay away from all believers who live idle lives and don't follow the tradition they received from us.

2 Thessalonians 3:6 NLT

Additional Notable Verses Concerning Traditions
Matthew 15:1–14; Mark 7:1–13; 1 Corinthians 11:2; Galatians 1:14; 2 Thessalonians 2:15

Trinity

The word *Trinity* is never actually used in the Bible. So why does the church believe strongly in something that God never even said? *Trinity* is really a summary word that is used to describe the Bible's teaching about God. The word itself is not important, but we must hold dear the truth that it describes.

The Scriptures teach us that there is a God, and that that God is one. There is no other God besides Him. In the New Testament we are introduced to Jesus Christ and the Holy Spirit, both of whom are God. We are then left with a dilemma. How can God be one, and yet be three at the same time? Exactly how the Trinity works is beyond human comprehension, but we can believe what the Scriptures teach, even without a perfect understanding.

Key Verses

As soon as Jesus was baptized, he went up out of the water. At that moment heaven was opened, and he saw the Spirit of God descending like a dove and alighting on him. And a voice from heaven said, "This is my Son, whom I love; with him I am well pleased."

Matthew 3:16–17 NIV

There is one body and one Spirit, and God called you to have one hope. There is one Lord, one faith, and one baptism. There is one God and Father of everything. He rules everything and is everywhere and is in everything.

Ephesians 4:4–6 NCV

Additional Notable Verses Concerning Trinity

Matthew 28:19; Romans 8:9; 1 Corinthians 12:3–6; 2 Corinthians 13:14; 1 Peter 1:2; Jude 1:20–21

Trouble

D. L. Moody was no stranger to trouble. He was a pastor in Chicago during the Great Chicago Fire, and he was a military chaplain during the bloody American Civil War. Yet despite these hardships, he said, "I have had more trouble with myself than with any other man."*

Moody's unique grasp of trouble was one that the Scriptures would largely agree with. God's Word says that trouble will come to all of us. No matter who you are, one day you will find yourself dealing with trouble in one form or another. Sometimes trouble comes to us and there is simply nothing that we could have done to avoid it. If we are honest, however, we would agree with Moody that we are the cause of much of our own trouble. Either way, God promises to help us when trouble comes.

Key Verses

According to what I have seen, those who plow iniquity and those who sow trouble harvest it. . . . For affliction does not come from the dust, nor does trouble sprout from the ground, for man is born for trouble, as sparks fly upward.

Job 4:8; 5:6–7 NASB

Call upon Me in the day of trouble; I will deliver you, and you shall glorify Me.

Psalm 50:15 NKJV

Additional Notable Verses Concerning Trouble

Numbers 33:55; Joshua 6:18; Judges 11:7; Psalm 9:9; 10:1; 20:1; 22:11; 25:18; 27:5; 32:7; 37:39; 41:1; 46:1; 54:7; 55:1–3; 73:2–5; 77:2; 78:49; 81:7; 86:7; 91:15; 107; 119:143; 120:1; 138:7; 142:2; 143:11; Proverbs 10:10; 11:8; 12:13, 21; 15:6; 24:2; 25:19; 31:7; Ecclesiastes 8:5–6; Jeremiah 2:27–28; 20:18; Nahum 1:7; Zephaniah 1:15; Matthew 6:34; Galatians 6:17; Hebrews 12:15

---

*Steve Brown, *Approaching God: Accepting the Invitation to Stand in the Presence of God* (New York: Howard Books, 2008), 49.

Truth

The idea that truth is relative is very popular in the world today. Truth is seen as something that is individual and flexible. If you believe that Jesus Christ is God's Son who paid the price for humanity's sins on the cross, that is fine; that is your truth. Someone else may believe in something else, and that is their truth. The problem with this philosophy is that anything could become the truth.

The Scriptures are very telling when it comes to truth. At Jesus' trial before His crucifixion, Pontius Pilate asked Jesus, "What is truth?" (John 18:38 NIV). This is an ironic question because he asked it of Jesus, who has revealed himself in the book of John as truth incarnate (14:6). The Bible tells us that truth definitely exists, it is revealed in God's Word, and it was revealed in the person of His Son.

Key Verses

He is the Rock, His work is perfect; for all His ways are justice, a God of truth and without injustice; righteous and upright is He.

Deuteronomy 32:4 NKJV

Only fear the Lord and serve Him in truth with all your heart; for consider what great things He has done for you.

1 Samuel 12:24 NASB

Jesus said to him, I am the Way and the Truth and the Life; no one comes to the Father except by (through) Me.

John 14:6 AMP

Additional Notable Verses Concerning Truth

Joshua 24:14; 1 Kings 2:4; 2 Kings 20:3; Psalm 51:6; 145:18; Proverbs 3:3; 12:17–22; 23:23; Jeremiah 5:3; Daniel 10:21; Zechariah 8:16; John 1:14, 17; 4:24; 8:31–59; 14:17; 16:13; 17:17–19; 18:33–38; Romans 2:2; 1 Corinthians 13:6; 2 Corinthians 4:2; 7:14; Galatians 3:1; Ephesians 4:25; 5:9; 6:14; Philippians 4:8; 1 Timothy 2:7; Titus 1:1

Unborn Children

The wonder of the sonogram gives us insight into the womb that the world did not have for thousands of years. Now you can watch your unborn child grow from the size of a small grain to a fully formed, ready-to-emerge-from-the-womb baby. Though the prophets and apostles of old were not equipped with sonograms, God revealed to them exactly what went on in the womb. An unborn child, even in the earliest stages of development, is just as much a child as one who is outside the womb. God himself takes credit for the act of creation that happens in the womb.

Key Verses

Your hands fashioned and made me, and now you have destroyed me altogether. Remember that you have made me like clay; and will you return me to the dust? Did you not pour me out like milk and curdle me like cheese? You clothed me with skin and flesh, and knit me together with bones and sinews.

Job 10:8–11 ESV

You made all the delicate, inner parts of my body and knit me together in my mother's womb. Thank you for making me so wonderfully complex! Your workmanship is marvelous—how well I know it. You watched me as I was being formed in utter seclusion, as I was woven together in the dark of the womb. You saw me before I was born. Every day of my life was recorded in your book. Every moment was laid out before a single day had passed.

Psalm 139:13–16 NLT

Additional Notable Verses Concerning Unborn Children

Genesis 1:26–27; 5:1–2; Exodus 21:22–25; Judges 13:7; Job 31:15; Jeremiah 1:5; Luke 1:15, 39–44; Galatians 1:15

Unity

Unity is the quality of many different and varying parts being combined into one whole and harmonious group. Unity is indispensable to a group's success. Sports teams, Fortune 500 companies, and political parties seek unity, sometimes at all costs. Rarely do any of these groups actually find lasting unity.

The Scriptures command the church to exhibit unity as true members of God's family. When we live in love and unity we resemble God the most. The world should look at people and know that they are Christians by the love and unity they possess with one another.

Key Verses

Behold, how good and how pleasant it is for brethren to dwell together in unity!
Psalm 133:1 NKJV

But I urge and entreat you, brethren, by the name of our Lord Jesus Christ, that all of you be in perfect harmony and full agreement in what you say, and that there be no dissensions or factions or divisions among you, but that you be perfectly united in your common understanding and in your opinions and judgments.
1 Corinthians 1:10 AMP

Beyond all these things put on love, which is the perfect bond of unity.
Colossians 3:14 NASB

Additional Notable Verses Concerning Unity
Ecclesiastes 4:9–12; Amos 3:3; John 17; Acts 4:32; Romans 12; 14:19; 15:1–6; 2 Corinthians 13:11; Ephesians 4:1–16; Philippians 1:27; 2:2; 1 Peter 3:8–9

Unwanted Pregnancies

Not every pregnancy is the result of meticulous family planning. There are plenty of times when a couple who may not be trying, or may even believe themselves to be past the point of bearing children, suddenly finds themselves expecting a baby.

The Bible's teaching on pregnancy extends even to those that are unplanned or unwanted. The clear teaching of Scripture is that pregnancies and the womb are the realm of Almighty God. Things like birth control may have their place, but ultimately God is sovereign over the womb.

Key Verses

Did not He who made me in the womb make them? Did not the same One fashion us in the womb?

Job 31:15 NKJV

Surely I was sinful at birth, sinful from the time my mother conceived me.

Psalm 51:5 NIV

Additional Notable Verses Concerning Unwanted Pregnancies

Genesis 1:20–27; Job 10:8–11; Psalm 139:13–16

Urban Ministry

God loves cities. Not because of the buildings, the streets, or the museums, but because cities are full of people, and God loves people. In the Scriptures God persistently and consistently reaches out to cities. In the Old Testament God sends Jonah to the ancient metropolis of Nineveh. Nineveh is a city filled with wicked people, but God sends Jonah chiefly because of the number of people in that great city. In the New Testament Jesus repeatedly goes to the cities to spread His message of repentance. After Jesus' ascension, the book of Acts reads much like an ancient atlas as the apostles preach the Gospel from city to city.

Key Verses

May there be abundance of grain in the land; on the tops of the mountains may it wave; may its fruit be like Lebanon; and may people blossom in the cities like the grass of the field!

Psalm 72:16 ESV

Thus says the Lord of hosts, the God of Israel, to all the exiles whom I have sent into exile from Jerusalem to Babylon, "Build houses and live in them; and plant gardens and eat their produce. Take wives and become the fathers of sons and daughters, and take wives for your sons and give your daughters to husbands, that they may bear sons and daughters; and multiply there and do not decrease. Seek the welfare of the city where I have sent you into exile, and pray to the Lord on its behalf; for in its welfare you will have welfare."

Jeremiah 29:4–7 NASB

Additional Notable Verses Concerning Urban Ministry

Genesis 18:16–33; Nehemiah 2; Psalm 31:21; 46:4; 48:1–8; 127:1; Proverbs 11:10–11; Jonah 1–4; Matthew 10; Luke 8:1; 9:1–6; 10:1–20; 13:22; Acts 1:8; Titus 1:5; Hebrews 11:9–10

Values

What a person values tells you a lot about that person and about a culture. Someone who values money over independence will choose to stay in a job with a good salary but little influence. What we value determines what we think and how we act.

Values are something on which God's Word places great importance. If we value what God values, then we honor and glorify Him. If we value anything other than what God values, we sin and invite great confusion and disaster into our lives.

Key Verses

Who may worship in your sanctuary, Lord? Who may enter your presence on your holy hill? Those who lead blameless lives and do what is right, speaking the truth from sincere hearts.

Psalm 15:1–2 NLT

Better the poor whose walk is blameless than a fool whose lips are perverse.

Proverbs 19:1 NIV

And one of the scribes came up and heard them disputing with one another, and seeing that he answered them well, asked him, "Which commandment is the most important of all?" Jesus answered, "The most important is, 'Hear, O Israel: The Lord our God, the Lord is one. And you shall love the Lord your God with all your heart and with all your soul and with all your mind and with all your strength.' The second is this: 'You shall love your neighbor as yourself.' There is no other commandment greater than these."

Mark 12:28–31 ESV

And just as you want men to do to you, you also do to them likewise.

Luke 6:31 NKJV

Additional Notable Verses Concerning Values

Exodus 20:1–17; Leviticus 11:45; 19:18; Ecclesiastes 3:11; Habakkuk 3:17–18; Matthew 5:48; 6; Luke 6:32–42; Romans 2:14–16; 13:10; Galatians 5:4

Violence

There are times, such as in self-defense, when violence is necessary. But when a group of people begins to love and enjoy violence, something has gone terribly wrong. Violence was one of the reasons that God judged the earth with the Flood in Noah's time. God is so opposed to violence that He was willing to destroy all of humanity and start over with just a handful of faithful followers. Violence is not something that God merely disapproves of; it is something that He promises to judge.

Key Verses

As far as God was concerned, the Earth had become a sewer; there was violence everywhere. God took one look and saw how bad it was, everyone corrupt and corrupting—life itself corrupt to the core.

God said to Noah, "It's all over. It's the end of the human race. The violence is everywhere; I'm making a clean sweep."

Genesis 6:11–13 THE MESSAGE

You have heard that it was said, "An eye for an eye, and a tooth for a tooth." But I tell you, don't stand up against an evil person. If someone slaps you on the right cheek, turn to him the other cheek also. If someone wants to sue you in court and take your shirt, let him have your coat also. If someone forces you to go with him one mile, go with him two miles. If a person asks you for something, give it to him. Don't refuse to give to someone who wants to borrow from you.

Matthew 5:38–42 NCV

Additional Notable Verses Concerning Violence

2 Samuel 22:3; Job 5:21–22; Psalm 7:16; 11:5; 27:12; 72:14; Proverbs 1:19; 3:31; 4:16–17; 10:6; 13:2; 16:29; 21:7; Isaiah 60:18; Jeremiah 22:3; Ezekiel 8:17; 12:19; Amos 3:10; Obadiah 1:10; Habakkuk 2:12; Matthew 11:12; 26:52–54

Vocation

What do you want to be when you grow up?" It is a question commonly addressed to children, who give some very creative answers. Children might reply that they want to be an astronaut, a firefighter, the president, a police officer, a teacher, and almost anything that you can think of. The beauty of childhood is that their answers do not consider things like taxes, salaries, benefits, or education. As a child, you do not have to consider all of the factors that will actually matter later when you make a decision regarding vocation.

There are many vocations and job types in the Bible. Some of those seem like fun (king), and others seem like they would be the last choice (shepherd). The Scriptures tell us, however, that all jobs are honorable if they are done as if God is your boss. Any vocation can be a good one if it is done to glorify God.

Key Verses

You shall generously give to him, and your heart shall not be grieved when you give to him, because for this thing the Lord your God will bless you in all your work and in all your undertakings.

Deuteronomy 15:10 NASB

May the favor of the Lord our God rest on us; establish the work of our hands for us—yes, establish the work of our hands.

Psalm 90:17 NIV

In all labor there is profit, but idle chatter leads only to poverty.

Proverbs 14:23 NKJV

Additional Notable Verses Concerning Vocation

Deuteronomy 24:14; Psalm 128:2; Proverbs 12:11; 18:9; Ecclesiastes 3:22; 4:9; John 5:17; 6:27; Acts 20:35; 1 Corinthians 4:12; 15:58; Colossians 3:23; 1 Thessalonians 4:11; 2 Thessalonians 3:10; 1 Timothy 4:10; Hebrews 6:10

War

In the fourth and fifth centuries AD, prominent theologian Augustine of Hippo pioneered his theory of just war. His theory essentially says that Christians should be pacifists who refuse to fight in their private lives. It is possible and justified, however, for Christians to lay aside their pacifism to protect those who are innocent and defenseless. The pursuit of peace is preeminent, even if it requires war.

Augustine's theory on just war is valuable, but it does not agree exactly with what the Bible tells us about war. We know from God's Word that at times war was permissible and even commanded by God. Beyond that, we know that governments have been ordained by God and that making war is a part of the role of government. Wars are ugly things, but at times life is ugly.

Key Verses

You can get the horses ready for battle, but it is the Lord who gives the victory.
Proverbs 21:31 NCV

It's better to be wise than strong; intelligence outranks muscle any day. Strategic planning is the key to warfare; to win, you need a lot of good counsel.
Proverbs 24:5–6 THE MESSAGE

Or what king, when he sets out to meet another king in battle, will not first sit down and consider whether he is strong enough with ten thousand men to encounter the one coming against him with twenty thousand? Or else, while the other is still far away, he sends a delegation and asks for terms of peace.
Luke 14:31–32 NASB

Where do wars and fights come from among you? Do they not come from your desires for pleasure that war in your members?
James 4:1 NKJV

Additional Notable Verses Concerning War

Exodus 17:16; Leviticus 26:7–8; Joshua 1–13; 2 Samuel 22:35; 1 Chronicles 5:22; 12; Psalm 46:9; 68:30; Ecclesiastes 3:8; 8:8; Matthew 24:6; 2 Corinthians 10:1–6; Ephesians 6:10–20; 1 Timothy 1:18

Wealth

Given the chance, most of us would choose being rich over being poor. You do not have to believe that money can buy you happiness, love, or righteousness to want to work hard and provide a nice life for yourself and those close to you.

Wealth and its attainment are a constant topic in the Bible. It may be a surprise to some, but the Scriptures do not prohibit having wealth. God's Word is, however, abundantly concerned with how wealth is obtained and used. Wealth that is obtained through dishonest and abusive means will not benefit its owner. And those who are wealthy should share with those in need.

Key Verses

The Lord makes poor and makes rich; he brings low and he exalts.

1 Samuel 2:7 ESV

The silver is mine, and the gold is mine, saith the Lord of hosts.

Haggai 2:8 KJV

Teach those who are rich in this world not to be proud and not to trust in their money, which is so unreliable. Their trust should be in God, who richly gives us all we need for our enjoyment. Tell them to use their money to do good. They should be rich in good works and generous to those in need, always being ready to share with others. By doing this they will be storing up their treasure as a good foundation for the future so that they may experience true life.

1 Timothy 6:17–19 NLT

Additional Notable Verses Concerning Wealth
Deuteronomy 8:11–18; Psalm 39:6; 49:10; 62:10; 73:12; Proverbs 10:22; 11:4; 13:7, 22; 15:27; 22:7; 23:4–5; 27:24; 28:11, 20; Ecclesiastes 4:8; 5:10–20; Jeremiah 9:23; Matthew 6:19–21; 19:16–30; Mark 10:23–25; 12:42–44; Luke 12:13–21; Ephesians 3:8; 1 Timothy 6:6–10; James 1:9–11; 2:1–7; 5:1–6; 1 John 3:17; Revelation 18

Weddings

American culture is obsessed with weddings. They are the subject of an increasing number of reality shows that are anything but real. The cost can run into the millions for celebrity weddings, though many of the marriages are over before the flowers are dead. Perhaps our society is so obsessed with weddings because, with a divorce rate near 50 percent, they happen so frequently.

Weddings and the marriages that result from them are of supreme importance to God. The Scriptures are not incredibly concerned with a wedding's order of service, the music that is played, how many attendants there are, or the colors of the decorations. God's desire for a wedding is that it be the beginning of a marriage of two people who are intent on glorifying Him through their union.

Key Verses

When a man has taken a new wife, he shall not go out to war or be charged with any business; he shall be free at home one year, and bring happiness to his wife whom he has taken.

Deuteronomy 24:5 NKJV

Come out to see King Solomon, young women of Jerusalem. He wears the crown his mother gave him on his wedding day, his most joyous day.

Song of Solomon 3:11 NLT

In the original creation, God made male and female to be together. Because of this, a man leaves father and mother, and in marriage he becomes one flesh with a woman—no longer two individuals, but forming a new unity. Because God created this organic union of the two sexes, no one should desecrate his art by cutting them apart.

Mark 10:6–9 THE MESSAGE

Additional Notable Verses Concerning Weddings

Genesis 2:18–24; Matthew 19:4–6; 22:1–14; 25:1–13; John 2:1–12; 1 Corinthians 7:1–16; 13; Ephesians 5:22–33; Colossians 3:18–19; Hebrews 13:4–7

Weight Control

Obesity has reached epidemic proportions in much of the civilized world. While some parts of the world are starving to death, other parts are eating themselves to death. It may seem like problems with weight are a modern phenomenon, but the truth is that, for a multitude of reasons, people have struggled to control their weight for thousands of years.

It is a sign of the Bible's practical nature that an issue like weight control is discussed on its pages as much as it is. In the Scriptures, gluttony is most definitely a sin. To struggle with one's weight is not unusual, but to give in and allow it to control your life is just as much a sin as drunkenness or adultery. The message of the Bible is not always popular, but Christians must decide whether they want to let the Holy Spirit control their lives, or their appetites.

Key Verses

Do not mix with winebibbers, or with gluttonous eaters of meat; for the drunkard and the glutton will come to poverty, and drowsiness will clothe a man with rags.

Proverbs 23:20–21 NKJV

He who keeps the law is a discerning son, but he who is a companion of gluttons humiliates his father.

Proverbs 28:7 NASB

So, whether you eat or drink, or whatever you do, do all to the glory of God.

1 Corinthians 10:31 ESV

Additional Notable Verses Concerning Weight Control

Deuteronomy 21:20; Proverbs 23:2; 25:16, 27; Matthew 11:19; Romans 12:1–2; 13:14; 1 Corinthians 6:19–20; 10:13; Philippians 3:17–21; 2 Timothy 3:1–9; 2 Peter 1:5–7

Widows

Thanks to modern advances in a multitude of areas, people today are living longer and longer, particularly when compared to the era in which the Bible was written. One consequence of shorter life spans was that there were many more widows in society. In a world in which the work force was dominated by men, being a widow was a dangerous proposition. Widows were under constant threat of being taken advantage of, particularly if they had no sons.

The constant fear and danger that was the everyday life of a widow was at the forefront of the mind of God. For God's children to stand by while those unfortunate enough to have lost a husband were taken advantage of was unconscionable. To attempt to take advantage of a widow was a direct affront to God and His Word, and it still is.

Key Verses

You shall not afflict any widow or orphan. If you afflict him at all, and if he does cry out to Me, I will surely hear his cry; and My anger will be kindled, and I will kill you with the sword, and your wives shall become widows and your children fatherless.

Exodus 22:22–24 NASB

The Lord tears down the house of the proud, but he protects the property of widows.

Proverbs 15:25 NLT

Religion that God the Father accepts as pure and without fault is this: caring for orphans or widows who need help, and keeping yourself free from the world's evil influence.

James 1:27 NCV

Additional Notable Verses Concerning Widows
Deuteronomy 10:17–18; 14:29; 24:17–22; 27:19; Psalm 68:5; 94:6; 146:9; Isaiah 1:17, 23; 10:1–2; Jeremiah 7:5–7; 22:3; 49:11; Zechariah 7:8–10; Malachi 3:5; Mark 12:42–43; Luke 2:36–38; Acts 6:1–7; Romans 7:3; 1 Timothy 5:1–16

Wisdom

People will go to amazing lengths to get something that they are desperate to own. In all of this seeking to obtain, however, wisdom is rarely the object of anyone's passion.

The lack of passion for wisdom is in ignorance of the Scriptures' teaching. The Bible teaches that wisdom is one of the most important things in the world to possess. If people do not have wisdom, they are urged to get it. They are to ask God for it, and they are to do what they can to find it on their own as well.

Key Verses

The fear of the Lord is the beginning of knowledge; fools despise wisdom and instruction.

Proverbs 1:7 ESV

Who is as the wise man? and who knoweth the interpretation of a thing? a man's wisdom maketh his face to shine, and the boldness of his face shall be changed.

Ecclesiastes 8:1 KJV

Don't fool yourself. Don't think that you can be wise merely by being up-to-date with the times. Be God's fool—that's the path to true wisdom. What the world calls smart, God calls stupid. It's written in Scripture,
He exposes the chicanery of the chic.
The Master sees through the smoke screens of the know-it-alls.

1 Corinthians 3:18–20 THE MESSAGE

But if any of you lacks wisdom, let him ask of God, who gives to all generously and without reproach, and it will be given to him. . . . But the wisdom from above is first pure, then peaceable, gentle, reasonable, full of mercy and good fruits, unwavering, without hypocrisy.

James 1:5; 3:17 NASB

Additional Notable Verses Concerning Wisdom

1 Kings 3; 4:29–34; Job 12:12–13; 36:5; Psalm 37:30; 51:6; 90:12; 111:10; Proverbs 2:1–15; 3:13–26; 4:5–9; 10:23; 12:15; 13:14–16; 17:27–28; 18:15; 19:20; 24:3–7; 29:3; Isaiah 29:14–16; Jeremiah 9:23–24; Daniel 1:17; Romans 11:33; 1 Corinthians 1:17–26; Ephesians 1:16–19; 5:15–17; Colossians 2:3; 3:16; James 3:13

Wives

A good wife is so important and such a blessing that when a man finds one the Bible tells us that credit must go to God himself for such a great gift. The Scriptures give wives God's expectations for them, but they make plain what a husband's role and expectations are as well.

Key Verses

A man's greatest treasure is his wife—she is a gift from the Lord.
Proverbs 18:22 CEV

Houses and wealth are inherited from parents, but a wise wife is a gift from the Lord.
Proverbs 19:14 NCV

Charm is deceptive, and beauty does not last; but a woman who fears the Lord will be greatly praised. Reward her for all she has done. Let her deeds publicly declare her praise.
Proverbs 31:30–31 NLT

Wives, in the same way submit yourselves to your own husbands so that, if any of them do not believe the word, they may be won over without words by the behavior of their wives, when they see the purity and reverence of your lives. Your beauty should not come from outward adornment, such as elaborate hairstyles and the wearing of gold jewelry or fine clothes. Rather, it should be that of your inner self, the unfading beauty of a gentle and quiet spirit, which is of great worth in God's sight. For this is the way the holy women of the past who put their hope in God used to adorn themselves They submitted themselves to their own husbands, like Sarah, who obeyed Abraham and called him her lord. You are her daughters if you do what is right and do not give way to fear.
1 Peter 3:1–6 NIV

Additional Notable Verses Concerning Wives

Proverbs 12:4; 21:9; 31:10–31; Romans 7:2–3; 1 Corinthians 7:3–5, 10–16, 39–40; Ephesians 5:22–33; Titus 2:4–5

Words

Because of the awesome power of words, the Bible constantly urges caution and wisdom when we speak. We are to speak words that are true, but our truth must be wrapped in love.

Key Verses

Pleasant words are a honeycomb, sweet to the soul and healing to the bones.

Proverbs 16:24 NASB

The words of a wise man's mouth are gracious, but the lips of a fool shall swallow him up; the words of his mouth begin with foolishness, and the end of his talk is raving madness. A fool also multiplies words. No man knows what is to be; who can tell him what will be after him?

Ecclesiastes 10:12–14 NKJV

Make a tree good and its fruit will be good, or make a tree bad and its fruit will be bad, for a tree is recognized by its fruit. You brood of vipers, how can you who are evil say anything good? For the mouth speaks what the heart is full of. A good man brings good things out of the good stored up in him, and an evil man brings evil things out of the evil stored up in him. But I tell you that everyone will have to give account on the day of judgment for every empty word they have spoken. For by your words you will be acquitted, and by your words you will be condemned.

Matthew 12:33–37 NIV

When you talk, do not say harmful things, but say what people need—words that will help others become stronger. Then what you say will do good to those who listen to you.

Ephesians 4:29 NCV

Additional Notable Verses Concerning Words

Psalm 19:14; Proverbs 6:1–5; 10:18–21; 11:12; 12:18; 13:3; 15:1–4, 23; 16:23–24; 17:27–28; 18:8, 21; 21:23; 25:11; 27:2; 29:20; Ecclesiastes 5:3; 12:9–12; Isaiah 55:11; Matthew 15:15–20; Luke 6:43–45; Romans 16:17–18; Ephesians 5:6; Colossians 3:8, 16; 2 Timothy 2:14; James 1:26; 3:1–12

World

The Scriptures affirm that God most definitely loves the entire world. But sometimes "the world" in Scripture refers to the pressure we feel to live like the lost around us.

Key Verses

He has made the earth by His power, He has established the world by His wisdom, and has stretched out the heavens at His discretion. When He utters His voice, there is a multitude of waters in the heavens: "And He causes the vapors to ascend from the ends of the earth. He makes lightning for the rain, He brings the wind out of His treasuries."

Jeremiah 10:12–13 NKJV

Therefore I urge you, brethren, by the mercies of God, to present your bodies a living and holy sacrifice, acceptable to God, which is your spiritual service of worship. And do not be conformed to this world, but be transformed by the renewing of your mind, so that you may prove what the will of God is, that which is good and acceptable and perfect.

Romans 12:1–2 NASB

Do not love this world nor the things it offers you, for when you love the world, you do not have the love of the Father in you. For the world offers only a craving for physical pleasure, a craving for everything we see, and pride in our achievements and possessions. These are not from the Father, but are from this world. And this world is fading away, along with everything that people crave. But anyone who does what pleases God will live forever.

1 John 2:15–17 NLT

Additional Notable Verses Concerning the World

Psalm 9:8; 18:15; 24:1; 33:8; 89:11; 90:2; 93:1; 96:10–13; 98:7–9; Isaiah 13:11; 26:9; 34:1; Jeremiah 51:5; Matthew 5:14; 16:26; 24:3–51; John 1:6–13; 3:16–21; 4:42; 6:1–59; 7:1–8; 8:1–30; 9:5; 12:20–50; 13:1; 14:15–31; 15:18–25; 16–17; 18:36–37; Romans 1:8; 3:1–19; 5:12–21; 1 Corinthians 1:18–31; 2:12; 5:9–11; 6:2; 11:32; 2 Corinthians 4:1–6; 5:12–21; Galatians 6:14; Ephesians 2:1–13; 6:12; Colossians 2:8; 1 Timothy 1:15; 6:7; Hebrews 1:1–3; James 4:1–6; 1 Peter 5:9; 1 John 2:1–2; 3:1–13; 4–5; Revelation 3:10; 11:15; 12:9

Worship

The Hebrew word *shachah,* which is translated "worship," literally means to bow down. This is a fantastic picture of what is meant by worship. There are many things that we may value, but according to the Bible, God is all that is worthy of our worship. If we worship something other than God, He will see to it that whatever is taking His place is removed.

Key Verses

Do not worship any other god, for the Lord, whose name is Jealous, is a jealous God.

Exodus 34:14 NIV

Ascribe to the Lord the glory due to His name; Worship the Lord in holy array.

Psalm 29:2 NASB

"Sir," the woman said, "you must be a prophet. So tell me, why is it that you Jews insist that Jerusalem is the only place of worship, while we Samaritans claim it is here at Mount Gerizim, where our ancestors worshiped?"

Jesus replied, "Believe me, dear woman, the time is coming when it will no longer matter whether you worship the Father on this mountain or in Jerusalem. You Samaritans know very little about the one you worship, while we Jews know all about him, for salvation comes through the Jews. But the time is coming—indeed it's here now—when true worshipers will worship the Father in spirit and in truth. The Father is looking for those who will worship him that way. For God is Spirit, so those who worship him must worship in spirit and in truth."

The woman said, "I know the Messiah is coming—the one who is called Christ. When he comes, he will explain everything to us."

Then Jesus told her, "I AM the Messiah!"

John 4:19–26 NLT

Additional Notable Verses Concerning Worship

Exodus 3:12; 20:4–6; 33:7–11; Deuteronomy 6:13; 8:19; 1 Kings 9:1–9; 1 Chronicles 16:29; Nehemiah 12:45; Psalm 2:11; 22:27; 29:2; 66:4; 81:9; 86:9; 95:6; 96:9; 99:5; 132:7; Isaiah 19:21–23; Daniel 3; Zechariah 14:16–17; Matthew 2:1–12; Romans 12:1–2; Philippians 3:1–4; Hebrews 12:28–29; Revelation 4

Worth

As Creator, God reserves the right to determine something's worth. Though our system of evaluating worth is sometimes out of whack, God's is not. God believed so strongly that humanity was worth saving that He sent His only Son to die for our sins. The price was high, but to God we were worth it.

Key Verses

The words of a good person are like pure silver, but the thoughts of an evil person are almost worthless.

Proverbs 10:20 CEV

Therefore I tell you, do not be anxious about your life, what you will eat or what you will drink, nor about your body, what you will put on. Is not life more than food, and the body more than clothing? Look at the birds of the air: they neither sow nor reap nor gather into barns, and yet your heavenly Father feeds them. Are you not of more value than they? And which of you by being anxious can add a single hour to his span of life? And why are you anxious about clothing? Consider the lilies of the field, how they grow: they neither toil nor spin, yet I tell you, even Solomon in all his glory was not arrayed like one of these. But if God so clothes the grass of the field, which today is alive and tomorrow is thrown into the oven, will he not much more clothe you, O you of little faith? Therefore do not be anxious, saying, "What shall we eat?" or "What shall we drink?" or "What shall we wear?" For the Gentiles seek after all these things, and your heavenly Father knows that you need them all. But seek first the kingdom of God and his righteousness, and all these things will be added to you.

Matthew 6:25–33 ESV

Additional Notable Verses Concerning Worth
Genesis 1:26–27; Psalm 139:13–16; Proverbs 31:10; Ephesians 1:13–14

Youth

Rumors of a fountain of youth persisted throughout the ancient world. The Greeks, the Aztecs, and the Spanish all had a few people who believed in this fabled fountain. Unfortunately for all those who spent time searching for it, the fountain does not exist. We would all love for youth to be bottled up and sold, but none of us can remain young forever.

As the Creator of all life, God has much to say about youth. Much of what the Scriptures say about youth revolves around not taking youth for granted and missing the opportunities that it presents. The common expression that "you are only young once" is most definitely true. God wants and expects people not to see youth as a detriment to serving Him, but as a time in life when they are full of energy and hope, ready to be used by God.

Key Verses

Rejoice, young man, during your childhood, and let your heart be pleasant during the days of young manhood. And follow the impulses of your heart and the desires of your eyes. Yet know that God will bring you to judgment for all these things. So, remove grief and anger from your heart and put away pain from your body, because childhood and the prime of life are fleeting.

Ecclesiastes 11:9–10 NASB

Let no one despise or think less of you because of your youth, but be an example (pattern) for the believers in speech, in conduct, in love, in faith, and in purity.

1 Timothy 4:12 AMP

Additional Notable Verses Concerning Youth

1 Samuel 17; Psalm 25:7; 71:5, 17; 88:15; 89:45; 103:5; 127:4; 129:1–2; Proverbs 1:1–6; 5:18–19; Ecclesiastes 12:1; Jeremiah 1:4–8; Ezekiel 16:60; Ephesians 6:1–4

More Insight From God's Word

Have you ever wanted to ask God what heaven is like? It turns out, he's already told us! The Bible is filled with passages that describe it. In this book, you will find all the scriptural references to heaven, as well as brief, clear explanations from trustworthy commentaries.

Everything the Bible Says About Heaven

How people deal with money matters to God. In this short volume, all the scriptural references to money have been collected and explained in a clear and concise format. Hear what God has to say about everything related to money, including working, saving, tithing—and more!

Everything the Bible Says About Money

Supernatural beings—both the good and bad— fascinate us because they are surrounded by mystery. This book includes every Scripture passage relating to angels and demons along with brief commentaries to help you develop a clear, biblical point of view.

Everything the Bible Says About Angels and Demons